CREATED BY **JOSS WHEDON**

BRYAN EDWARD **HILL**   GLEB **MELNIKOV**   GABRIEL **CASSATA**   ROMAN **TITOV**

ANGEL ™

VOLUME ONE **BEING HUMAN**

Series Designers
Grace Park & **Scott Newman**

Collection Designer
Scott Newman

Assistant Editor
Gavin Gronenthal

Associate Editor
Jonathan Manning

Editor
Jeanine Schaefer

Special Thanks to **Sierra Hahn,
Dafna Pleban, Becca J. Sadowsky,**
and **Nicole Spiegel**, & **Carol Roeder**

Ross Richie CEO & Founder
Joy Huffman CFO
Matt Gagnon Editor-in-Chief
Filip Sablik President, Publishing & Marketing
Stephen Christy President, Development
Lance Kreiter Vice President, Licensing & Merchandising
Arune Singh Vice President, Marketing
Bryce Carlson Vice President, Editorial & Creative Strategy
Scott Newman Manager, Production Design
Kate Henning Manager, Operations
Spencer Simpson Manager, Sales
Elyse Strandberg Manager, Finance
Sierra Hahn Executive Editor
Jeanine Schaefer Executive Editor
Dafna Pleban Senior Editor
Shannon Watters Senior Editor
Eric Harburn Senior Editor
Chris Rosa Editor
Matthew Levine Editor
Sophie Philips-Roberts Associate Editor
Amanda LaFranco Associate Editor
Gavin Gronenthal Assistant Editor

Michael Moccio Assistant Editor
Gwen Waller Assistant Editor
Allyson Gronowitz Assistant Editor
Jillian Crab Design Coordinator
Michelle Ankley Design Coordinator
Kara Leopard Production Designer
Marie Krupina Production Designer
Grace Park Production Designer
Chelsea Roberts Production Design Assistant
Samantha Knapp Production Design Assistant
Paola Capalla Senior Accountant
José Meza Live Events Lead
Stephanie Hocutt Digital Marketing Lead
Esther Kim Marketing Coordinator
Cat O'Grady Digital Marketing Coordinator
Amanda Lawson Marketing Assistant
Holly Aitchison Digital Sales Coordinator
Morgan Perry Retail Sales Coordinator
Megan Christopher Operations Coordinator
Rodrigo Hernandez Mailroom Assistant
Zipporah Smith Operations Assistant
Breanna Sarpy Executive Assistant

ANGEL Volume One, October 2019. Published by BOOM!
Studios, a division of Boom Entertainment, Inc. Angel ™ & ©
Twentieth Century Fox Film Corporation. All rights reserved.
Originally published in single magazine form as ANGEL No.
0-4. ™ & © Twentieth Century Fox Film Corporation. All
rights reserved. BOOM! Studios™ and the BOOM! Studios
logo are trademarks of Boom Entertainment, Inc., registered
in various countries and categories. All characters, events,
and institutions depicted herein are fictional. Any similarity
between any of the names, characters, persons, events,
and/or institutions in this publication to actual names,
characters, and persons, whether living or dead, events, and/
or institutions is unintended and purely coincidental. BOOM!
Studios does not read or accept unsolicited submissions of
ideas, stories, or artwork.

BOOM! Studios, 5670 Wilshire Boulevard, Suite 400, Los
Angeles, CA 90036-5679. Printed in Canada. First Printing.

ISBN: 978-1-68415-471-5, eISBN: 978-1-64144-588-7

20th Anniversary Edition:
ISBN: 978-1-68415-470-8, eISBN: 978-1-64144-587-0

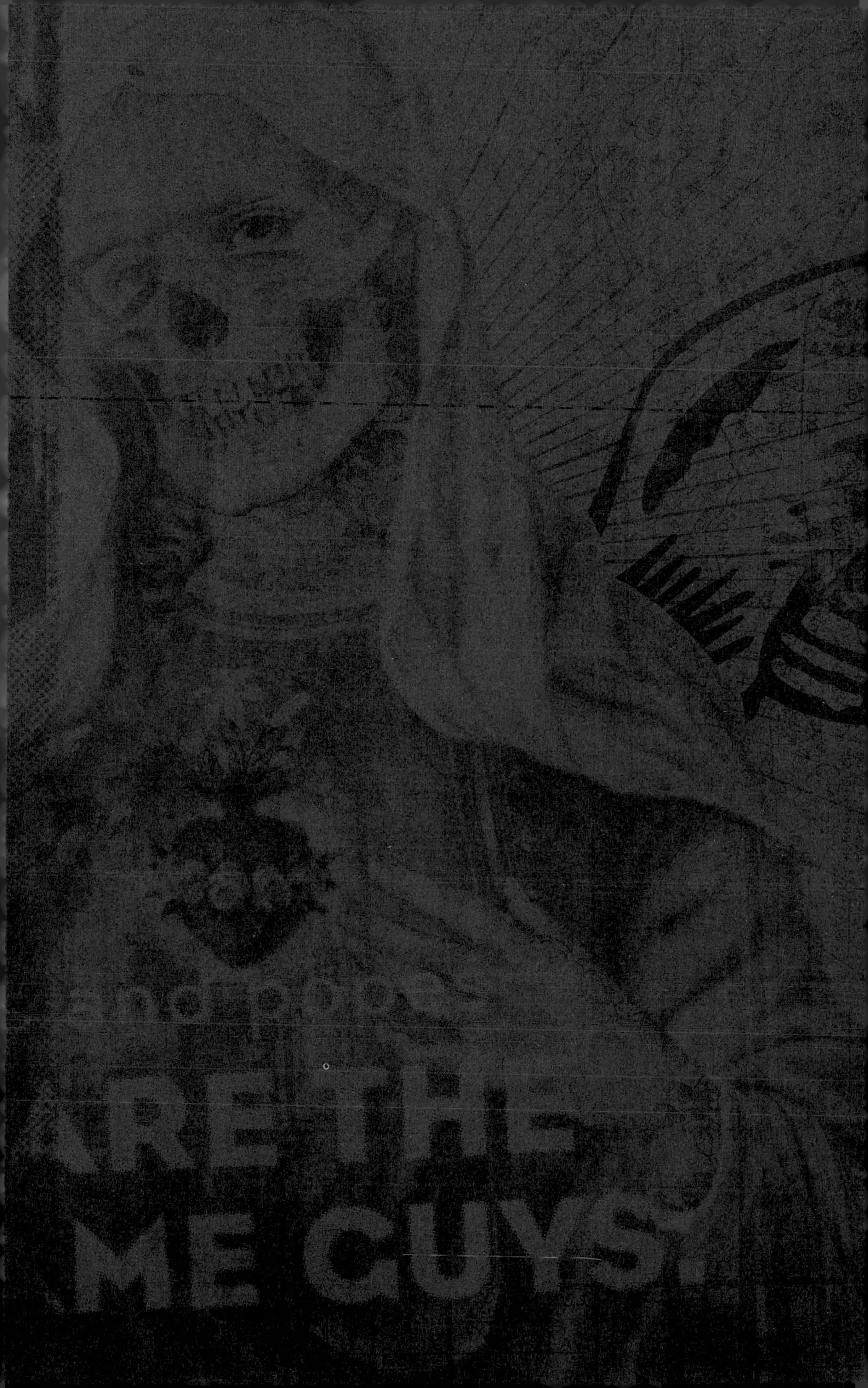
RE THE
ME GUYS!

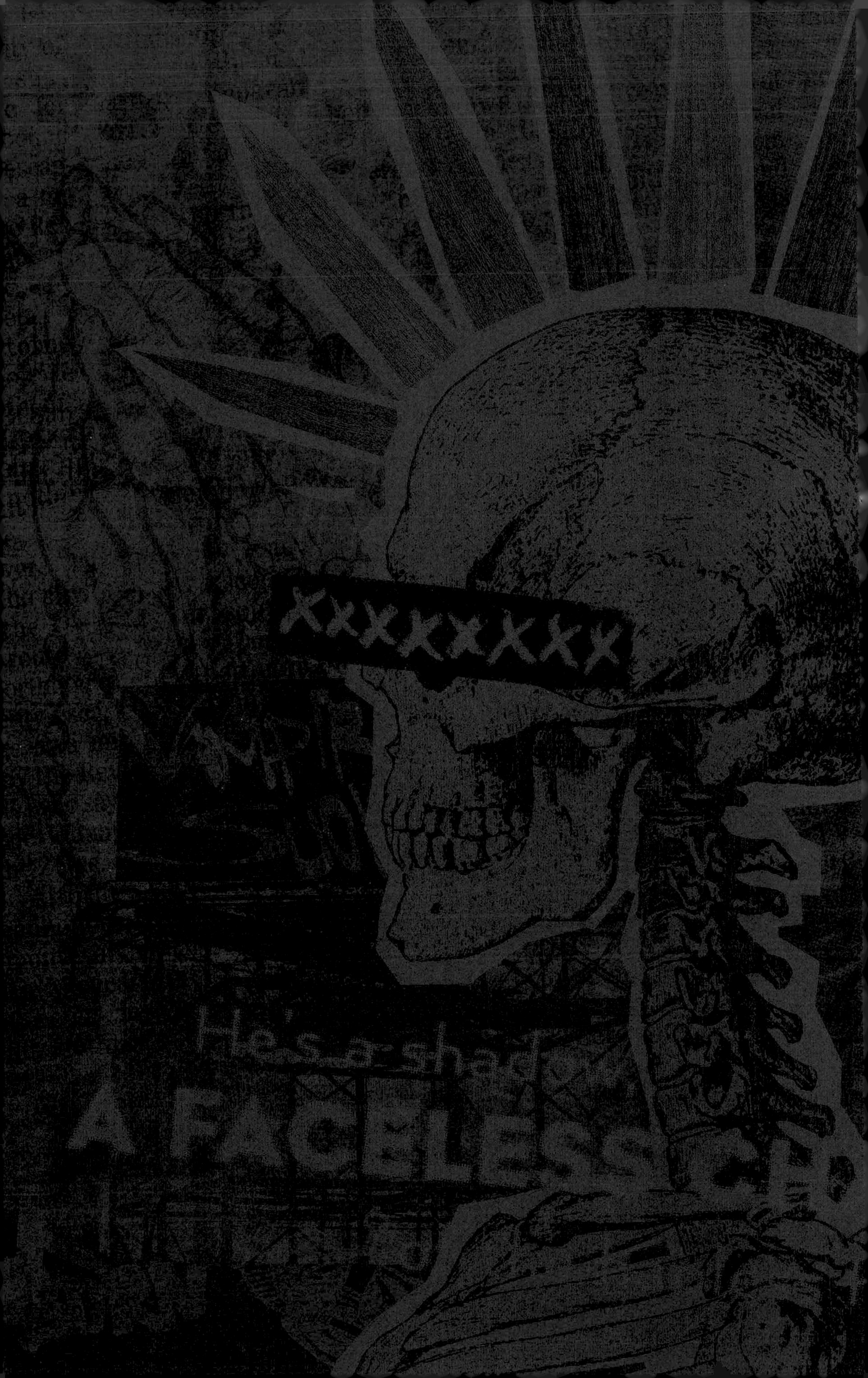
A FACELESS

Created by
Joss Whedon

Written by
Bryan Edward Hill

Illustrated by
Gleb Melnikov

Colored by
Gabriel Cassata
Prologue, Chapters One and Two
Roman Titov
Chapters Three and Four

Lettered by
Ed Dukeshire

Cover by
Dan Panosian

20th Anniversary Cover by
Scott Newman

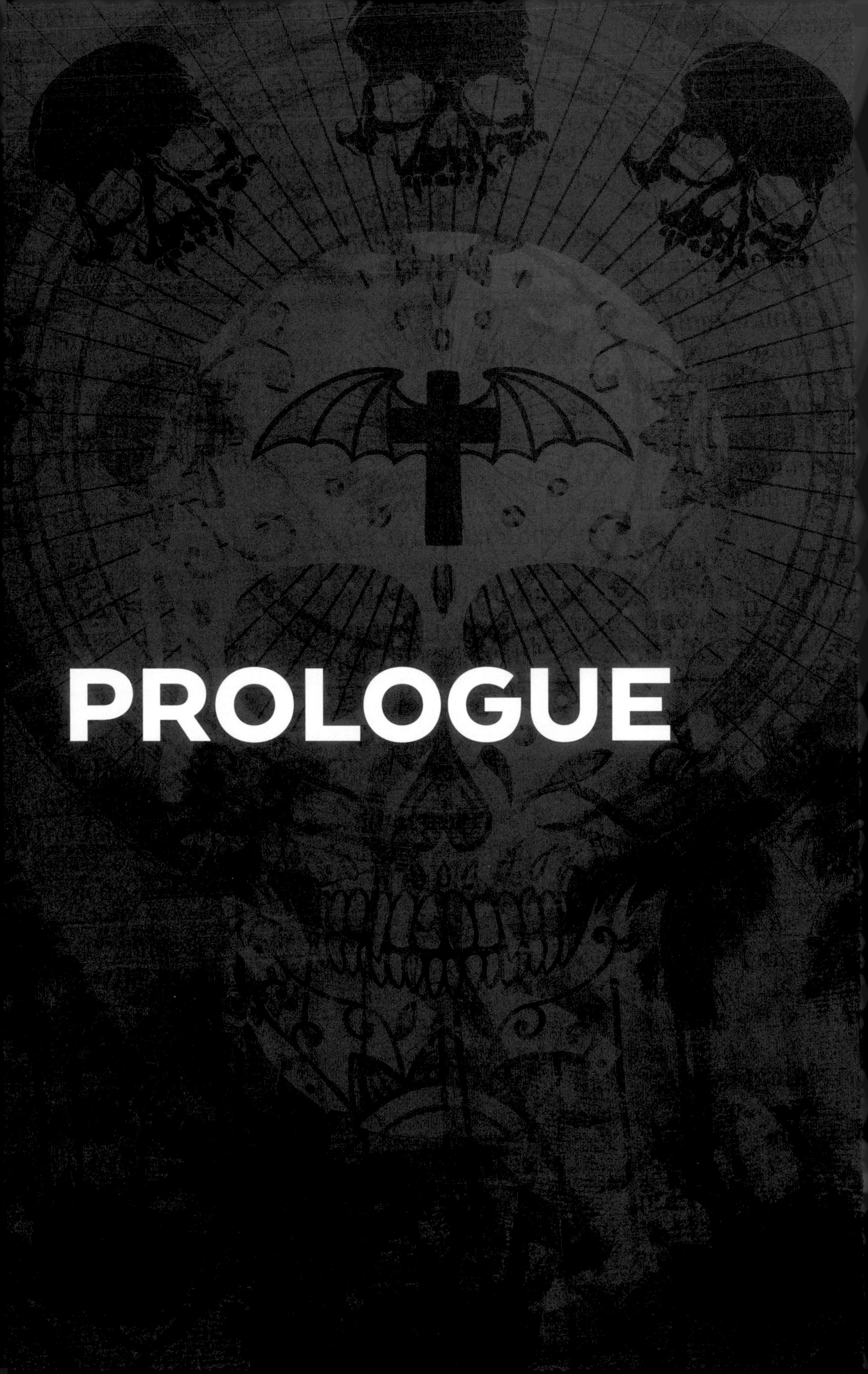

PROLOGUE

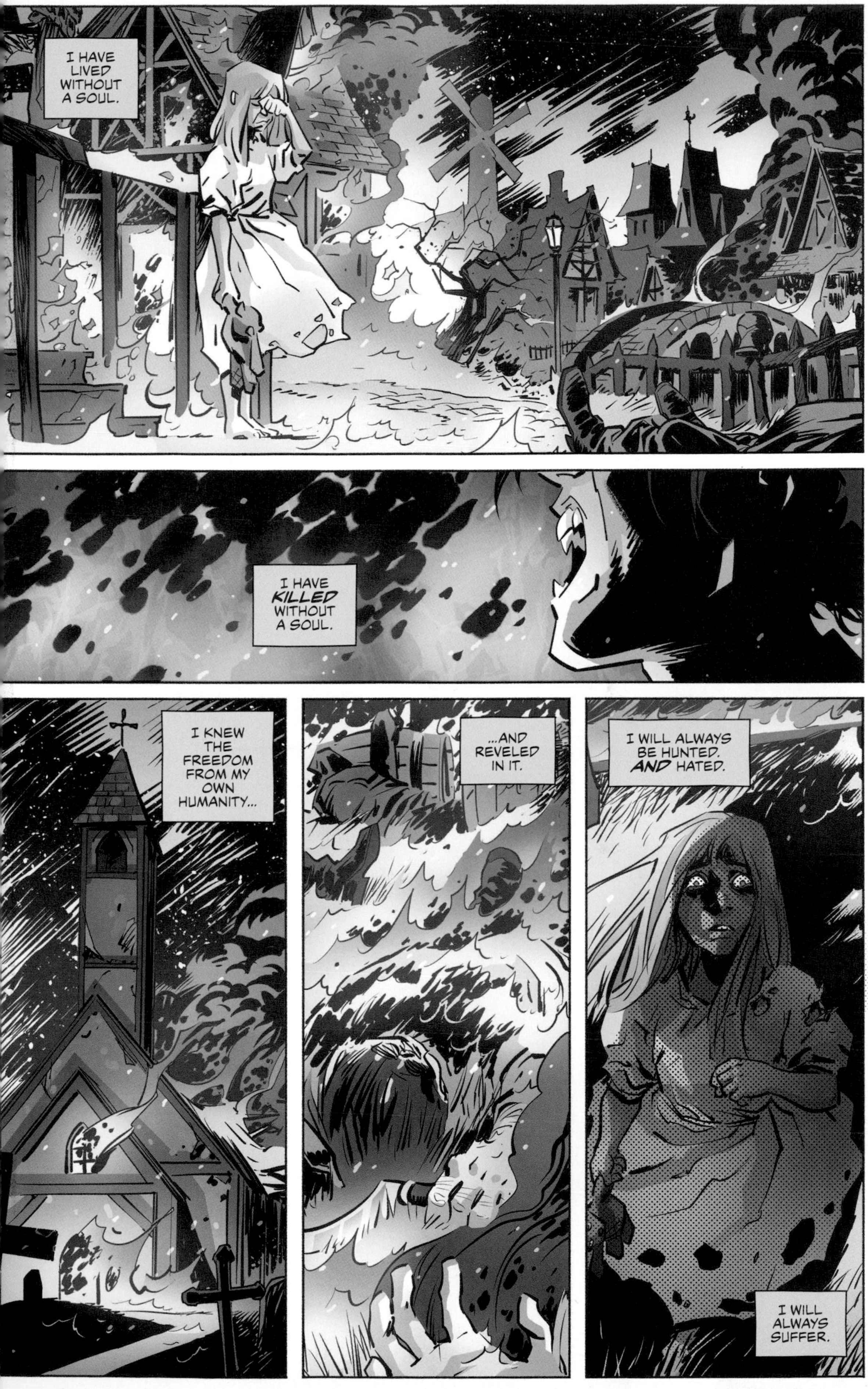

I HAVE LIVED WITHOUT A SOUL.
I HAVE KILLED WITHOUT A SOUL.
I KNEW THE FREEDOM FROM MY OWN HUMANITY...
...AND REVELED IN IT.
I WILL ALWAYS BE HUNTED. AND HATED.
I WILL ALWAYS SUFFER.

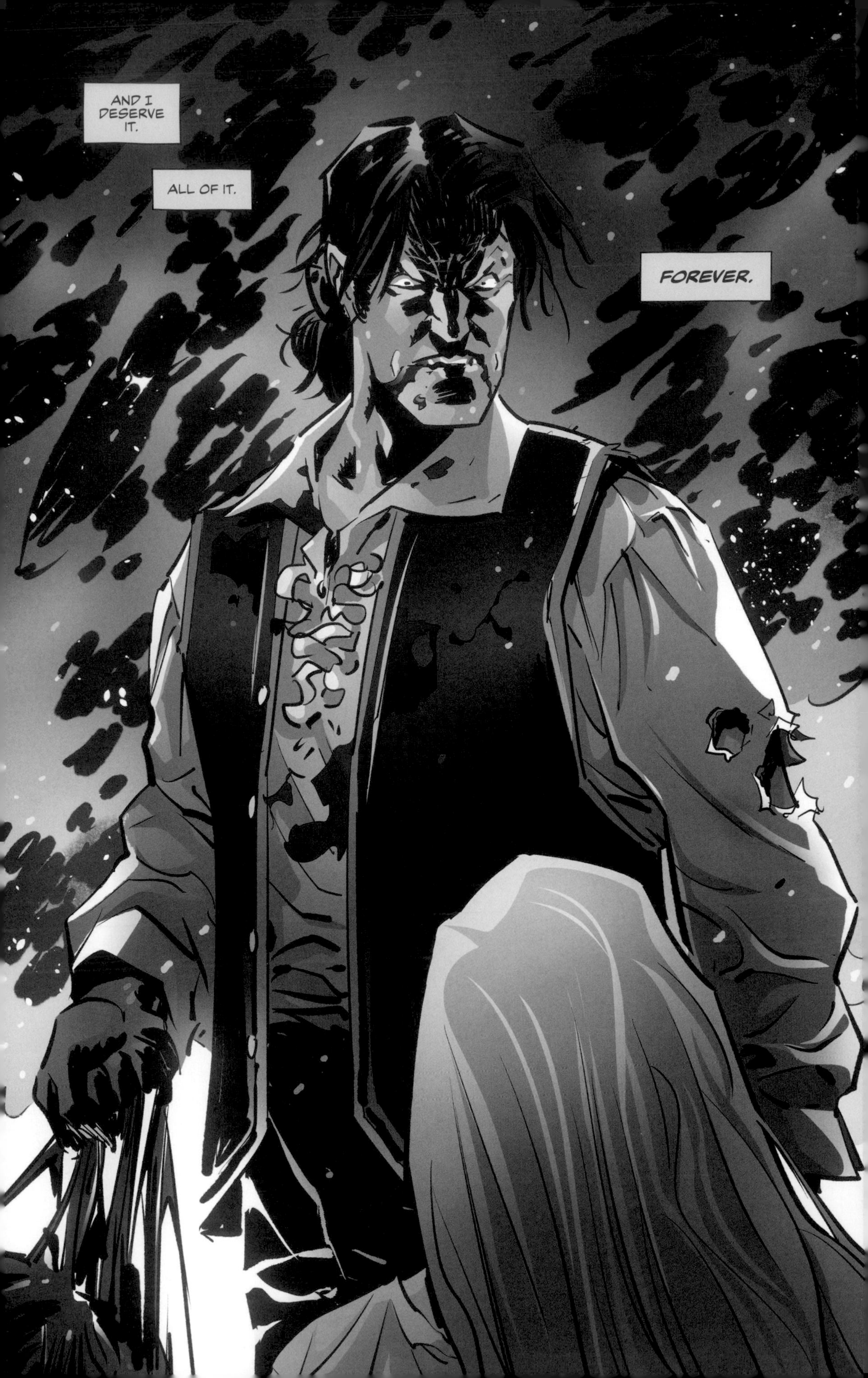
AND I DESERVE IT.
ALL OF IT.
FOREVER.

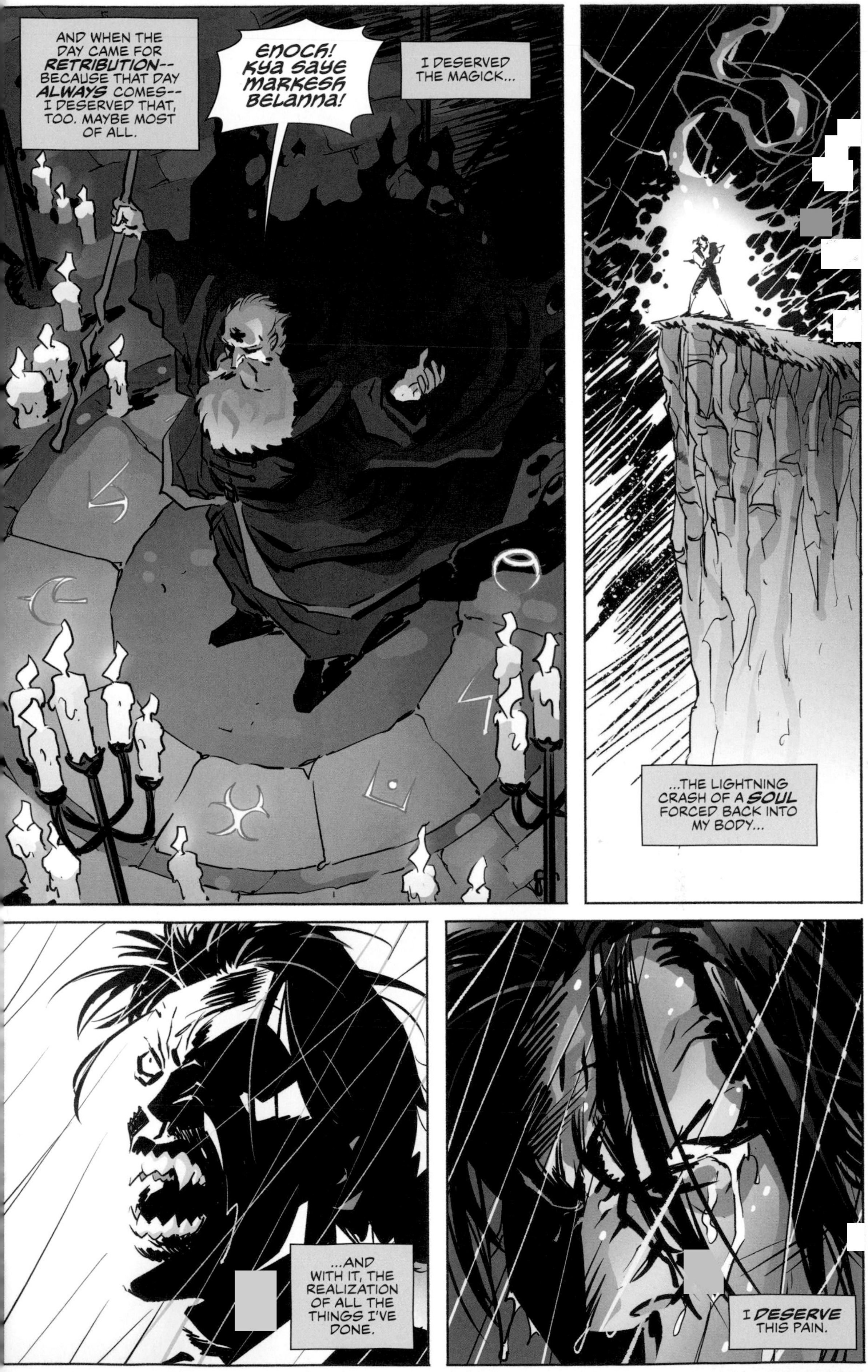
AND WHEN THE DAY CAME FOR RETRIBUTION-- BECAUSE THAT DAY ALWAYS COMES-- I DESERVED THAT, TOO. MAYBE MOST OF ALL.
ENOCH! KYA SAYE MARKESH BELANNA!
I DESERVED THE MAGICK...
...THE LIGHTNING CRASH OF A SOUL FORCED BACK INTO MY BODY...
...AND WITH IT, THE REALIZATION OF ALL THE THINGS I'VE DONE.
I DESERVE THIS PAIN.

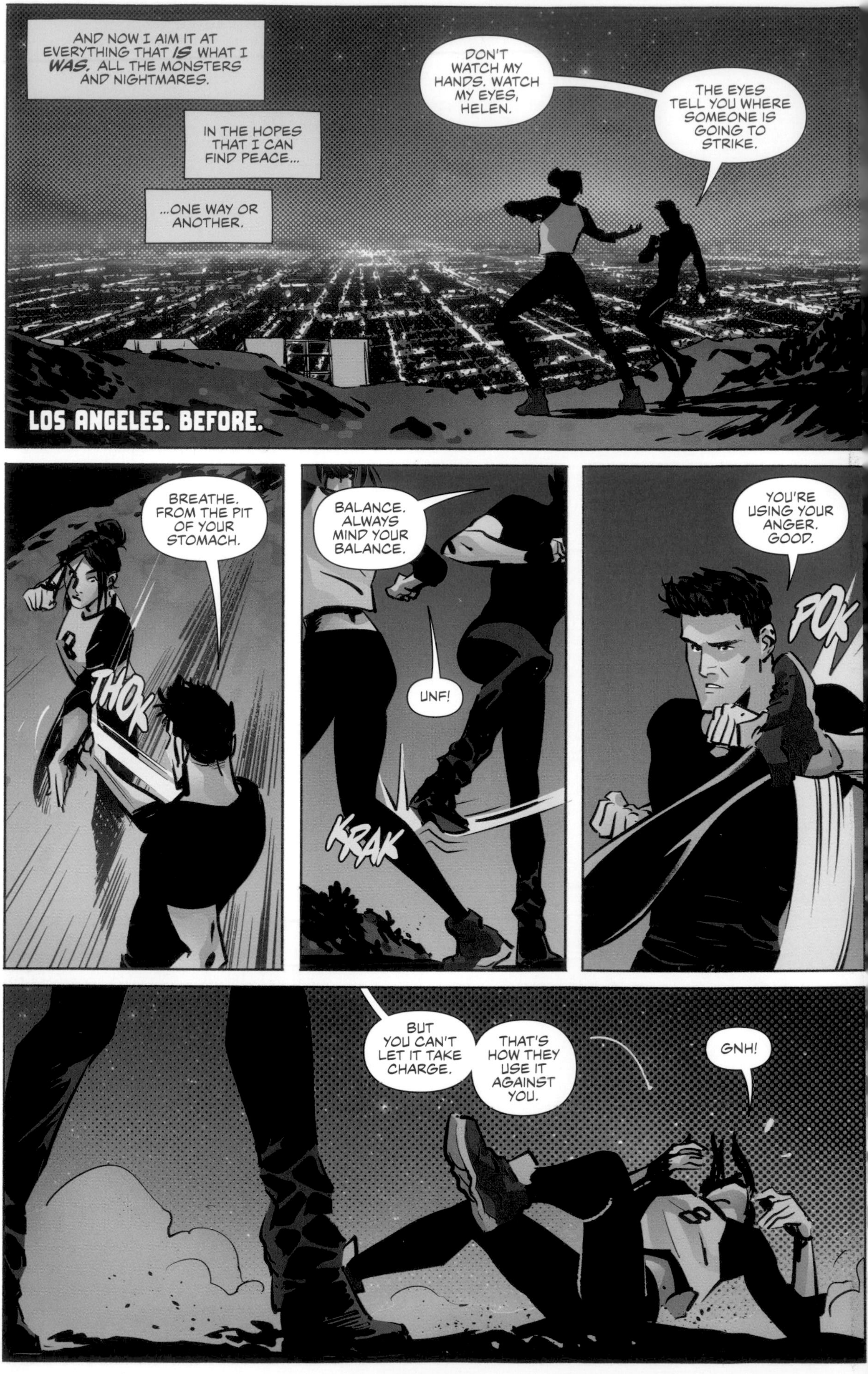
AND NOW I AIM IT AT EVERYTHING THAT *IS* WHAT I *WAS.* ALL THE MONSTERS AND NIGHTMARES.
IN THE HOPES THAT I CAN FIND PEACE...
...ONE WAY OR ANOTHER.
DON'T WATCH MY HANDS. WATCH MY EYES, HELEN.
THE EYES TELL YOU WHERE SOMEONE IS GOING TO STRIKE.
LOS ANGELES. BEFORE.
BREATHE. FROM THE PIT OF YOUR STOMACH.
THOK
BALANCE. ALWAYS MIND YOUR BALANCE.
UNF!
KRAK
YOU'RE USING YOUR ANGER. GOOD.
POK
BUT YOU CAN'T LET IT TAKE CHARGE.
THAT'S HOW THEY USE IT AGAINST YOU.
GNH!

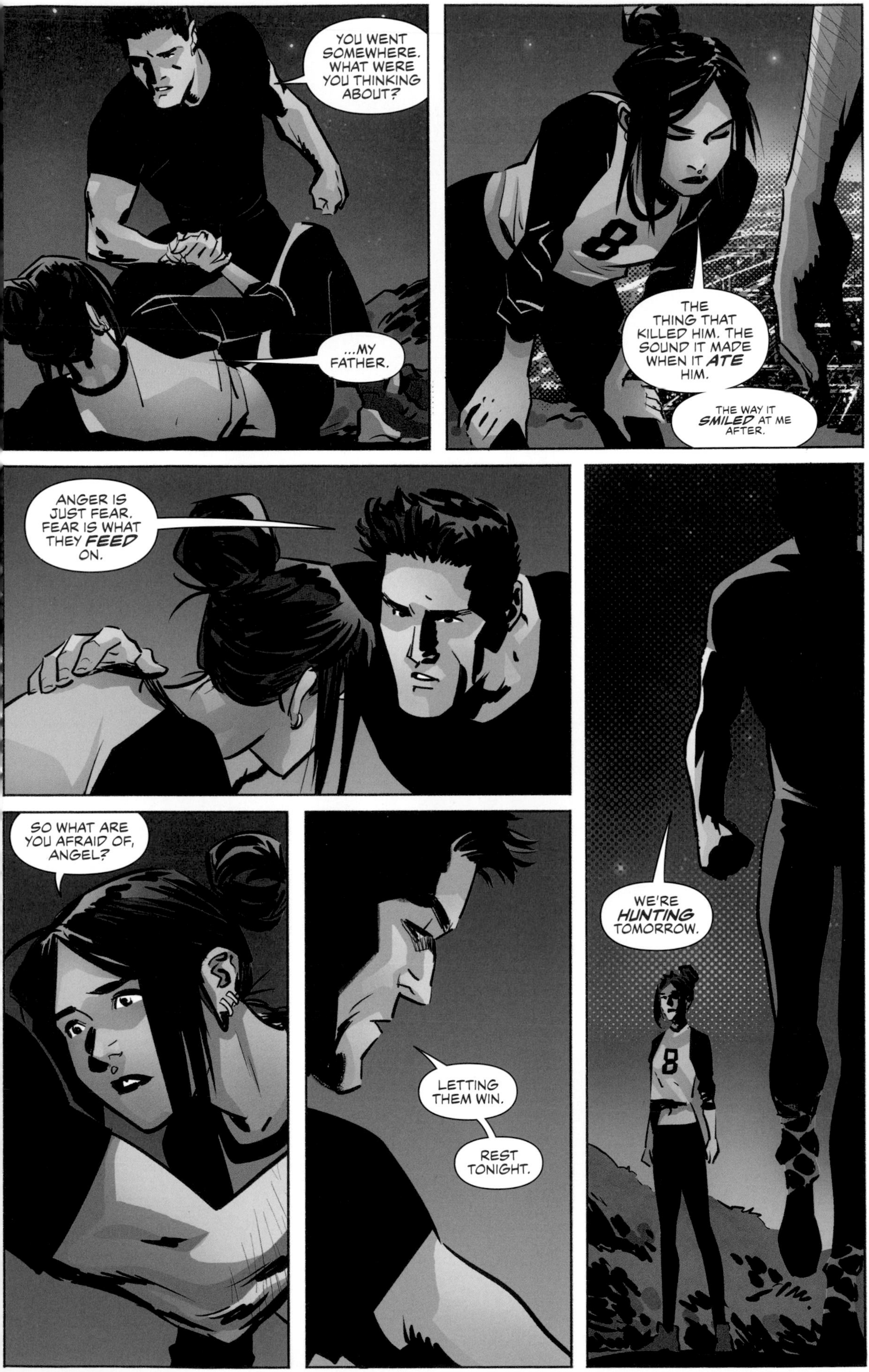
YOU WENT SOMEWHERE. WHAT WERE YOU THINKING ABOUT?
...MY FATHER.
THE THING THAT KILLED HIM. THE SOUND IT MADE WHEN IT ATE HIM.
THE WAY IT SMILED AT ME AFTER.
ANGER IS JUST FEAR. FEAR IS WHAT THEY FEED ON.
SO WHAT ARE YOU AFRAID OF, ANGEL?
LETTING THEM WIN.
REST TONIGHT.
WE'RE HUNTING TOMORROW.

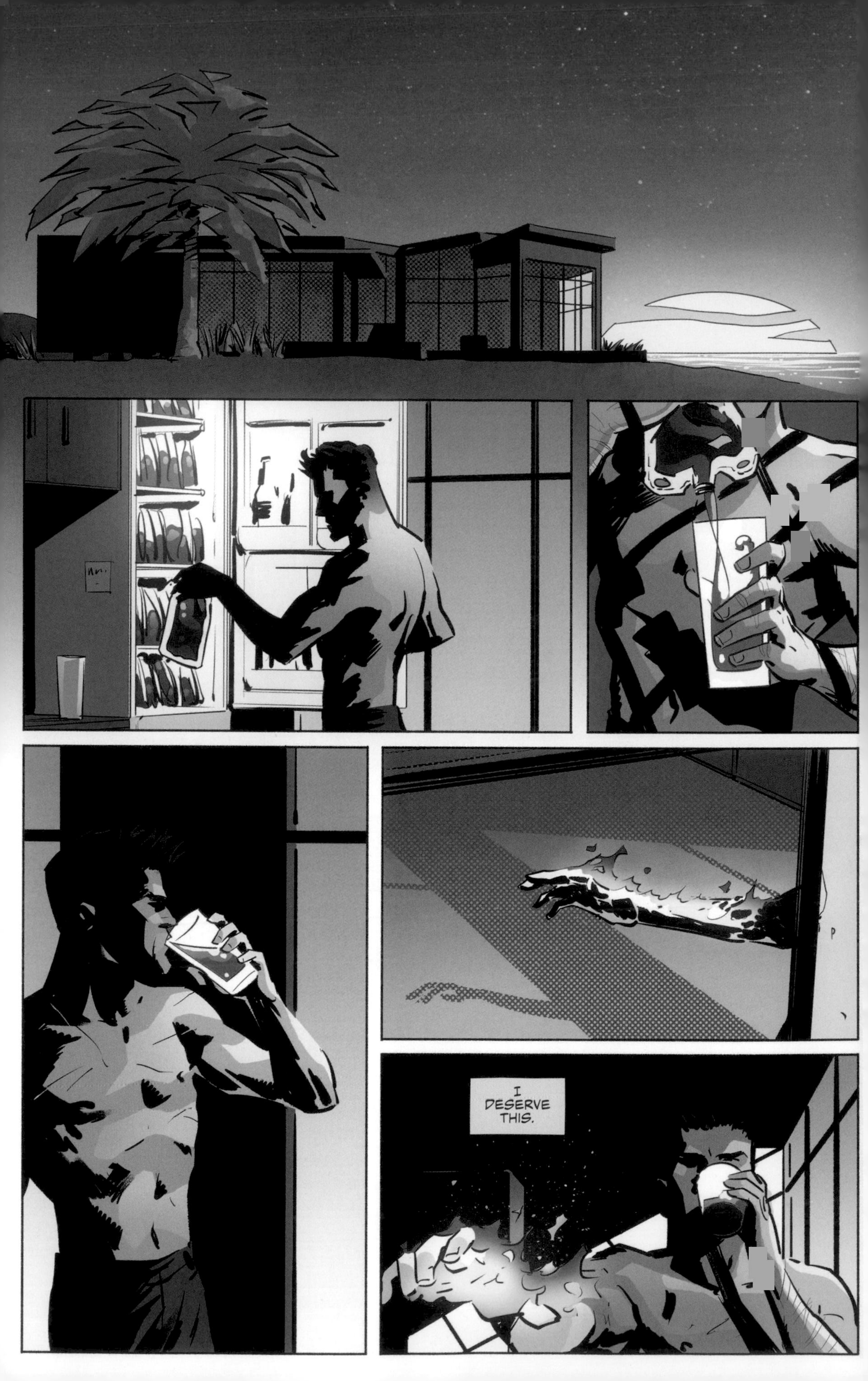
I DESERVE THIS.

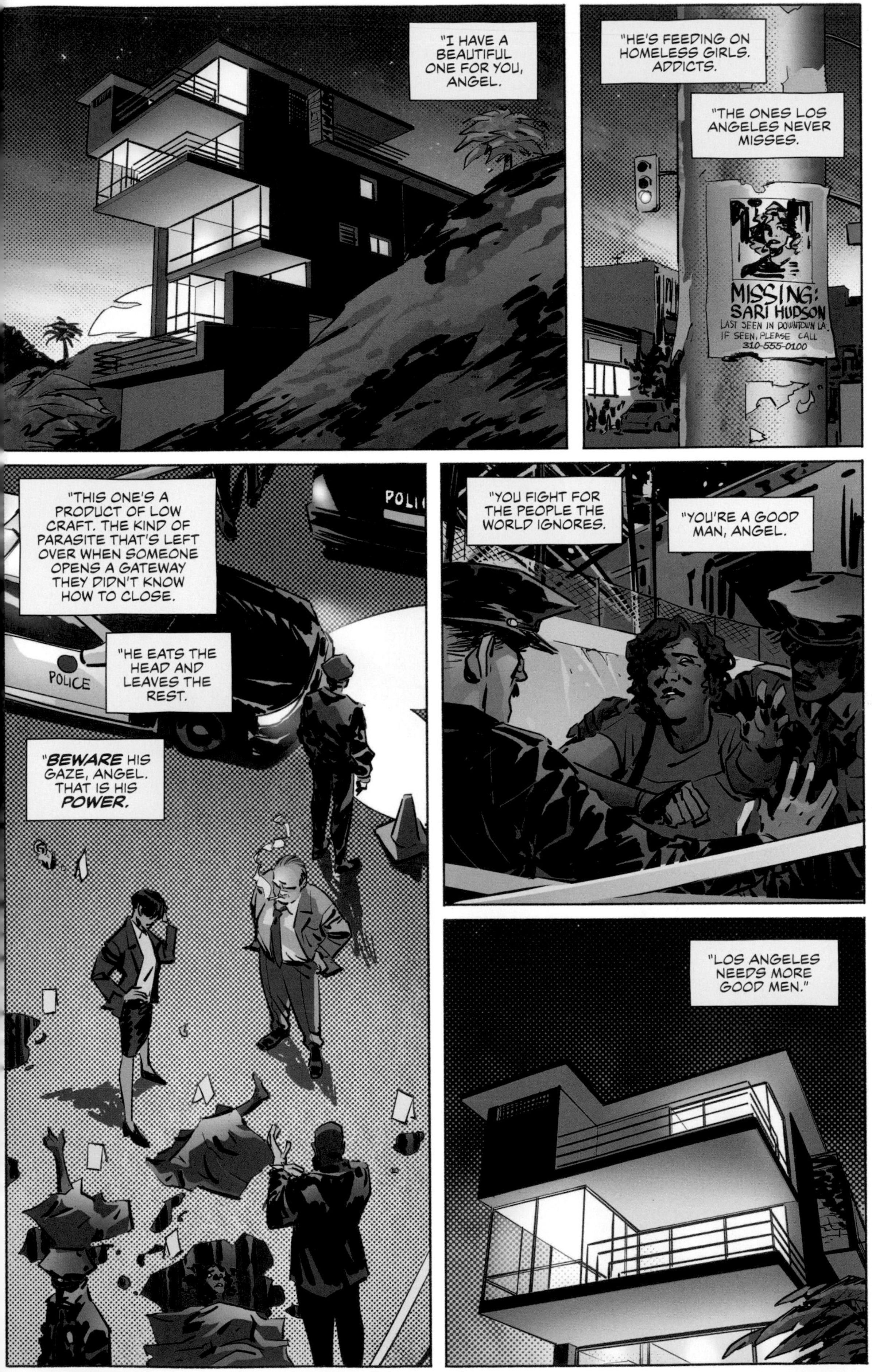
"I HAVE A BEAUTIFUL ONE FOR YOU, ANGEL.
"HE'S FEEDING ON HOMELESS GIRLS. ADDICTS.
"THE ONES LOS ANGELES NEVER MISSES.
MISSING: SARI HUDSON
LAST SEEN IN DOWNTOWN LA
IF SEEN, PLEASE CALL 310-555-0100
"THIS ONE'S A PRODUCT OF LOW CRAFT. THE KIND OF PARASITE THAT'S LEFT OVER WHEN SOMEONE OPENS A GATEWAY THEY DIDN'T KNOW HOW TO CLOSE.
POLICE
"HE EATS THE HEAD AND LEAVES THE REST.
"***BEWARE*** HIS GAZE, ANGEL. THAT IS HIS ***POWER.***
"YOU FIGHT FOR THE PEOPLE THE WORLD IGNORES.
"YOU'RE A GOOD MAN, ANGEL.
"LOS ANGELES NEEDS MORE GOOD MEN."

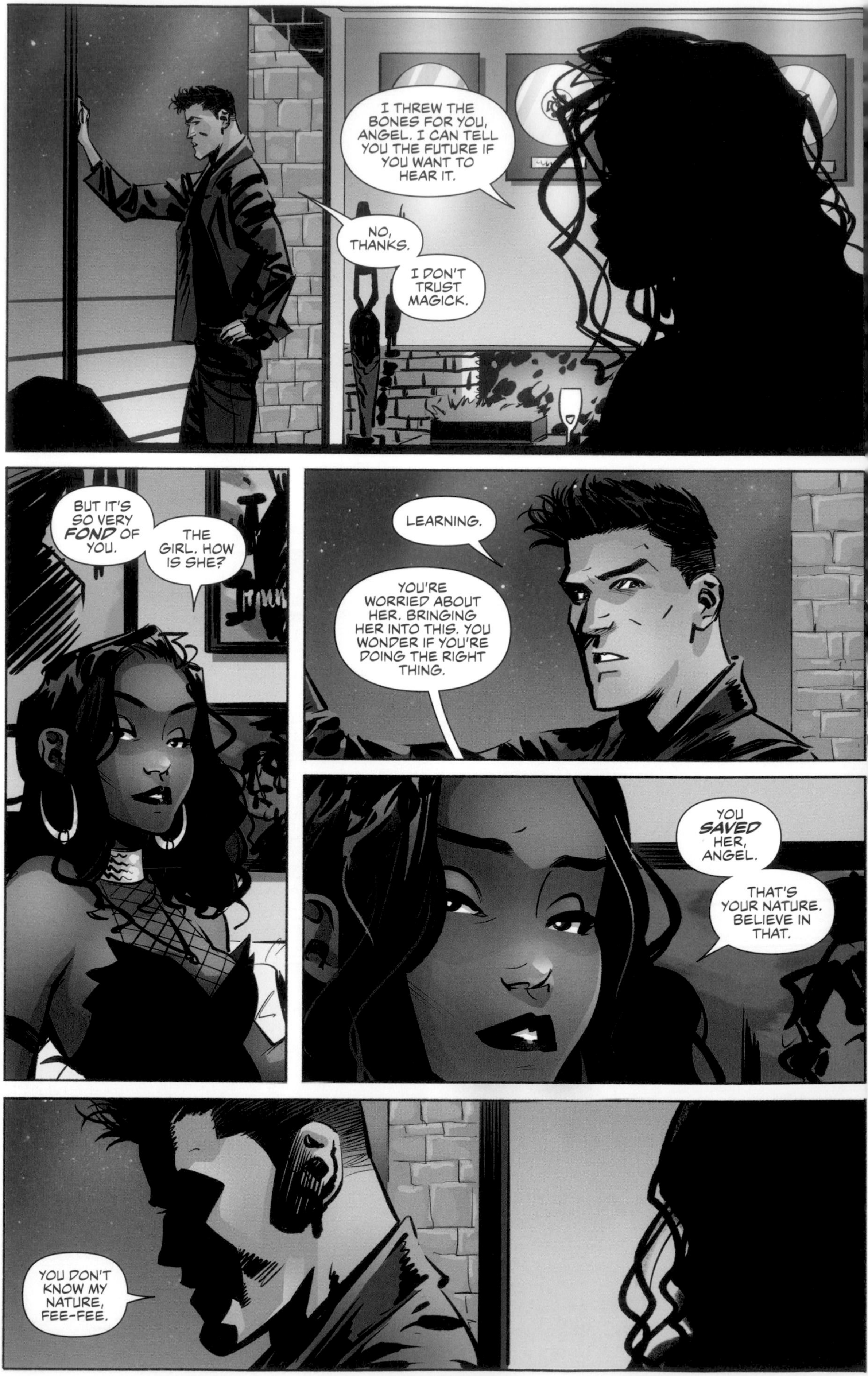

I THREW THE BONES FOR YOU, ANGEL. I CAN TELL YOU THE FUTURE IF YOU WANT TO HEAR IT.
NO, THANKS.
I DON'T TRUST MAGICK.
BUT IT'S SO VERY FOND OF YOU.
THE GIRL. HOW IS SHE?
LEARNING.
YOU'RE WORRIED ABOUT HER. BRINGING HER INTO THIS. YOU WONDER IF YOU'RE DOING THE RIGHT THING.
YOU SAVED HER, ANGEL.
THAT'S YOUR NATURE. BELIEVE IN THAT.
YOU DON'T KNOW MY NATURE, FEE-FEE.

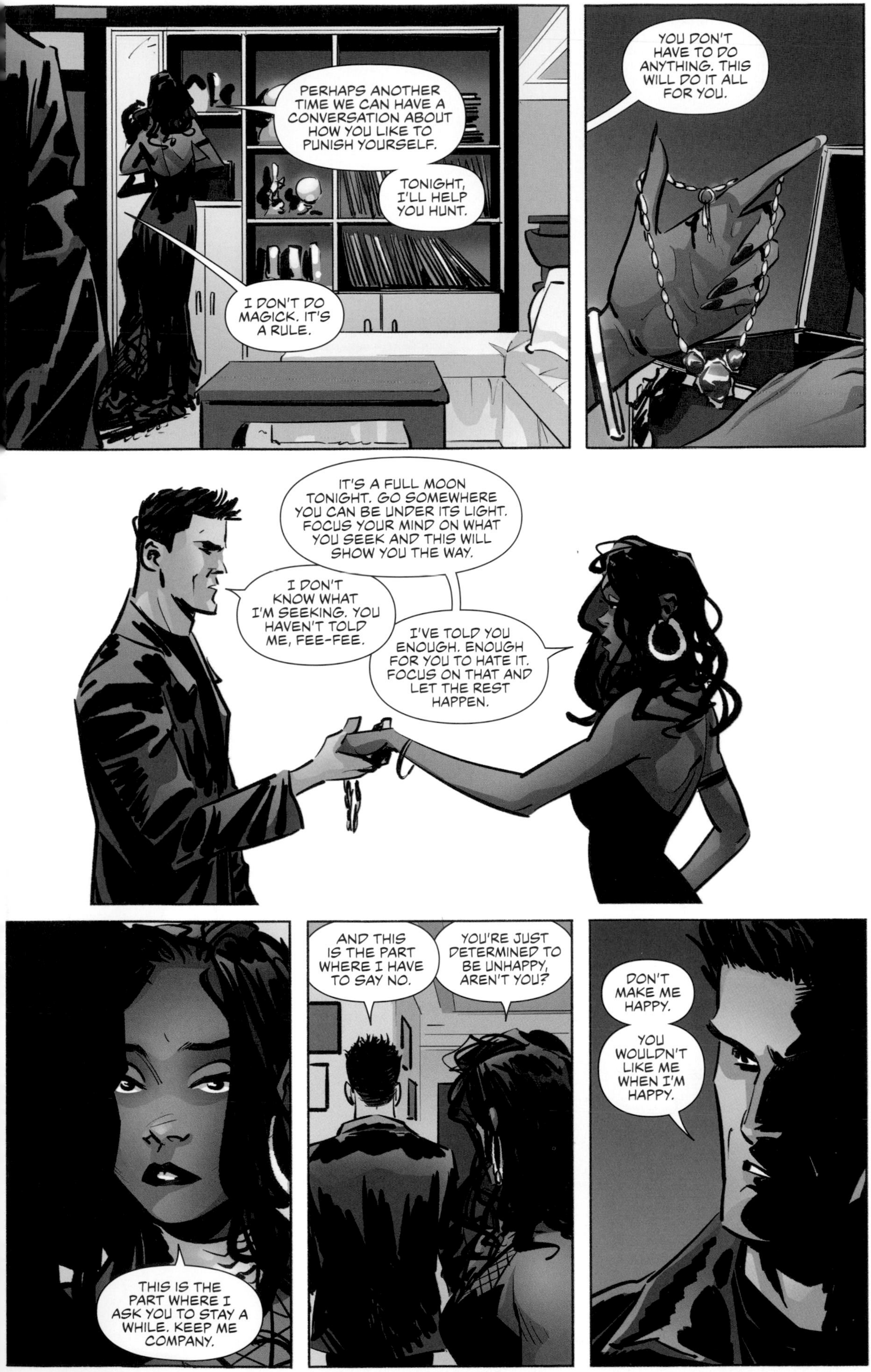
PERHAPS ANOTHER TIME WE CAN HAVE A CONVERSATION ABOUT HOW YOU LIKE TO PUNISH YOURSELF.
TONIGHT, I'LL HELP YOU HUNT.
I DON'T DO MAGICK. IT'S A RULE.
YOU DON'T HAVE TO DO ANYTHING. THIS WILL DO IT ALL FOR YOU.
IT'S A FULL MOON TONIGHT. GO SOMEWHERE YOU CAN BE UNDER ITS LIGHT. FOCUS YOUR MIND ON WHAT YOU SEEK AND THIS WILL SHOW YOU THE WAY.
I DON'T KNOW WHAT I'M SEEKING. YOU HAVEN'T TOLD ME, FEE-FEE.
I'VE TOLD YOU ENOUGH. ENOUGH FOR YOU TO HATE IT. FOCUS ON THAT AND LET THE REST HAPPEN.
THIS IS THE PART WHERE I ASK YOU TO STAY A WHILE. KEEP ME COMPANY.
AND THIS IS THE PART WHERE I HAVE TO SAY NO.
YOU'RE JUST DETERMINED TO BE UNHAPPY, AREN'T YOU?
DON'T MAKE ME HAPPY.
YOU WOULDN'T LIKE ME WHEN I'M HAPPY.

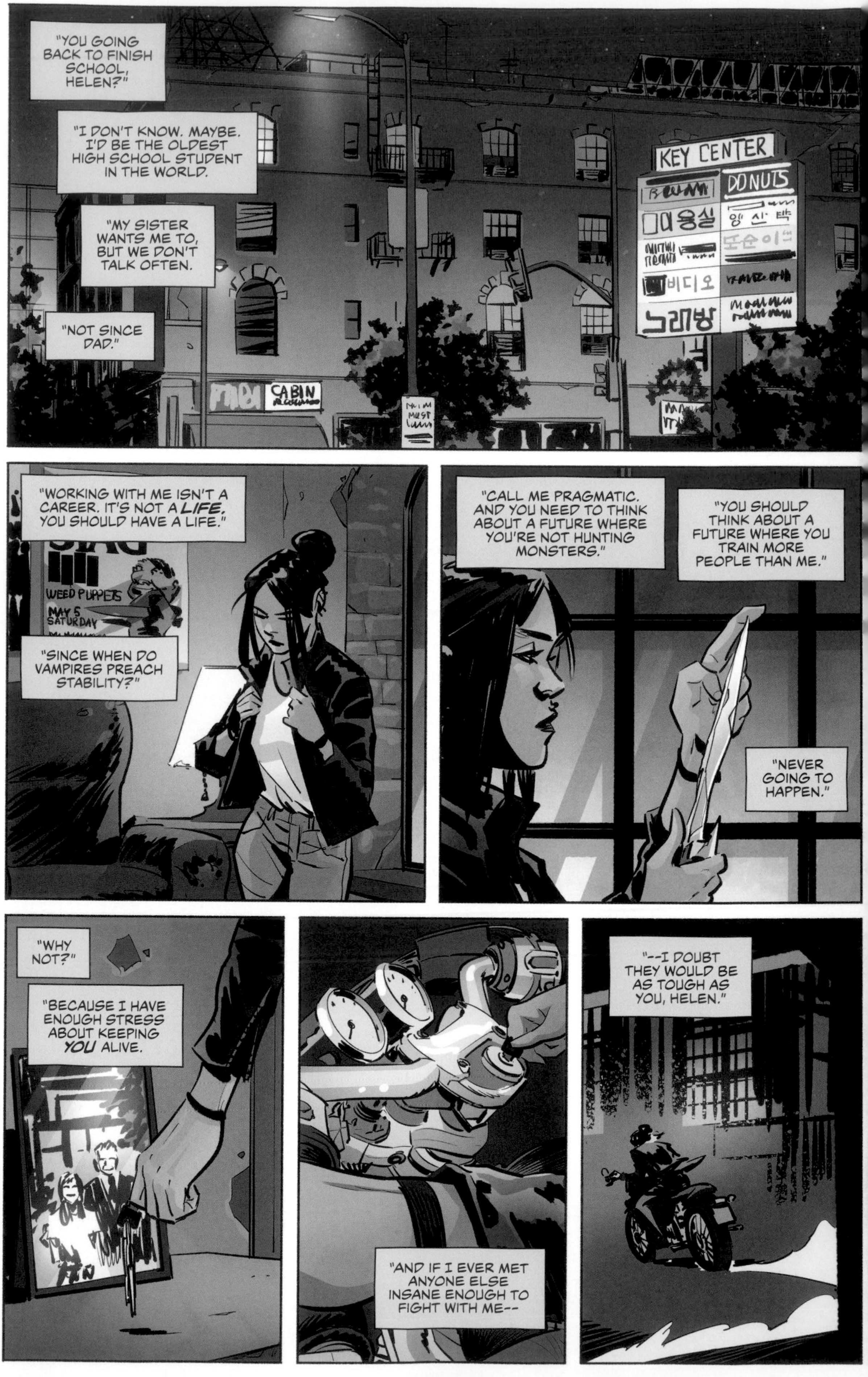
"YOU GOING BACK TO FINISH SCHOOL, HELEN?"
"I DON'T KNOW. MAYBE. I'D BE THE OLDEST HIGH SCHOOL STUDENT IN THE WORLD.
"MY SISTER WANTS ME TO, BUT WE DON'T TALK OFTEN.
"NOT SINCE DAD."
KEY CENTER
DONUTS
미용실
비디오
노래방
CABIN
"WORKING WITH ME ISN'T A CAREER. IT'S NOT A ***LIFE.*** YOU SHOULD HAVE A LIFE."
WEED PUPPETS
MAY 5 SATURDAY
"SINCE WHEN DO VAMPIRES PREACH STABILITY?"
"CALL ME PRAGMATIC. AND YOU NEED TO THINK ABOUT A FUTURE WHERE YOU'RE NOT HUNTING MONSTERS."
"YOU SHOULD THINK ABOUT A FUTURE WHERE YOU TRAIN MORE PEOPLE THAN ME."
"NEVER GOING TO HAPPEN."
"WHY NOT?"
"BECAUSE I HAVE ENOUGH STRESS ABOUT KEEPING ***YOU*** ALIVE.
"AND IF I EVER MET ANYONE ELSE INSANE ENOUGH TO FIGHT WITH ME--
"--I DOUBT THEY WOULD BE AS TOUGH AS YOU, HELEN."

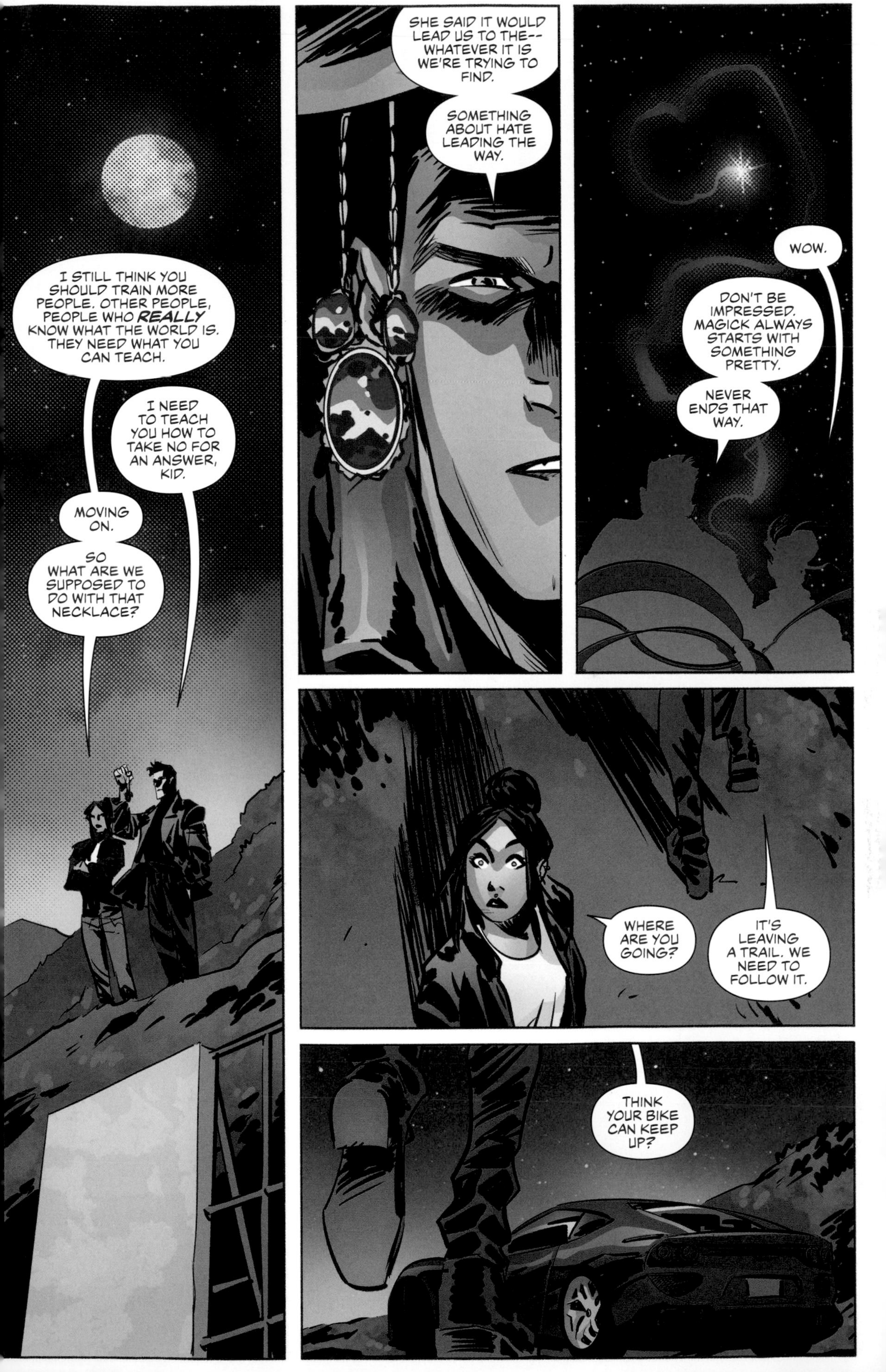
I STILL THINK YOU SHOULD TRAIN MORE PEOPLE. OTHER PEOPLE, PEOPLE WHO *REALLY* KNOW WHAT THE WORLD IS. THEY NEED WHAT YOU CAN TEACH.
I NEED TO TEACH YOU HOW TO TAKE NO FOR AN ANSWER, KID.
MOVING ON.
SO WHAT ARE WE SUPPOSED TO DO WITH THAT NECKLACE?
SHE SAID IT WOULD LEAD US TO THE-- WHATEVER IT IS WE'RE TRYING TO FIND.
SOMETHING ABOUT HATE LEADING THE WAY.
WOW.
DON'T BE IMPRESSED. MAGICK ALWAYS STARTS WITH SOMETHING PRETTY.
NEVER ENDS THAT WAY.
WHERE ARE YOU GOING?
IT'S LEAVING A TRAIL. WE NEED TO FOLLOW IT.
THINK YOUR BIKE CAN KEEP UP?

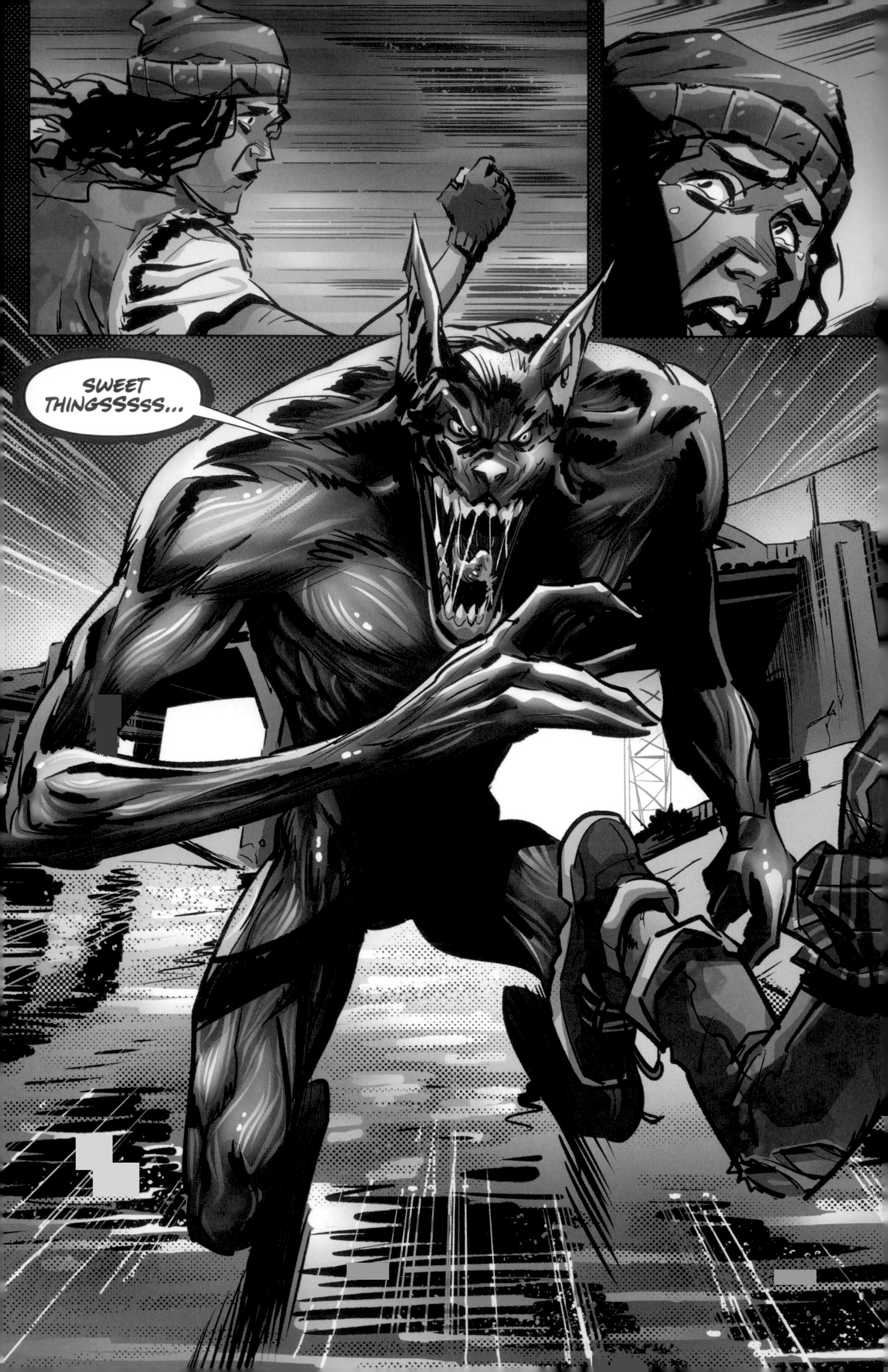
SWEET THINGSSSSS...

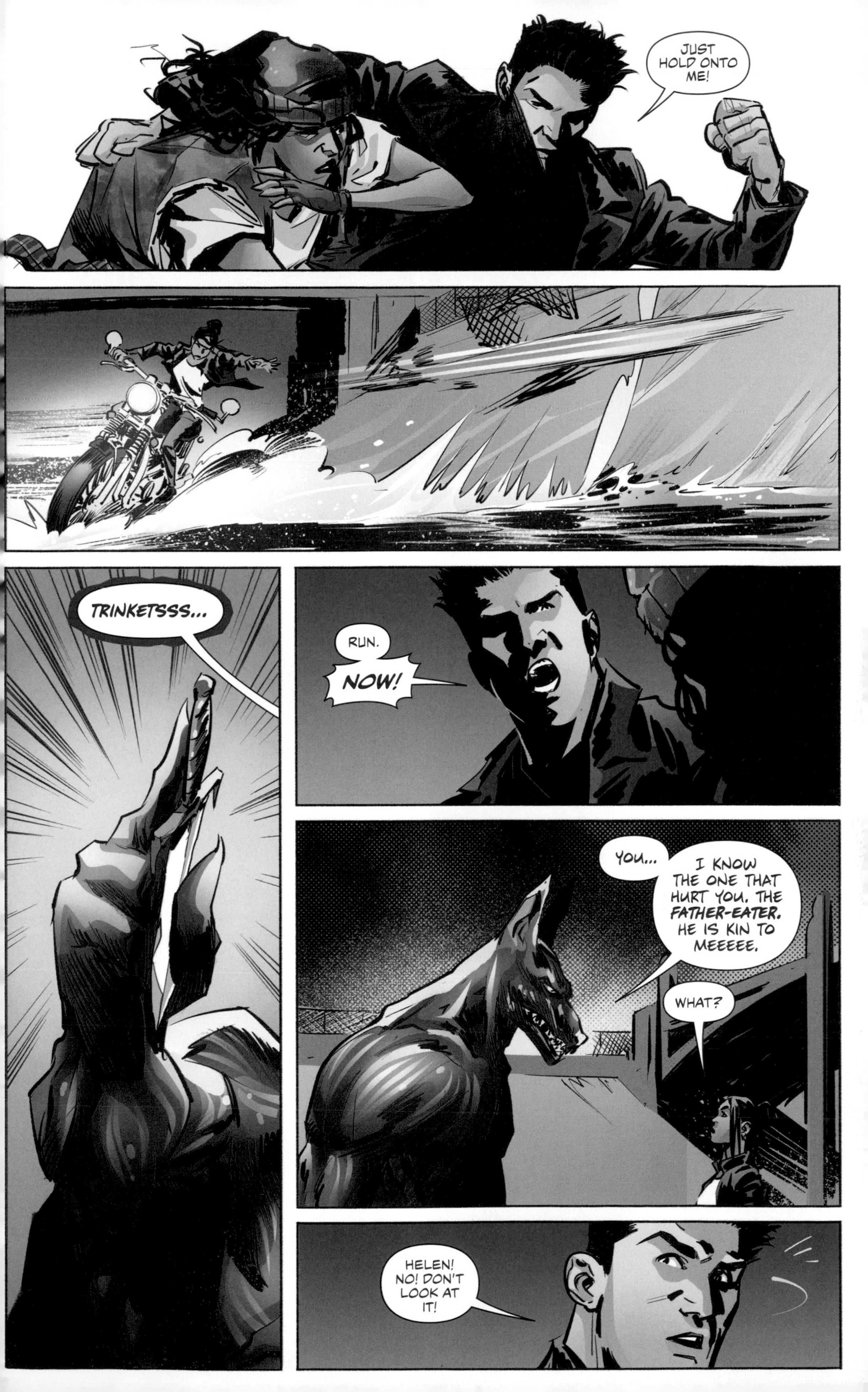
JUST HOLD ONTO ME!
TRINKETSSS...
RUN.
NOW!
YOU...
I KNOW THE ONE THAT HURT YOU. THE FATHER-EATER. HE IS KIN TO MEEEEE.
WHAT?
HELEN! NO! DON'T LOOK AT IT!

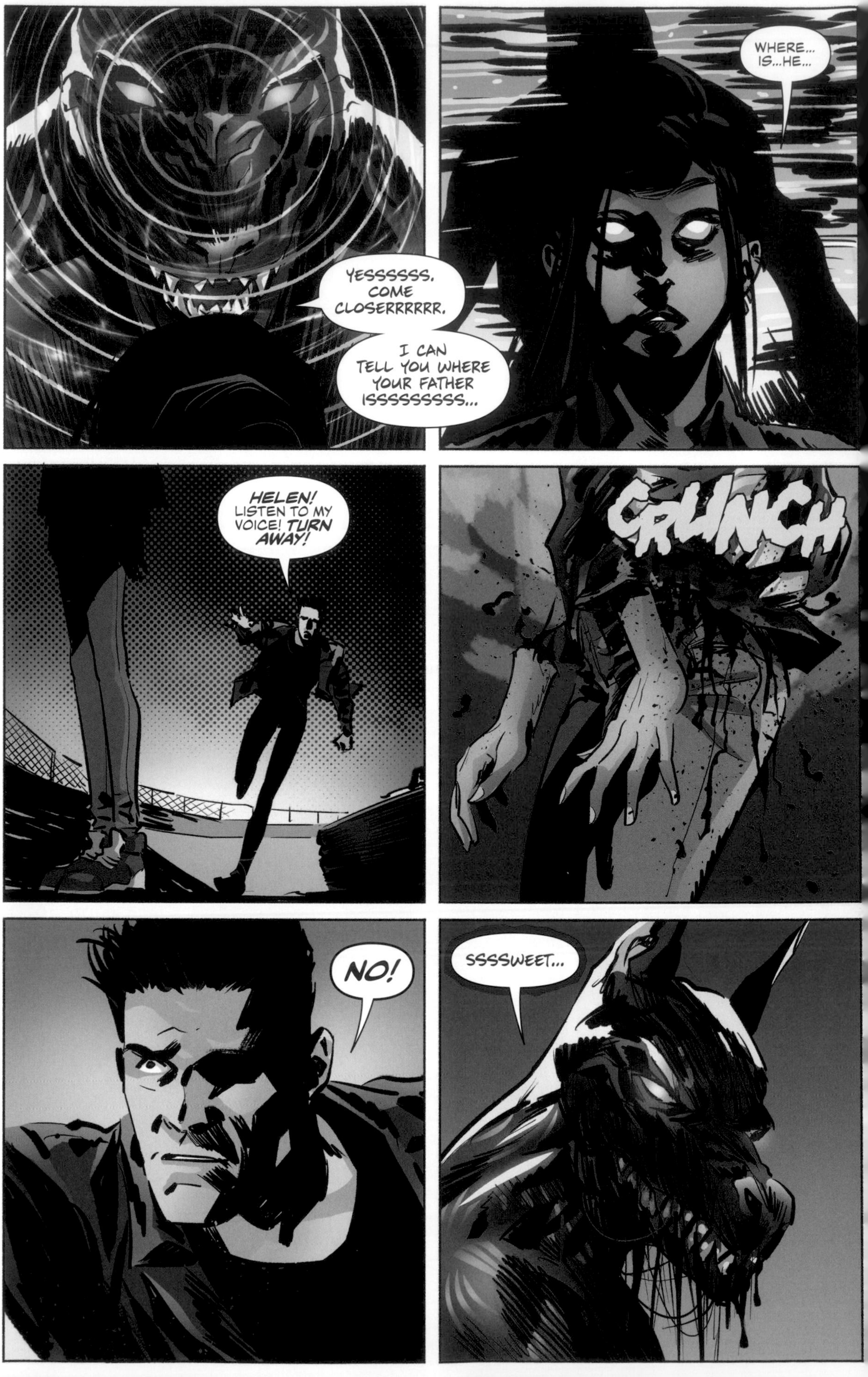
YESSSSSS. COME CLOSERRRRRR.
I CAN TELL YOU WHERE YOUR FATHER ISSSSSSSSS...
WHERE... IS...HE...
HELEN! LISTEN TO MY VOICE! TURN AWAY!
CRUNCH
NO!
SSSSWEET...

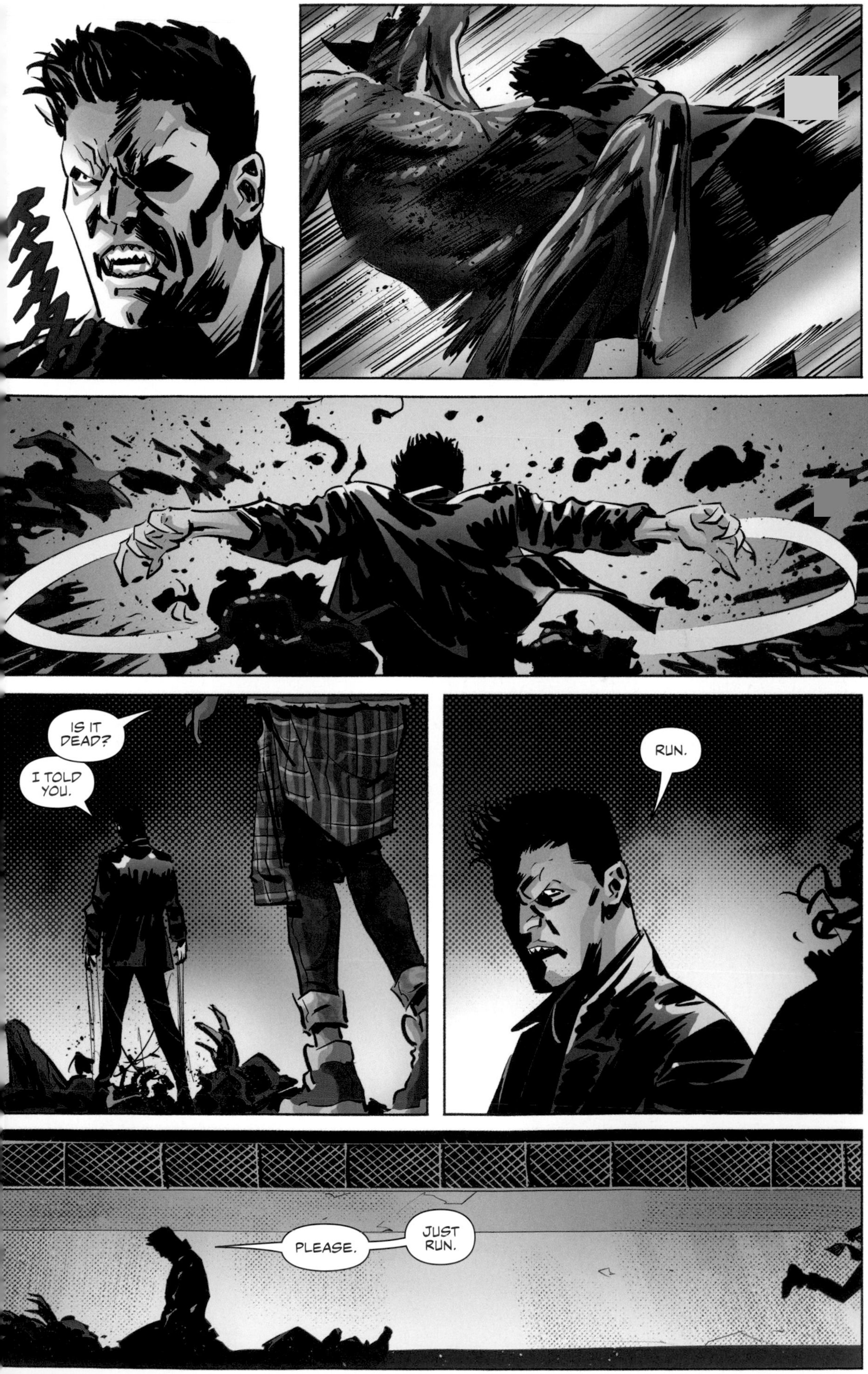

IS IT DEAD?
I TOLD YOU.
RUN.
PLEASE.
JUST RUN.

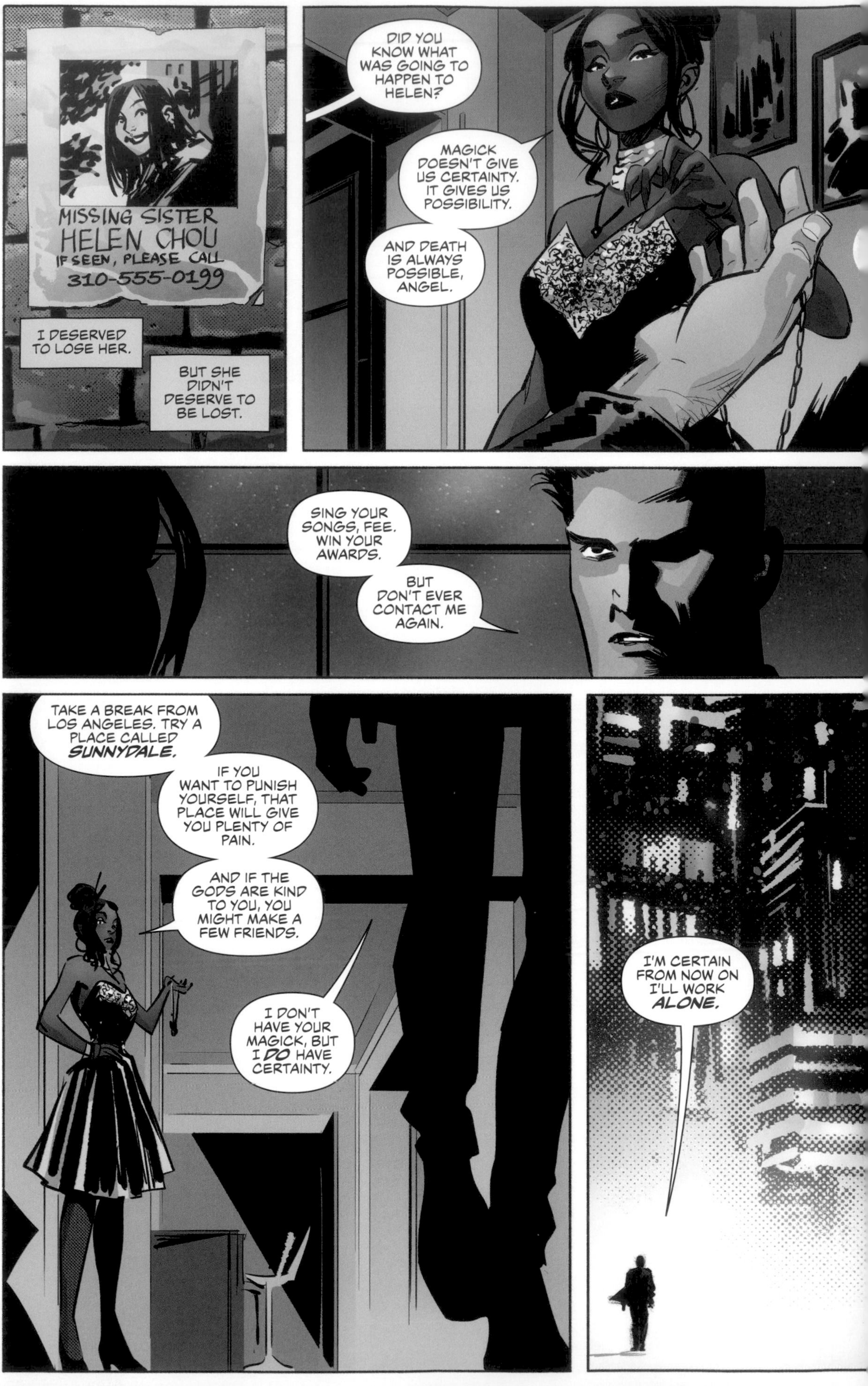
MISSING SISTER
HELEN CHOU
IF SEEN, PLEASE CALL
310-555-0199
I DESERVED TO LOSE HER.
BUT SHE DIDN'T DESERVE TO BE LOST.
DID YOU KNOW WHAT WAS GOING TO HAPPEN TO HELEN?
MAGICK DOESN'T GIVE US CERTAINTY. IT GIVES US POSSIBILITY.
AND DEATH IS ALWAYS POSSIBLE, ANGEL.
SING YOUR SONGS, FEE. WIN YOUR AWARDS.
BUT DON'T EVER CONTACT ME AGAIN.
TAKE A BREAK FROM LOS ANGELES. TRY A PLACE CALLED SUNNYDALE.
IF YOU WANT TO PUNISH YOURSELF, THAT PLACE WILL GIVE YOU PLENTY OF PAIN.
AND IF THE GODS ARE KIND TO YOU, YOU MIGHT MAKE A FEW FRIENDS.
I DON'T HAVE YOUR MAGICK, BUT I DO HAVE CERTAINTY.
I'M CERTAIN FROM NOW ON I'LL WORK ALONE.

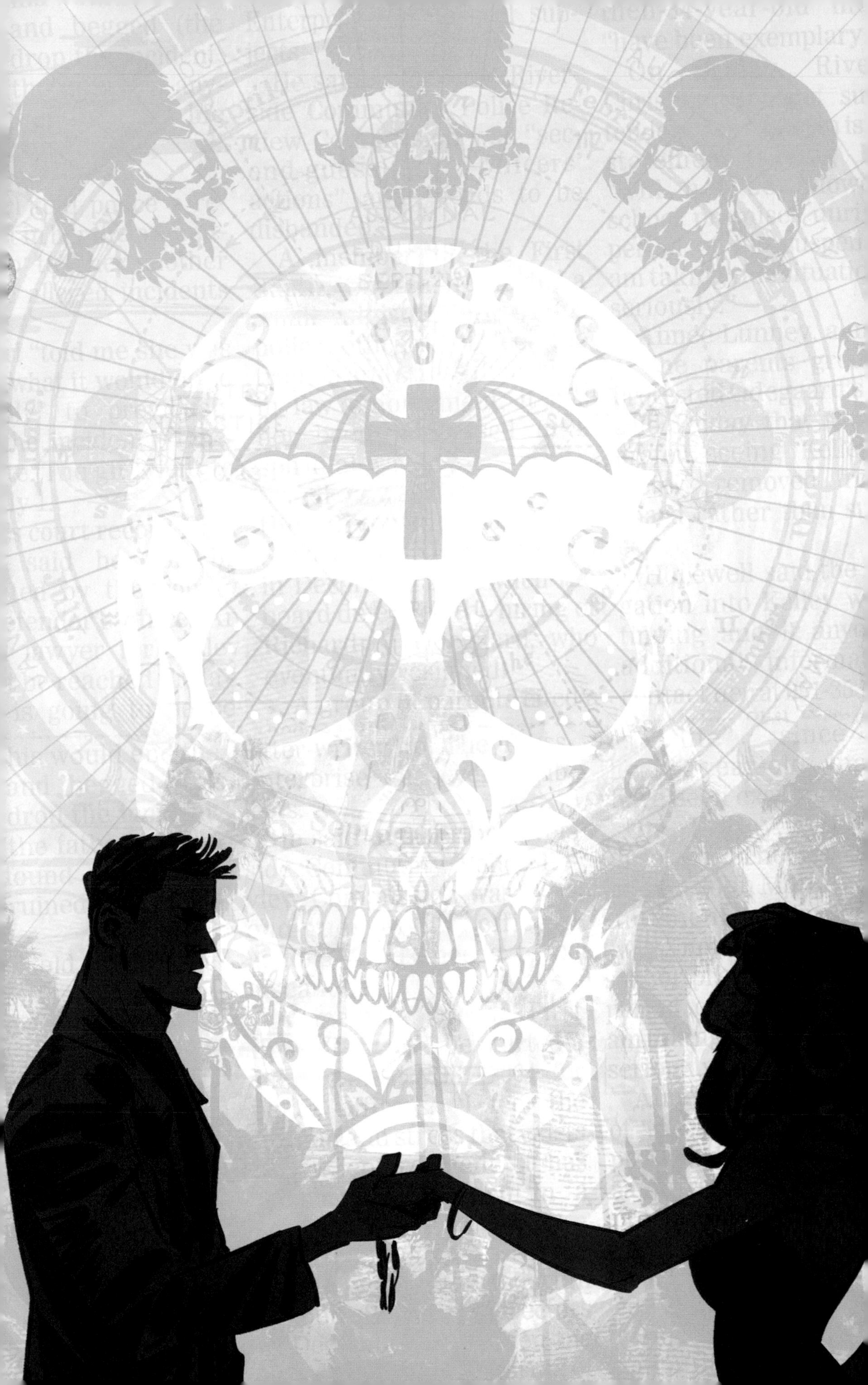

CHAPTER
ONE

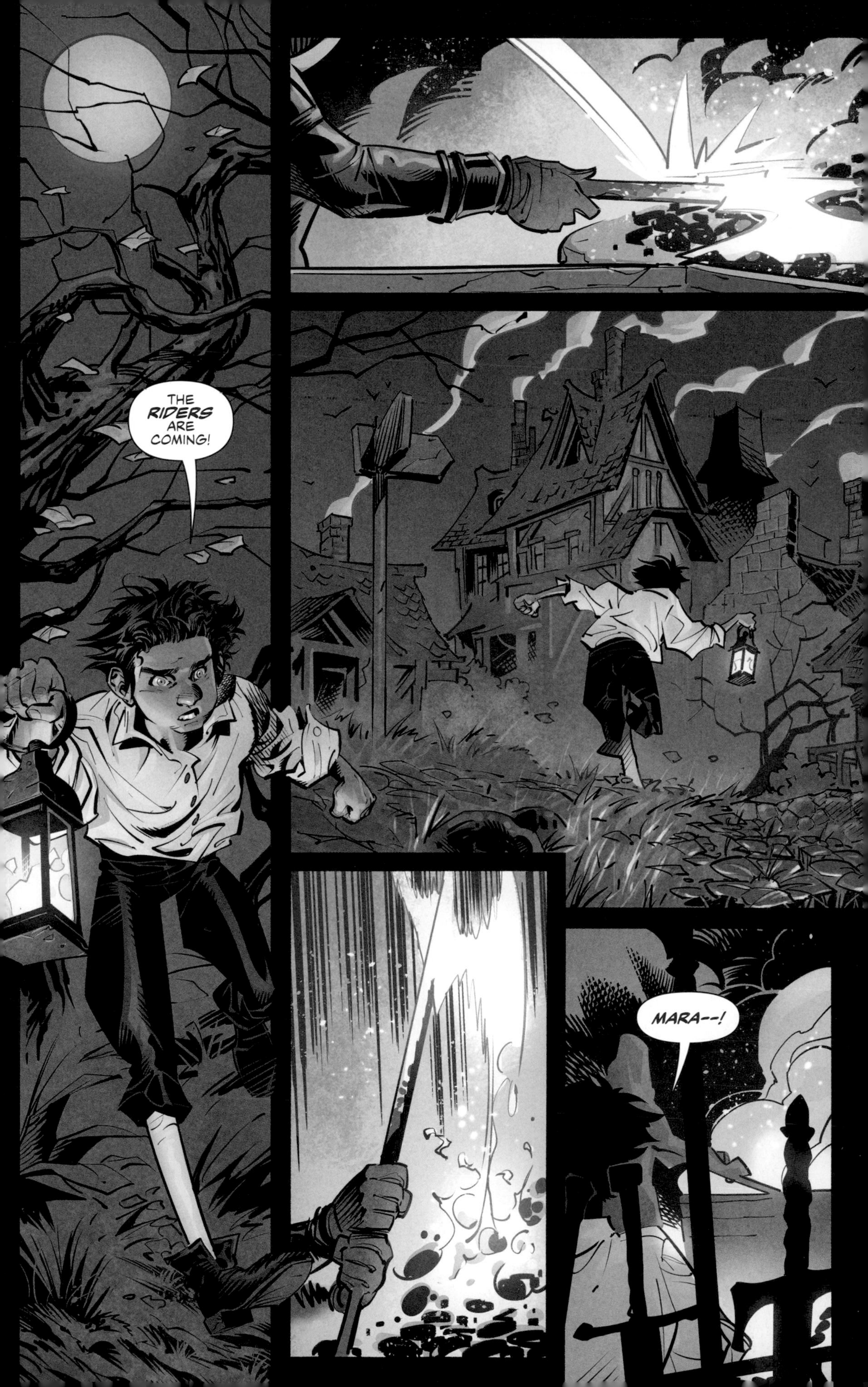
THE *RIDERS* ARE COMING!
MARA--!

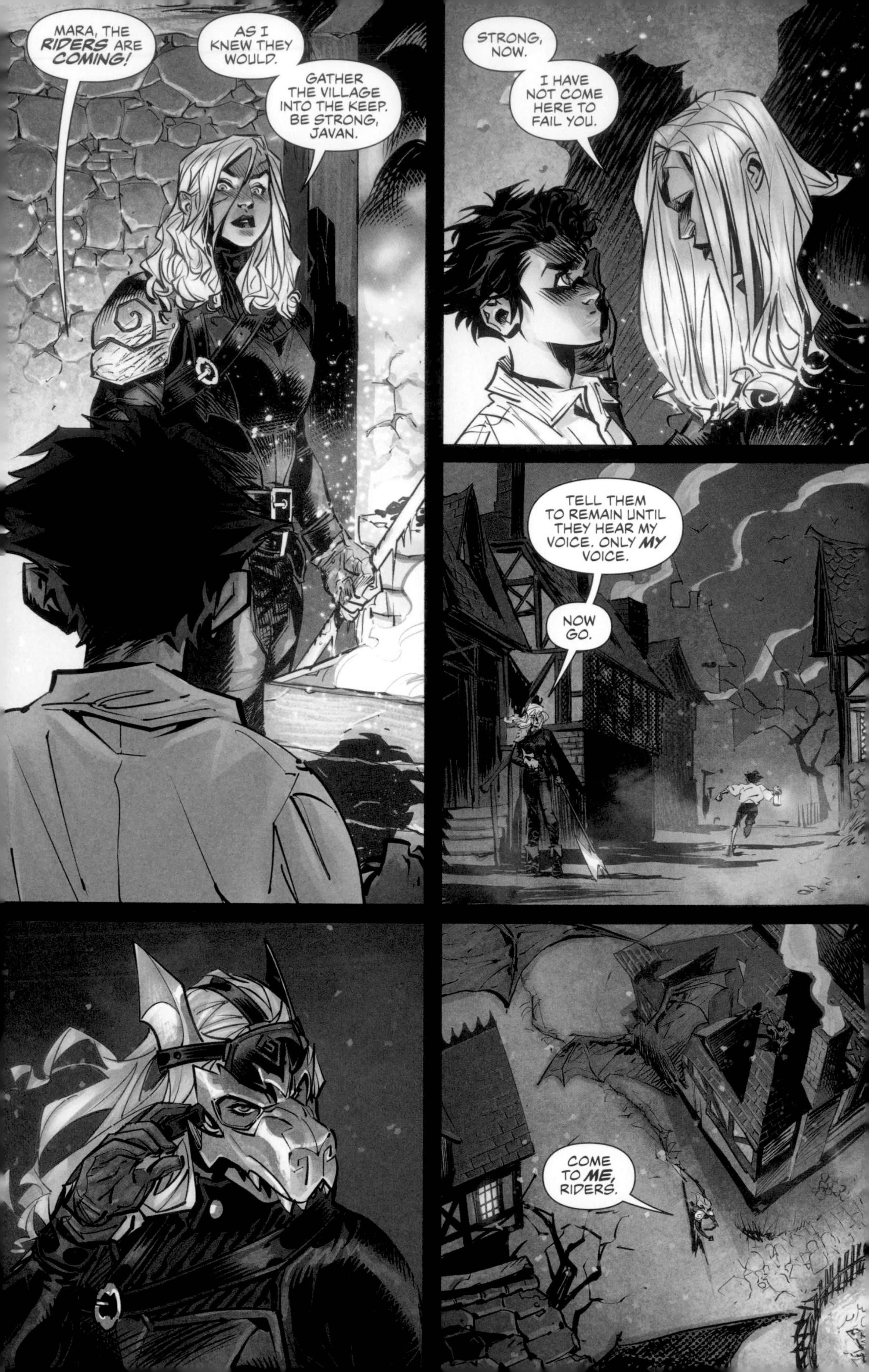
MARA, THE RIDERS ARE COMING!
AS I KNEW THEY WOULD.
GATHER THE VILLAGE INTO THE KEEP. BE STRONG, JAVAN.
STRONG, NOW.
I HAVE NOT COME HERE TO FAIL YOU.
TELL THEM TO REMAIN UNTIL THEY HEAR MY VOICE. ONLY MY VOICE.
NOW GO.
COME TO ME, RIDERS.

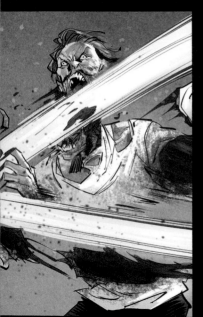

PESTE!

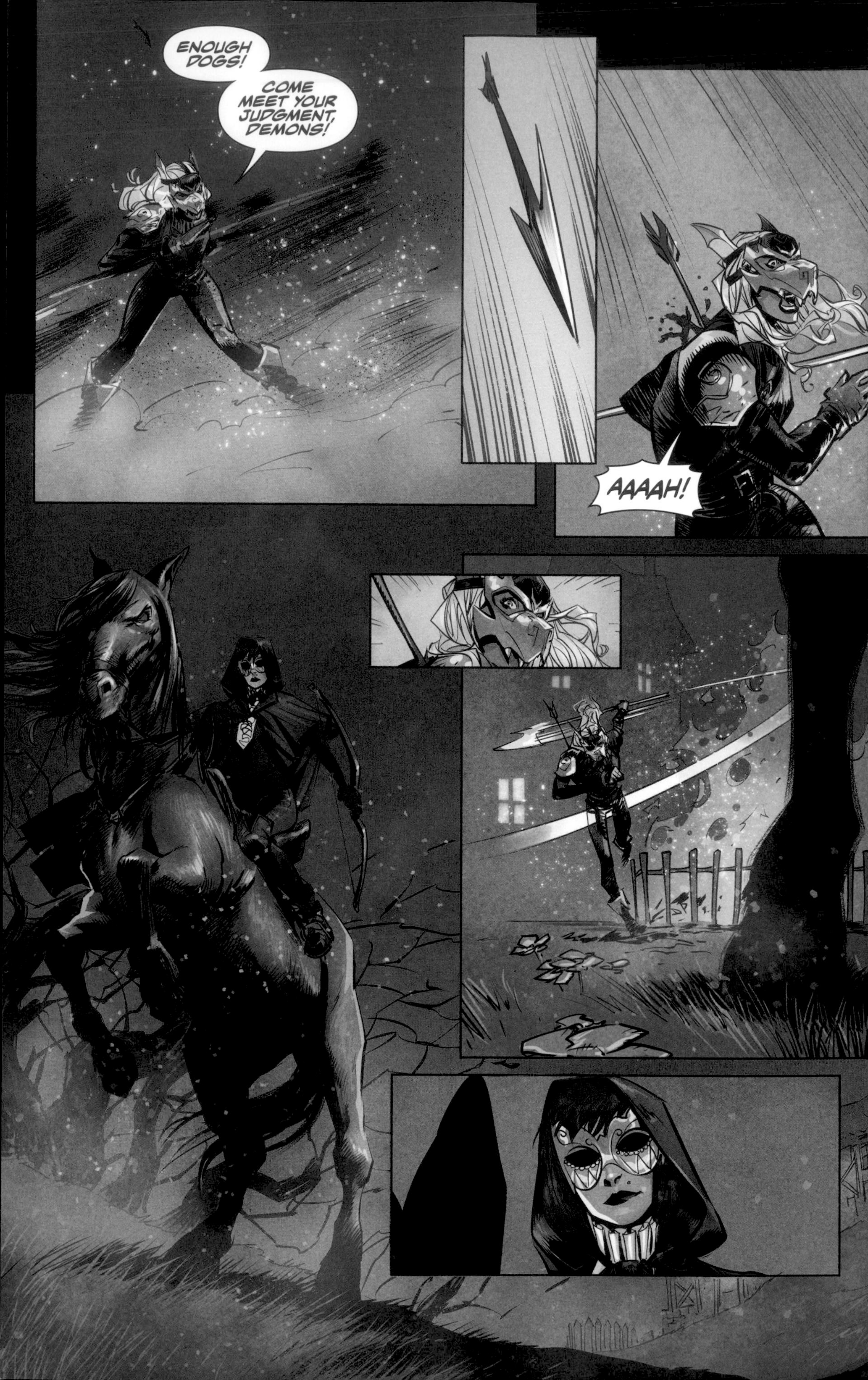

ENOUGH DOGS!
COME MEET YOUR JUDGMENT, DEMONS!
AAAAH!

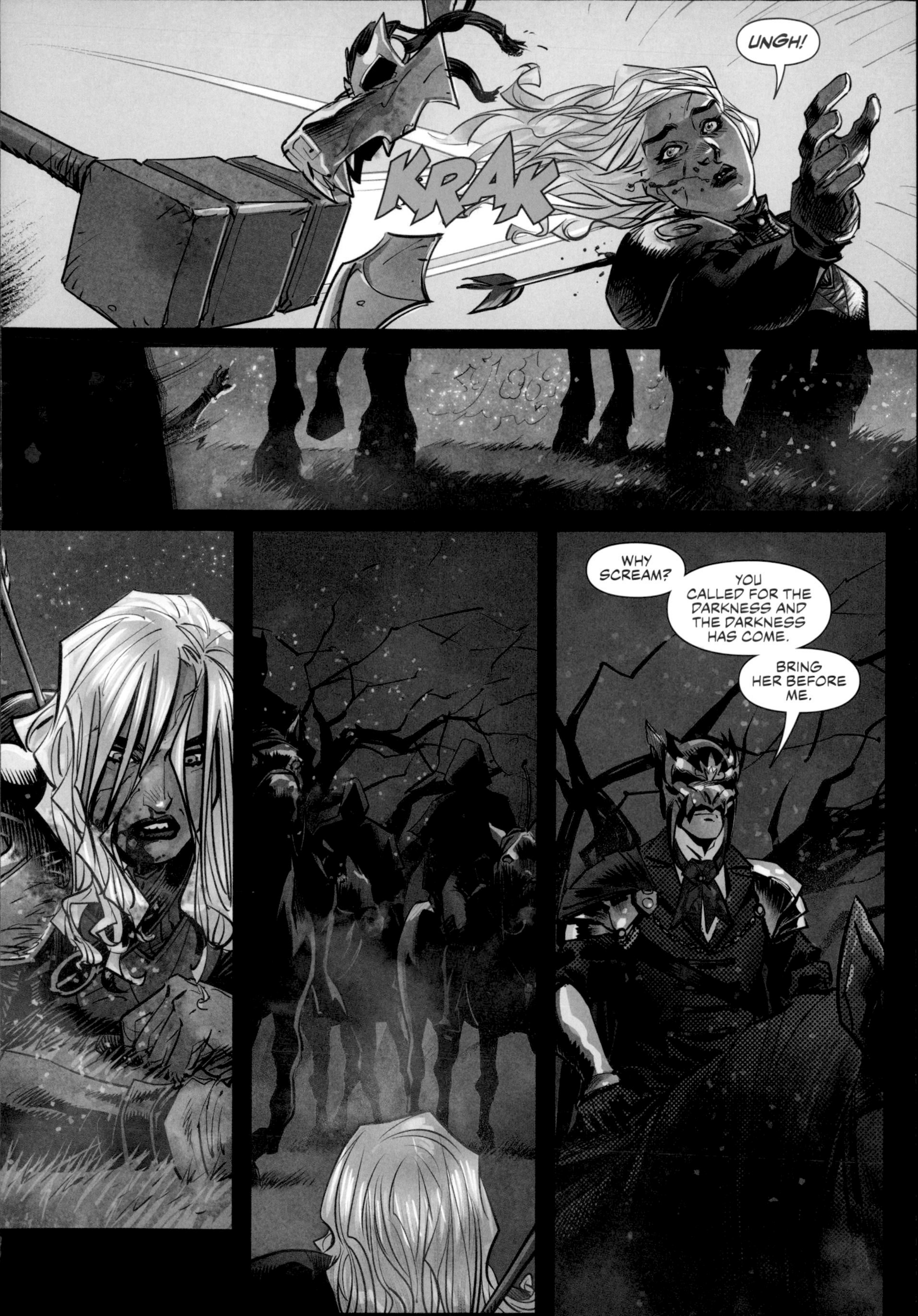
UNGH!
KRAK
WHY SCREAM?
YOU CALLED FOR THE DARKNESS AND THE DARKNESS HAS COME.
BRING HER BEFORE ME.

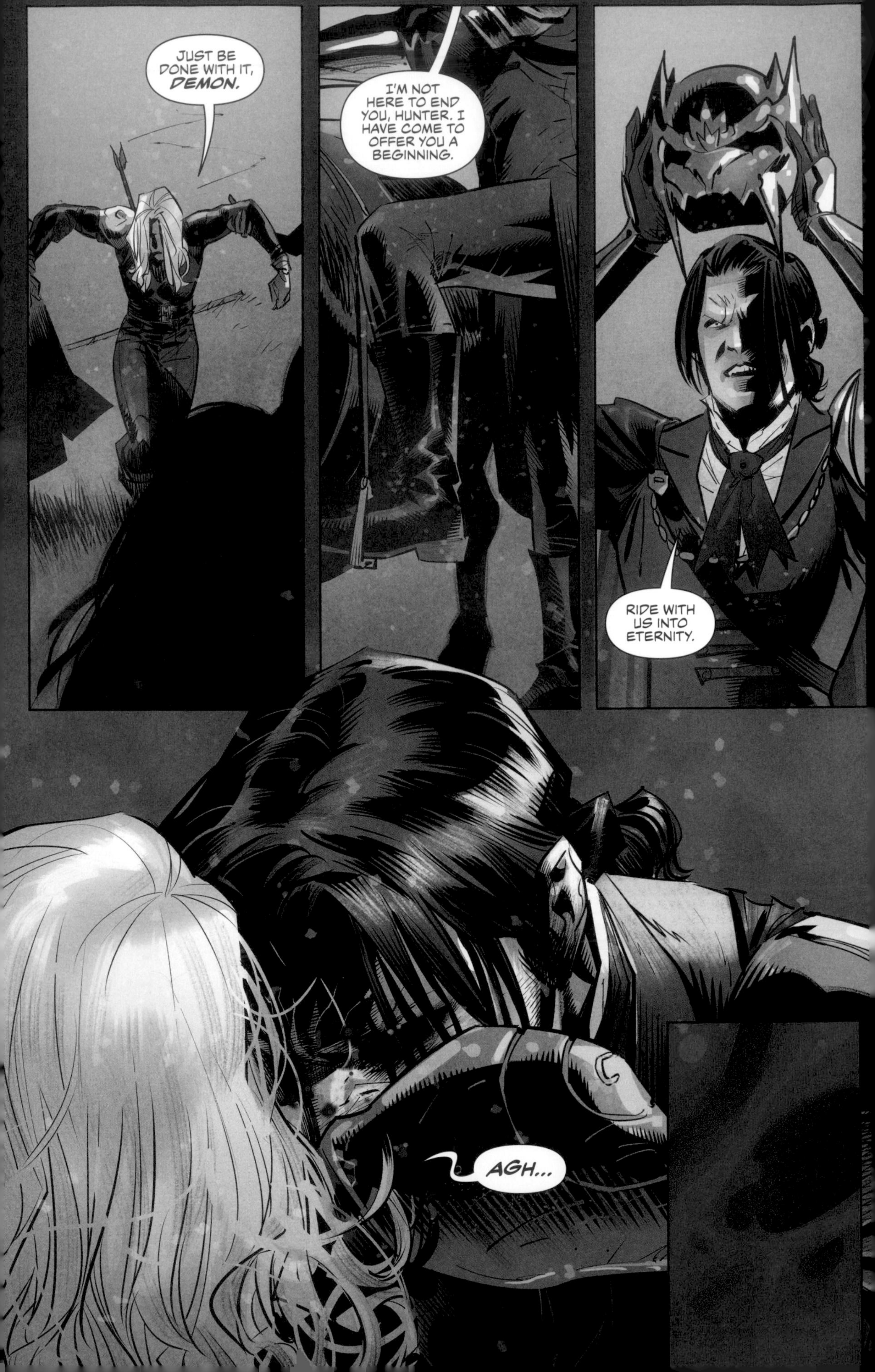
JUST BE DONE WITH IT, *DEMON.*
I'M NOT HERE TO END YOU, HUNTER. I HAVE COME TO OFFER YOU A BEGINNING.
RIDE WITH US INTO ETERNITY.
AGH...

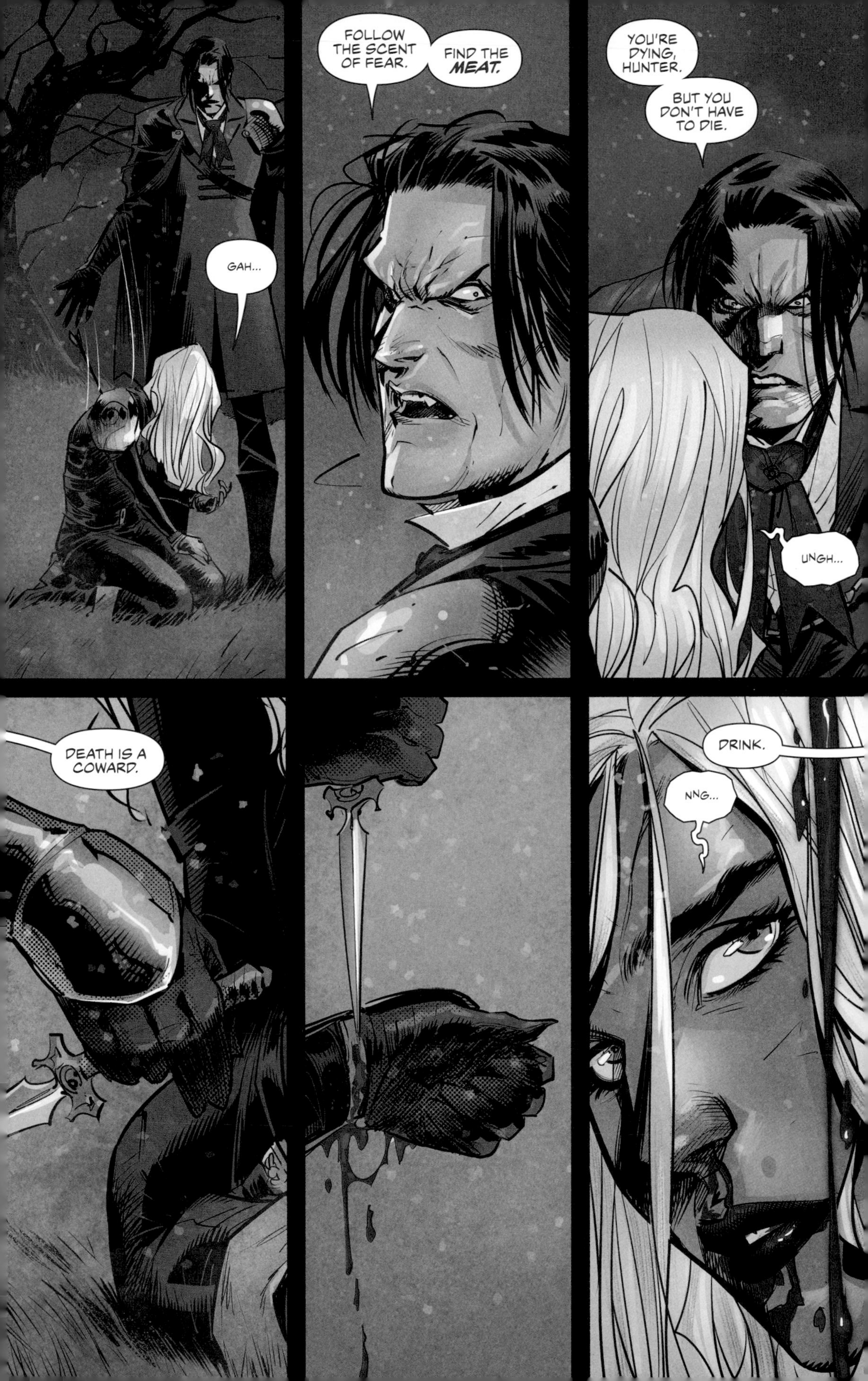
GAH...
FOLLOW THE SCENT OF FEAR.
FIND THE *MEAT.*
YOU'RE DYING, HUNTER.
BUT YOU DON'T HAVE TO DIE.
UNGH...
DEATH IS A COWARD.
DRINK.
NNG...

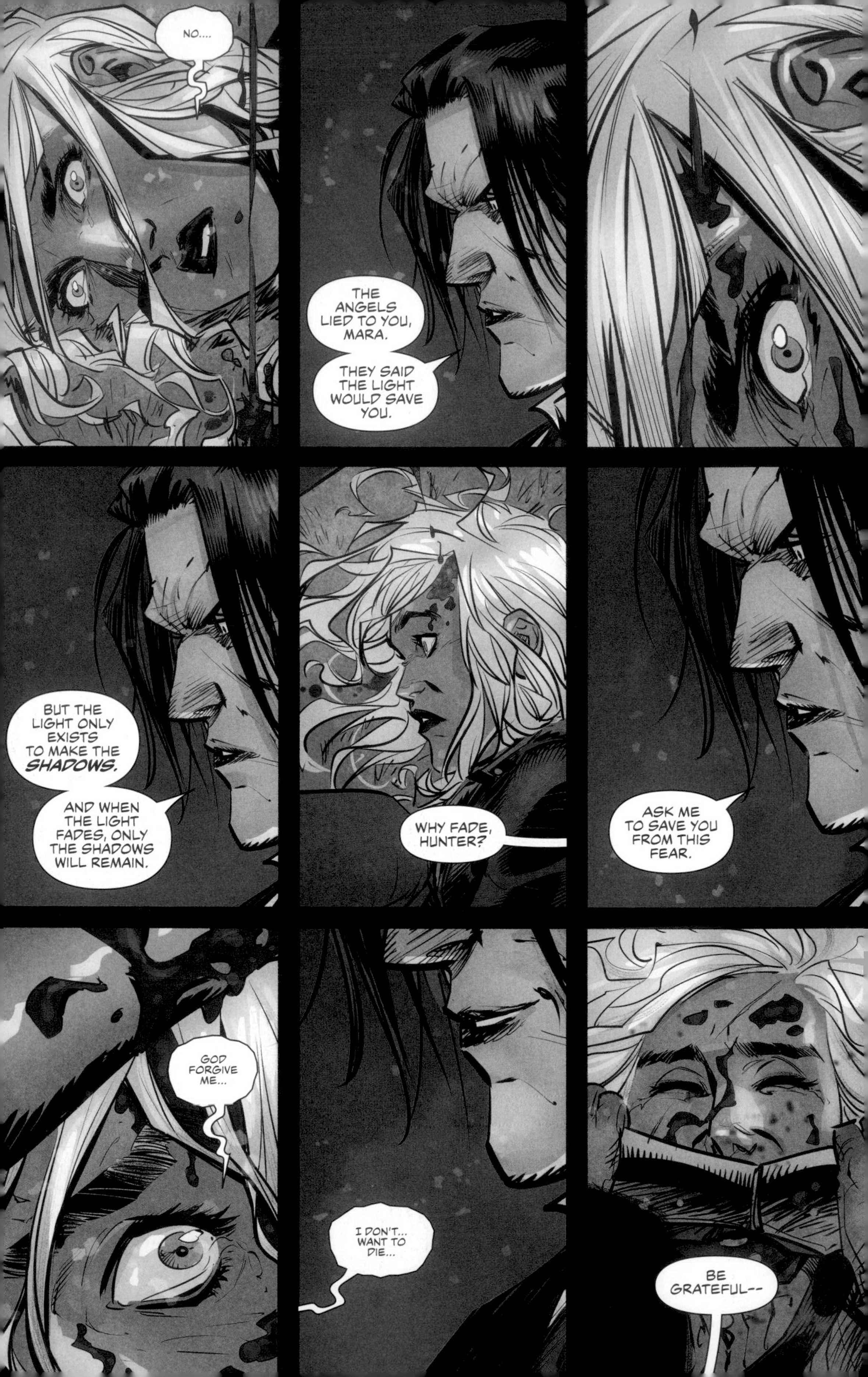
NO....
THE ANGELS LIED TO YOU, MARA.
THEY SAID THE LIGHT WOULD SAVE YOU.
BUT THE LIGHT ONLY EXISTS TO MAKE THE SHADOWS.
AND WHEN THE LIGHT FADES, ONLY THE SHADOWS WILL REMAIN.
WHY FADE, HUNTER?
ASK ME TO SAVE YOU FROM THIS FEAR.
GOD FORGIVE ME...
I DON'T... WANT TO DIE...
BE GRATEFUL--

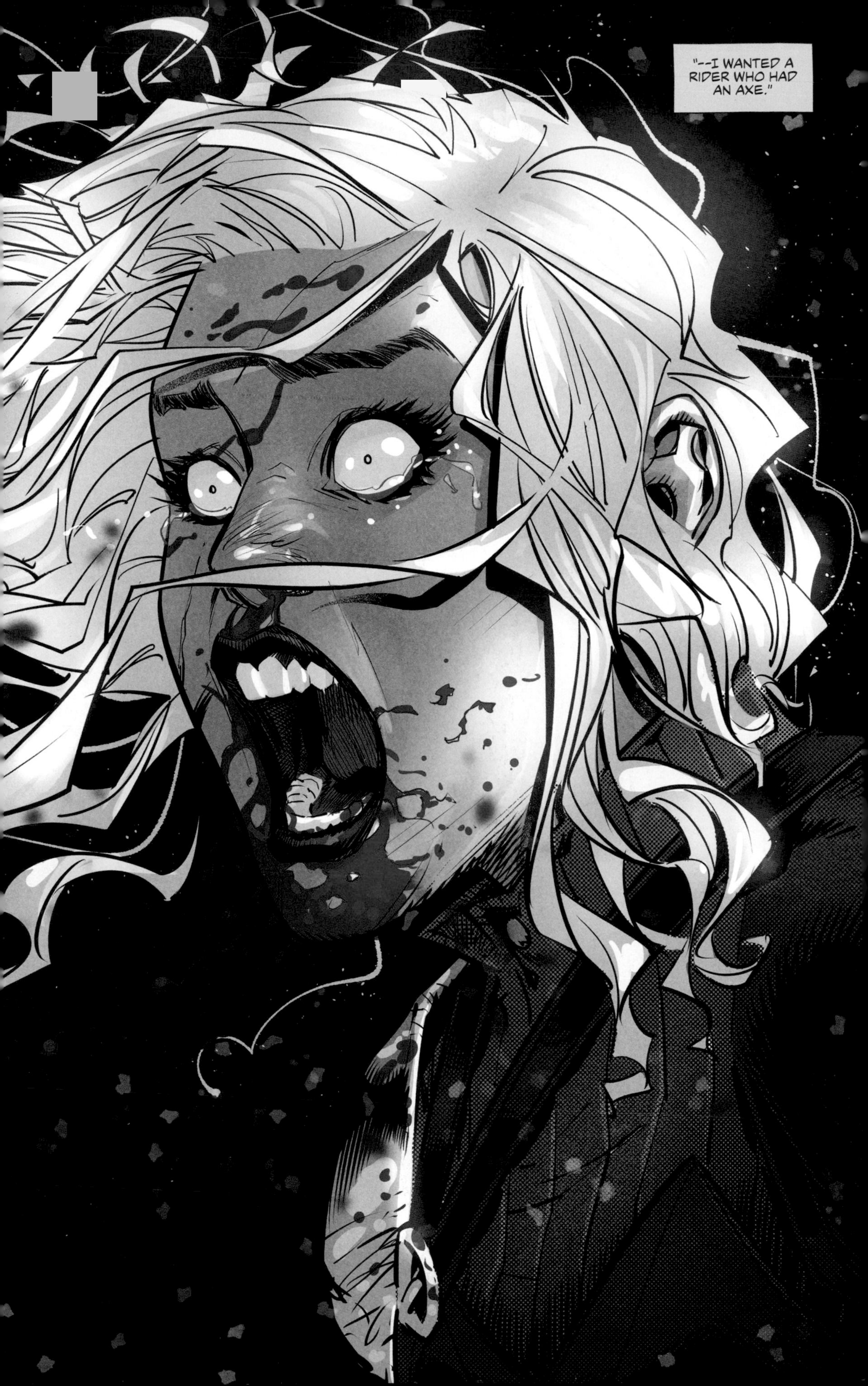
"--I WANTED A RIDER WHO HAD AN AXE."

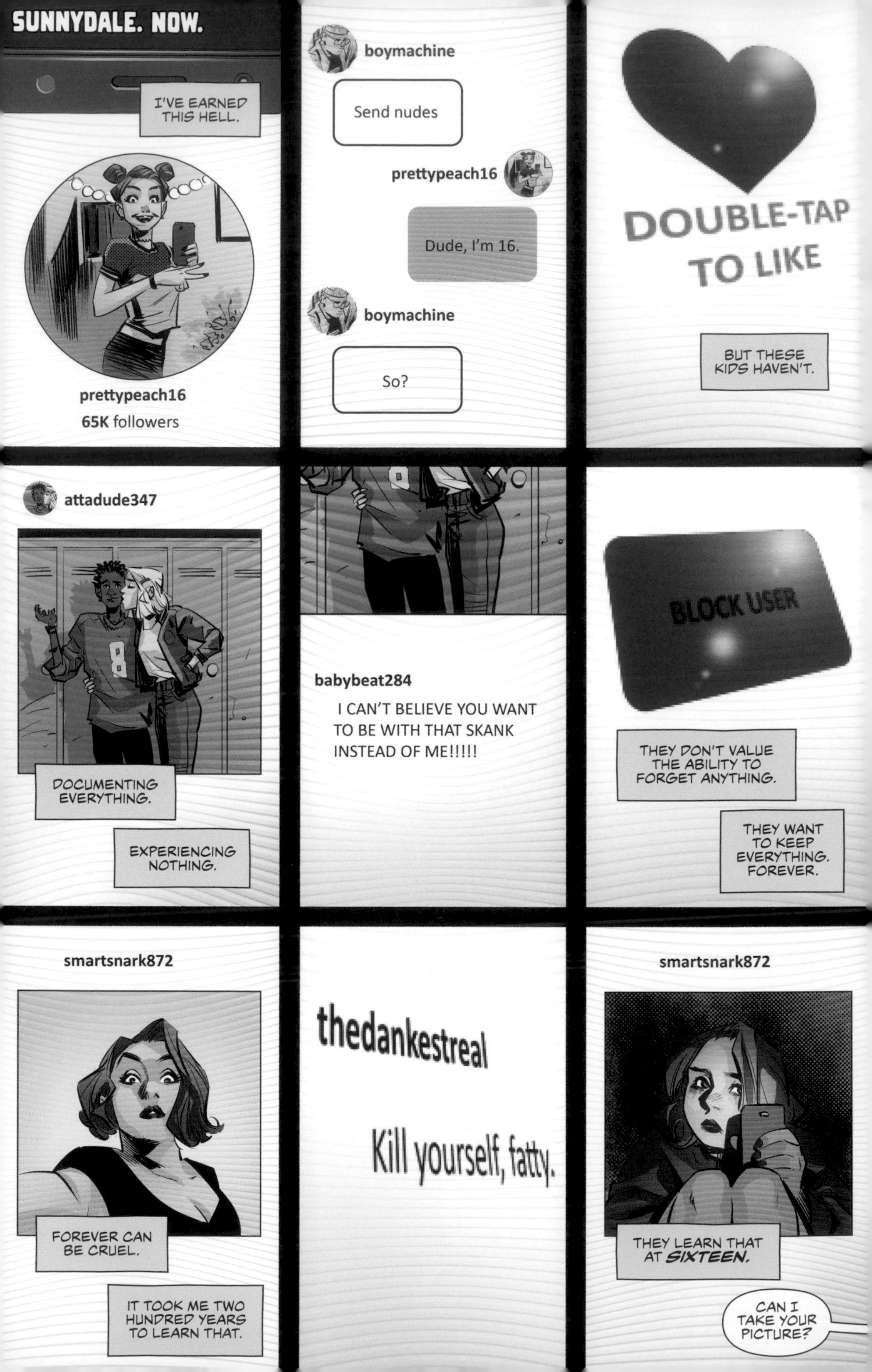
SUNNYDALE. NOW.
I'VE EARNED THIS HELL.
prettypeach16
65K followers
boymachine
Send nudes
prettypeach16
Dude, I'm 16.
boymachine
So?
DOUBLE-TAP TO LIKE
BUT THESE KIDS HAVEN'T.
attadude347
DOCUMENTING EVERYTHING.
EXPERIENCING NOTHING.
babybeat284
I CAN'T BELIEVE YOU WANT TO BE WITH THAT SKANK INSTEAD OF ME!!!!!
BLOCK USER
THEY DON'T VALUE THE ABILITY TO FORGET ANYTHING.
THEY WANT TO KEEP EVERYTHING. FOREVER.
smartsnark872
FOREVER CAN BE CRUEL.
IT TOOK ME TWO HUNDRED YEARS TO LEARN THAT.
thedankestreal
Kill yourself, fatty.
smartsnark872
THEY LEARN THAT AT SIXTEEN.
CAN I TAKE YOUR PICTURE?

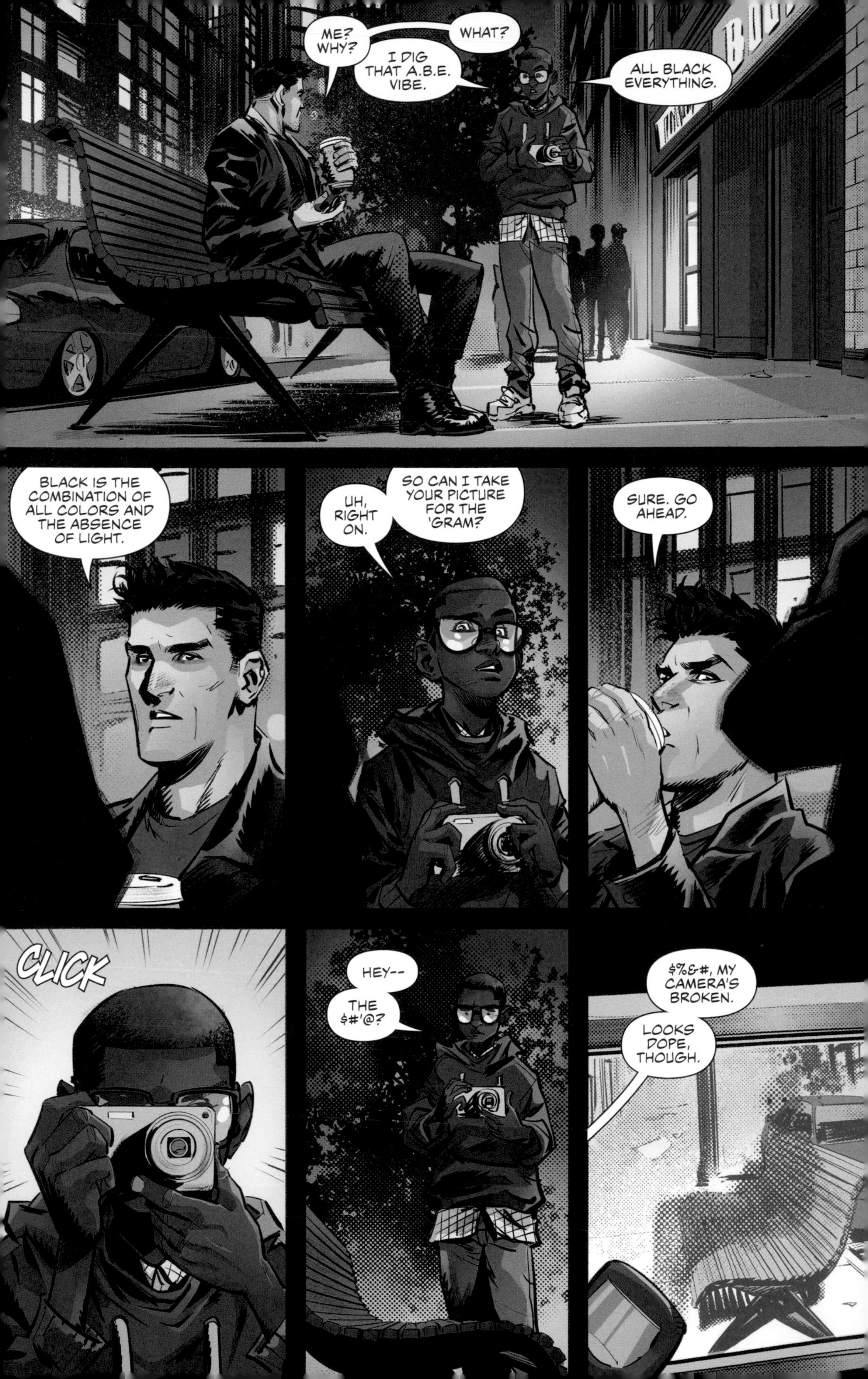

WHAT?
ME? WHY?
I DIG THAT A.B.E. VIBE.
ALL BLACK EVERYTHING.
BLACK IS THE COMBINATION OF ALL COLORS AND THE ABSENCE OF LIGHT.
UH, RIGHT ON.
SO CAN I TAKE YOUR PICTURE FOR THE 'GRAM?
SURE. GO AHEAD.
CLICK
HEY--
THE $#'@?
$%&#, MY CAMERA'S BROKEN.
LOOKS DOPE, THOUGH.

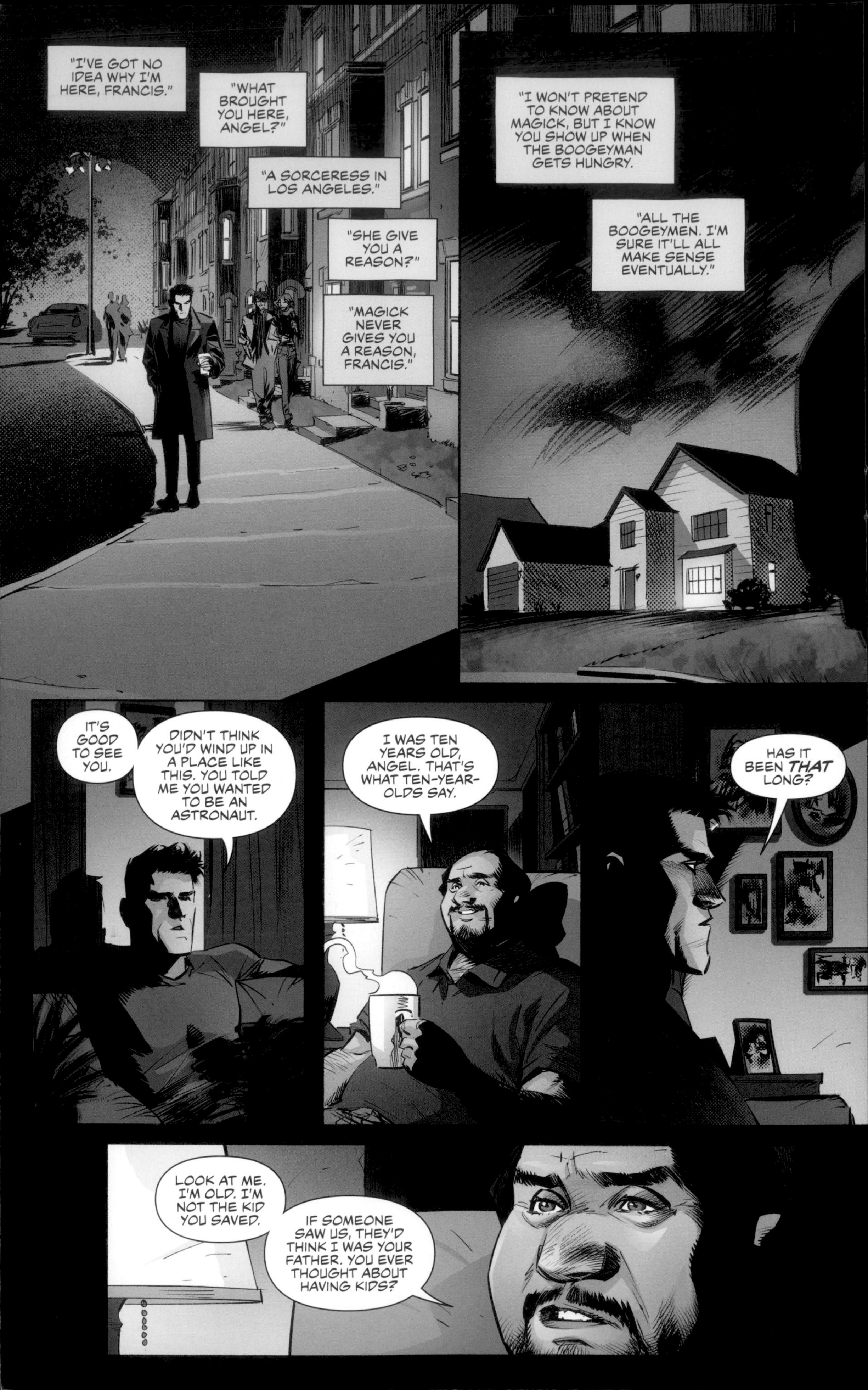
"I'VE GOT NO IDEA WHY I'M HERE, FRANCIS."
"WHAT BROUGHT YOU HERE, ANGEL?"
"A SORCERESS IN LOS ANGELES."
"SHE GIVE YOU A REASON?"
"MAGICK NEVER GIVES YOU A REASON, FRANCIS."
"I WON'T PRETEND TO KNOW ABOUT MAGICK, BUT I KNOW YOU SHOW UP WHEN THE BOOGEYMAN GETS HUNGRY.
"ALL THE BOOGEYMEN. I'M SURE IT'LL ALL MAKE SENSE EVENTUALLY."
IT'S GOOD TO SEE YOU.
DIDN'T THINK YOU'D WIND UP IN A PLACE LIKE THIS. YOU TOLD ME YOU WANTED TO BE AN ASTRONAUT.
I WAS TEN YEARS OLD, ANGEL. THAT'S WHAT TEN-YEAR-OLDS SAY.
HAS IT BEEN *THAT* LONG?
LOOK AT ME. I'M OLD. I'M NOT THE KID YOU SAVED.
IF SOMEONE SAW US, THEY'D THINK I WAS YOUR FATHER. YOU EVER THOUGHT ABOUT HAVING KIDS?

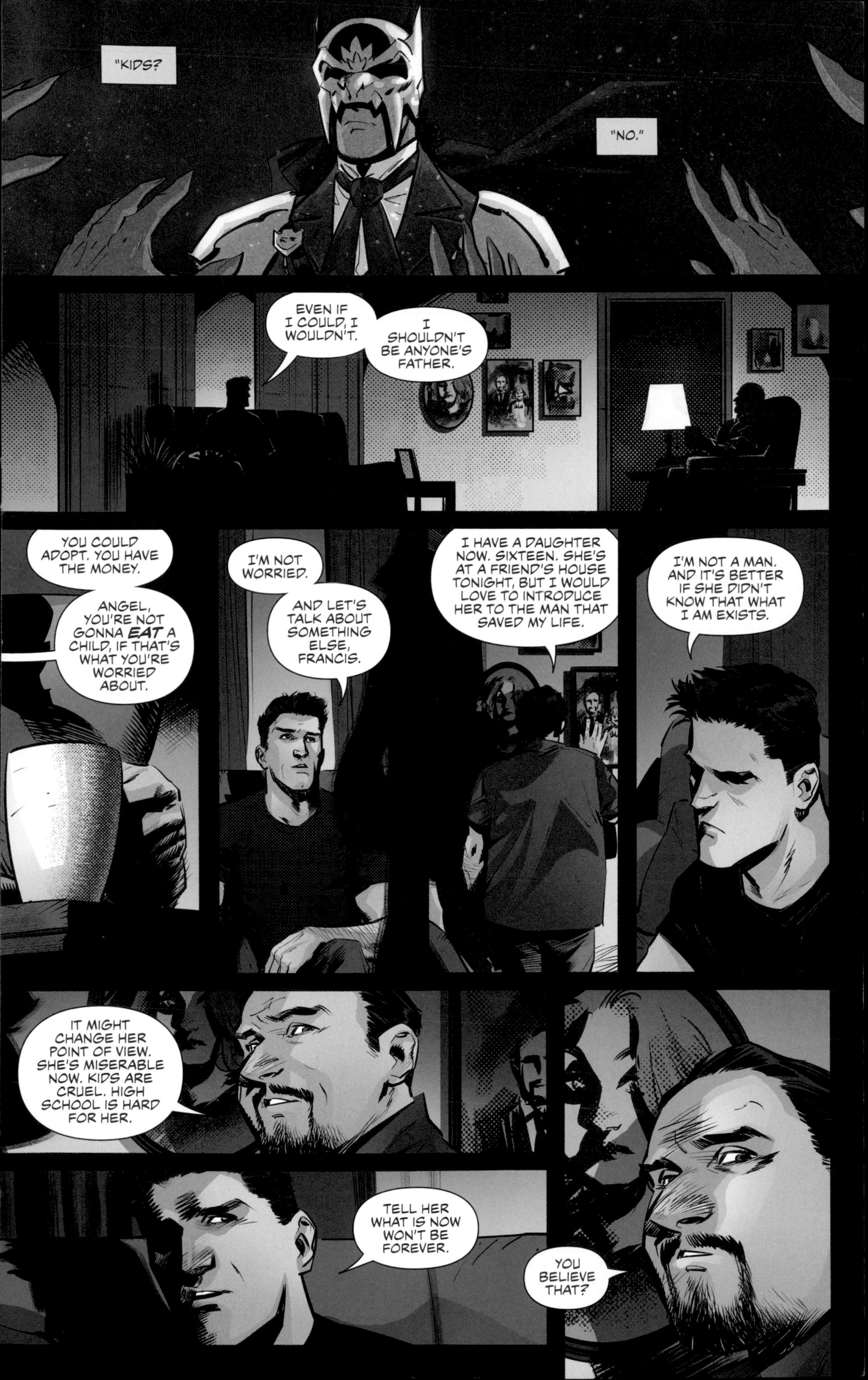
"KIDS?
"NO."
EVEN IF I COULD, I WOULDN'T.
I SHOULDN'T BE ANYONE'S FATHER.
YOU COULD ADOPT. YOU HAVE THE MONEY.
ANGEL, YOU'RE NOT GONNA EAT A CHILD, IF THAT'S WHAT YOU'RE WORRIED ABOUT.
I'M NOT WORRIED.
AND LET'S TALK ABOUT SOMETHING ELSE, FRANCIS.
I HAVE A DAUGHTER NOW. SIXTEEN. SHE'S AT A FRIEND'S HOUSE TONIGHT, BUT I WOULD LOVE TO INTRODUCE HER TO THE MAN THAT SAVED MY LIFE.
I'M NOT A MAN. AND IT'S BETTER IF SHE DIDN'T KNOW THAT WHAT I AM EXISTS.
IT MIGHT CHANGE HER POINT OF VIEW. SHE'S MISERABLE NOW. KIDS ARE CRUEL. HIGH SCHOOL IS HARD FOR HER.
TELL HER WHAT IS NOW WON'T BE FOREVER.
YOU BELIEVE THAT?

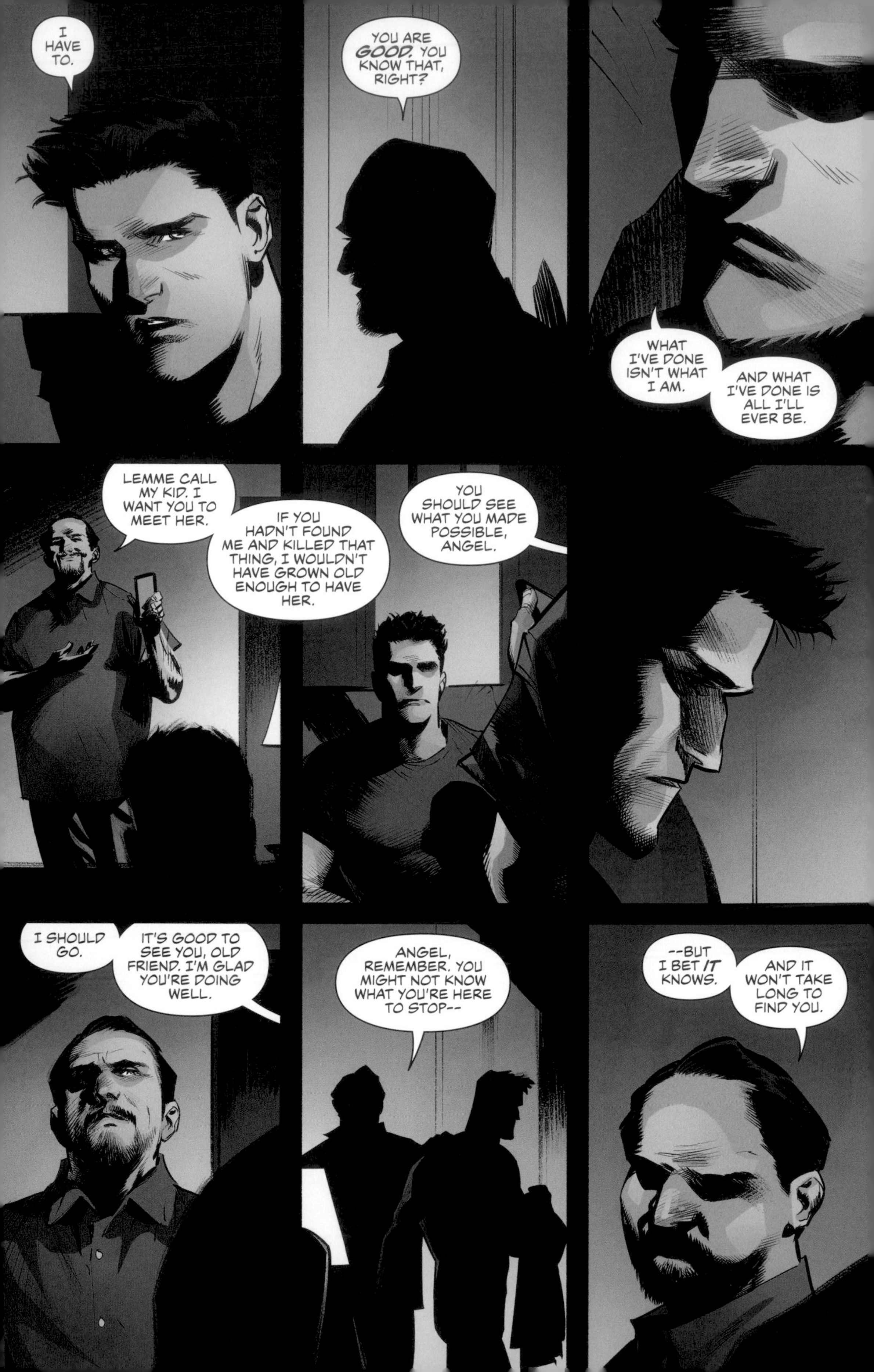
I HAVE TO.
YOU ARE GOOD. YOU KNOW THAT, RIGHT?
WHAT I'VE DONE ISN'T WHAT I AM.
AND WHAT I'VE DONE IS ALL I'LL EVER BE.
LEMME CALL MY KID. I WANT YOU TO MEET HER.
IF YOU HADN'T FOUND ME AND KILLED THAT THING, I WOULDN'T HAVE GROWN OLD ENOUGH TO HAVE HER.
YOU SHOULD SEE WHAT YOU MADE POSSIBLE, ANGEL.
I SHOULD GO.
IT'S GOOD TO SEE YOU, OLD FRIEND. I'M GLAD YOU'RE DOING WELL.
ANGEL, REMEMBER. YOU MIGHT NOT KNOW WHAT YOU'RE HERE TO STOP--
--BUT I BET IT KNOWS.
AND IT WON'T TAKE LONG TO FIND YOU.

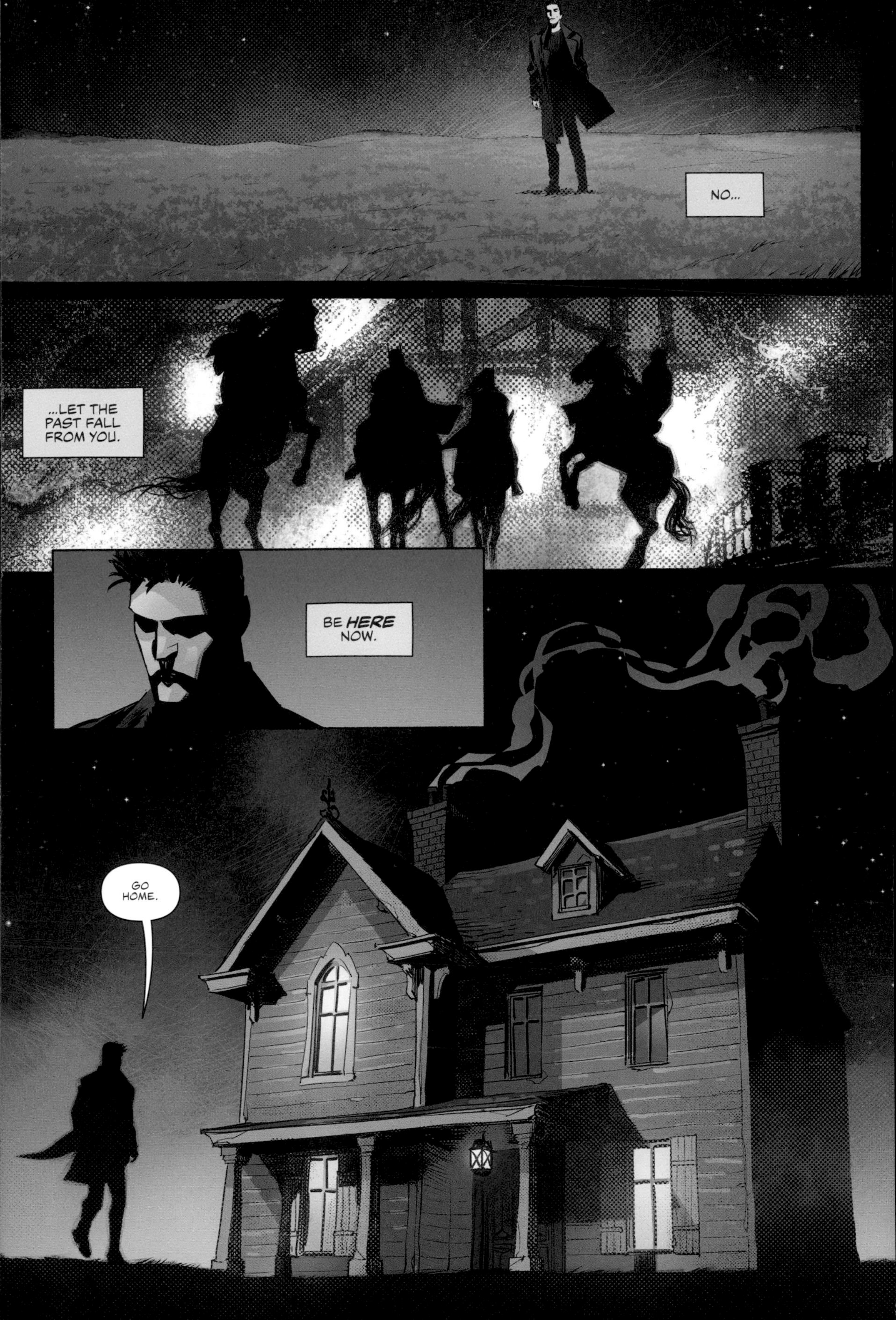
NO...
...LET THE PAST FALL FROM YOU.
BE *HERE* NOW.
GO HOME.

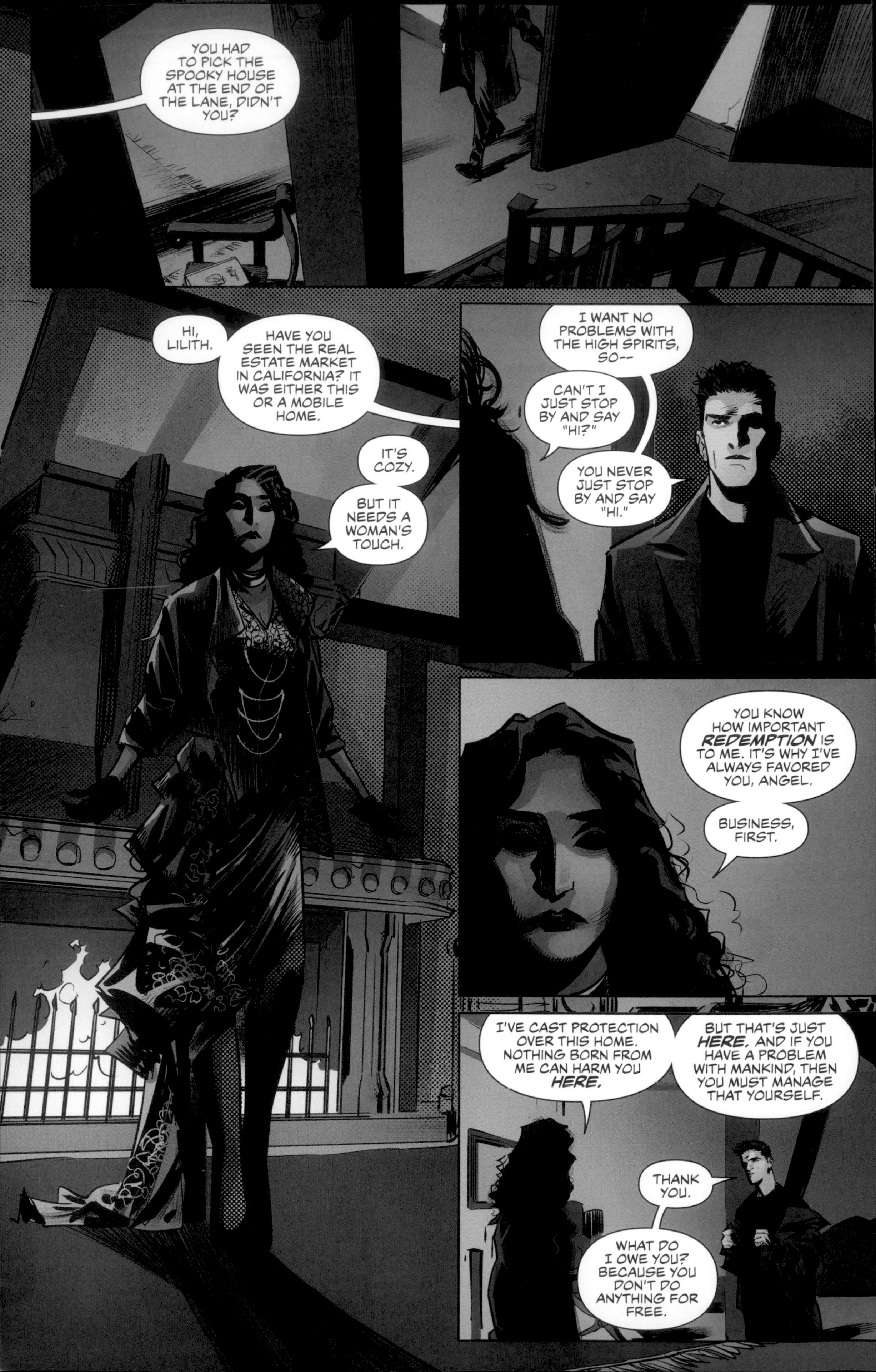
YOU HAD TO PICK THE SPOOKY HOUSE AT THE END OF THE LANE, DIDN'T YOU?
HI, LILITH.
HAVE YOU SEEN THE REAL ESTATE MARKET IN CALIFORNIA? IT WAS EITHER THIS OR A MOBILE HOME.
IT'S COZY.
BUT IT NEEDS A WOMAN'S TOUCH.
I WANT NO PROBLEMS WITH THE HIGH SPIRITS, SO--
CAN'T I JUST STOP BY AND SAY "HI?"
YOU NEVER JUST STOP BY AND SAY "HI."
YOU KNOW HOW IMPORTANT REDEMPTION IS TO ME. IT'S WHY I'VE ALWAYS FAVORED YOU, ANGEL.
BUSINESS, FIRST.
I'VE CAST PROTECTION OVER THIS HOME. NOTHING BORN FROM ME CAN HARM YOU HERE.
BUT THAT'S JUST HERE. AND IF YOU HAVE A PROBLEM WITH MANKIND, THEN YOU MUST MANAGE THAT YOURSELF.
THANK YOU.
WHAT DO I OWE YOU? BECAUSE YOU DON'T DO ANYTHING FOR FREE.

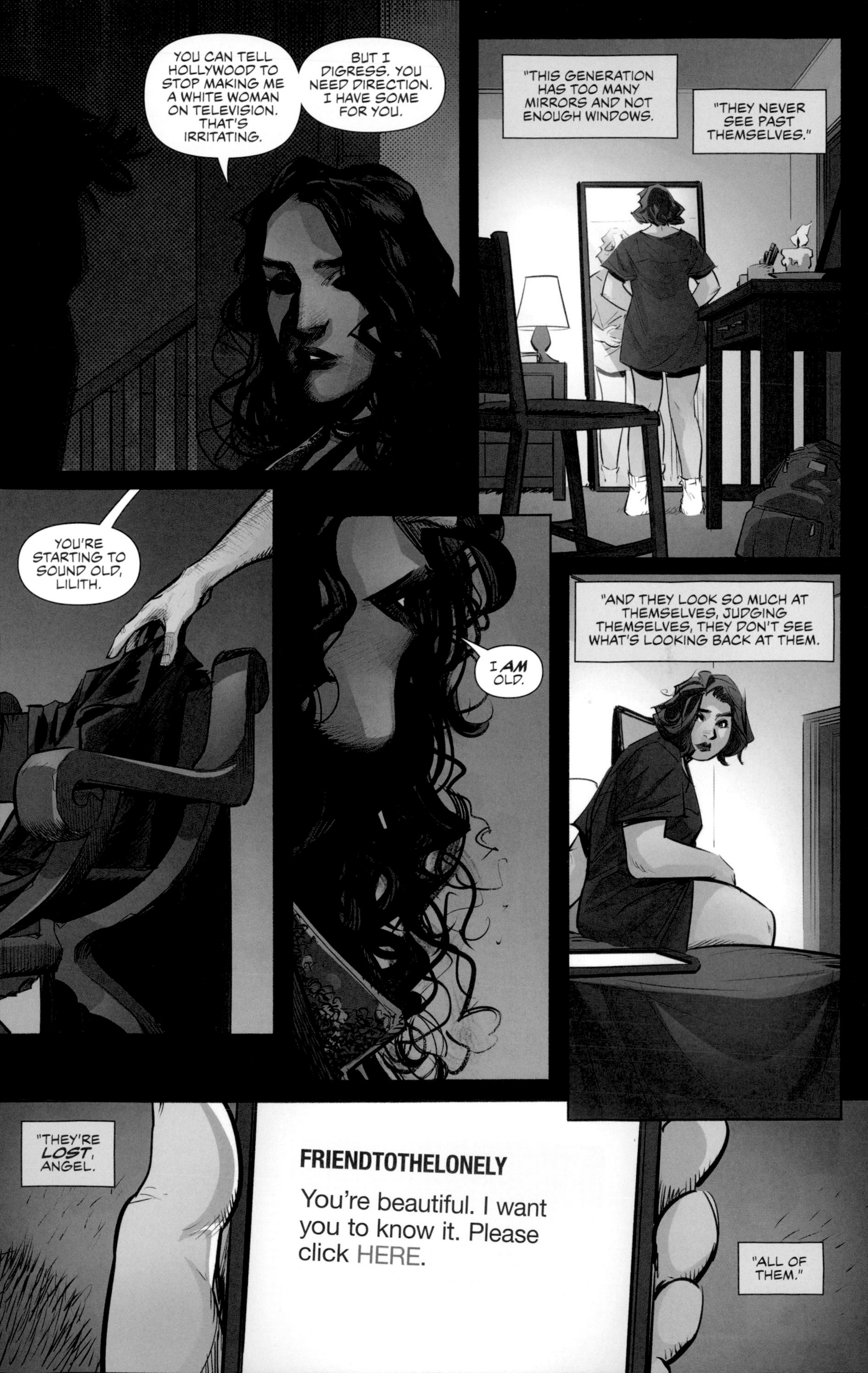
YOU CAN TELL HOLLYWOOD TO STOP MAKING ME A WHITE WOMAN ON TELEVISION. THAT'S IRRITATING.
BUT I DIGRESS. YOU NEED DIRECTION. I HAVE SOME FOR YOU.
"THIS GENERATION HAS TOO MANY MIRRORS AND NOT ENOUGH WINDOWS.
"THEY NEVER SEE PAST THEMSELVES."
YOU'RE STARTING TO SOUND OLD, LILITH.
I *AM* OLD.
"AND THEY LOOK SO MUCH AT THEMSELVES, JUDGING THEMSELVES, THEY DON'T SEE WHAT'S LOOKING BACK AT THEM.
"THEY'RE *LOST*, ANGEL.
FRIENDTOTHELONELY
You're beautiful. I want you to know it. Please click HERE.
"ALL OF THEM."

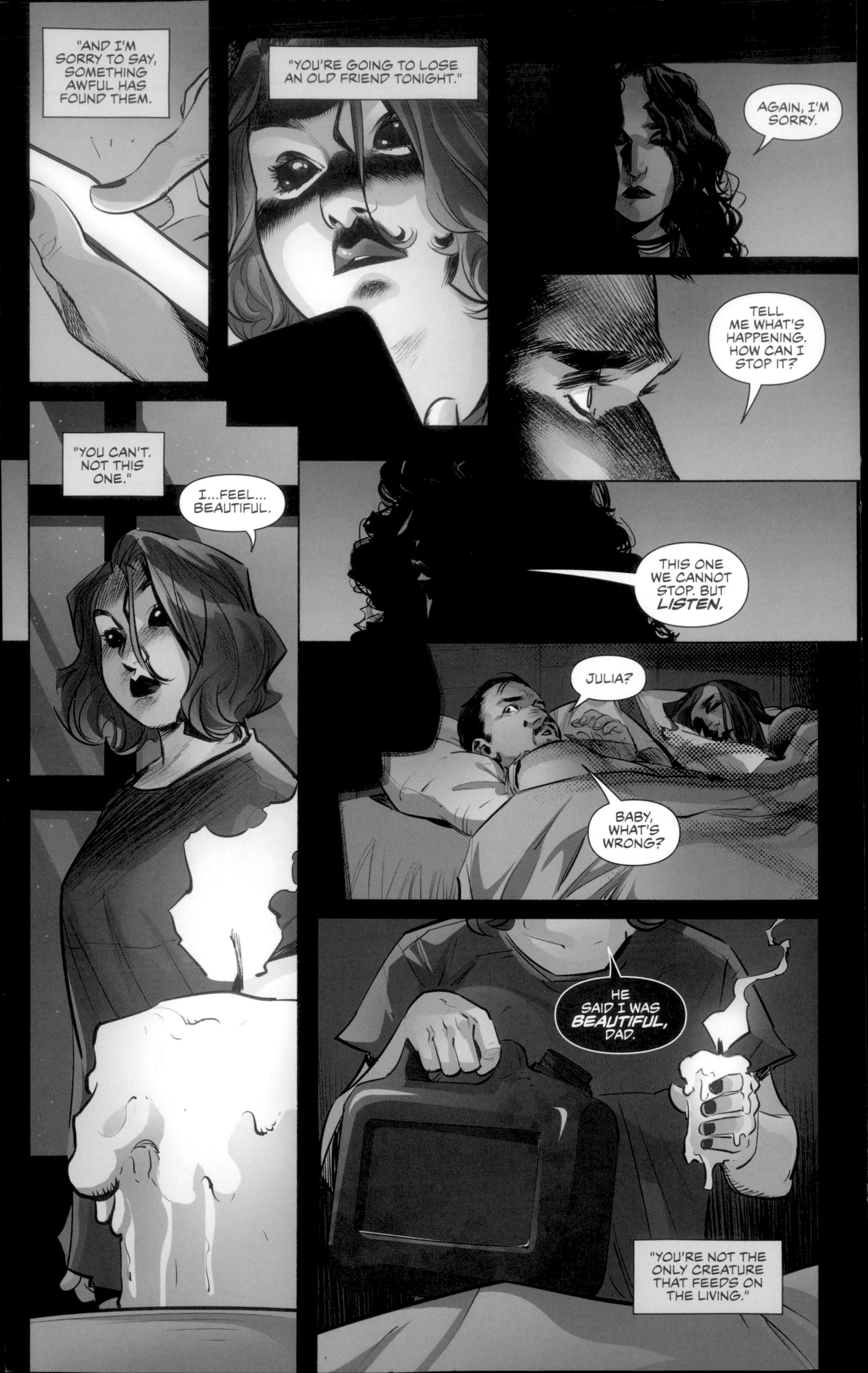
"AND I'M SORRY TO SAY, SOMETHING AWFUL HAS FOUND THEM.
"YOU'RE GOING TO LOSE AN OLD FRIEND TONIGHT."
AGAIN, I'M SORRY.
TELL ME WHAT'S HAPPENING. HOW CAN I STOP IT?
"YOU CAN'T. NOT THIS ONE."
I...FEEL... BEAUTIFUL.
THIS ONE WE CANNOT STOP. BUT *LISTEN.*
JULIA?
BABY, WHAT'S WRONG?
HE SAID I WAS *BEAUTIFUL,* DAD.
"YOU'RE NOT THE ONLY CREATURE THAT FEEDS ON THE LIVING."

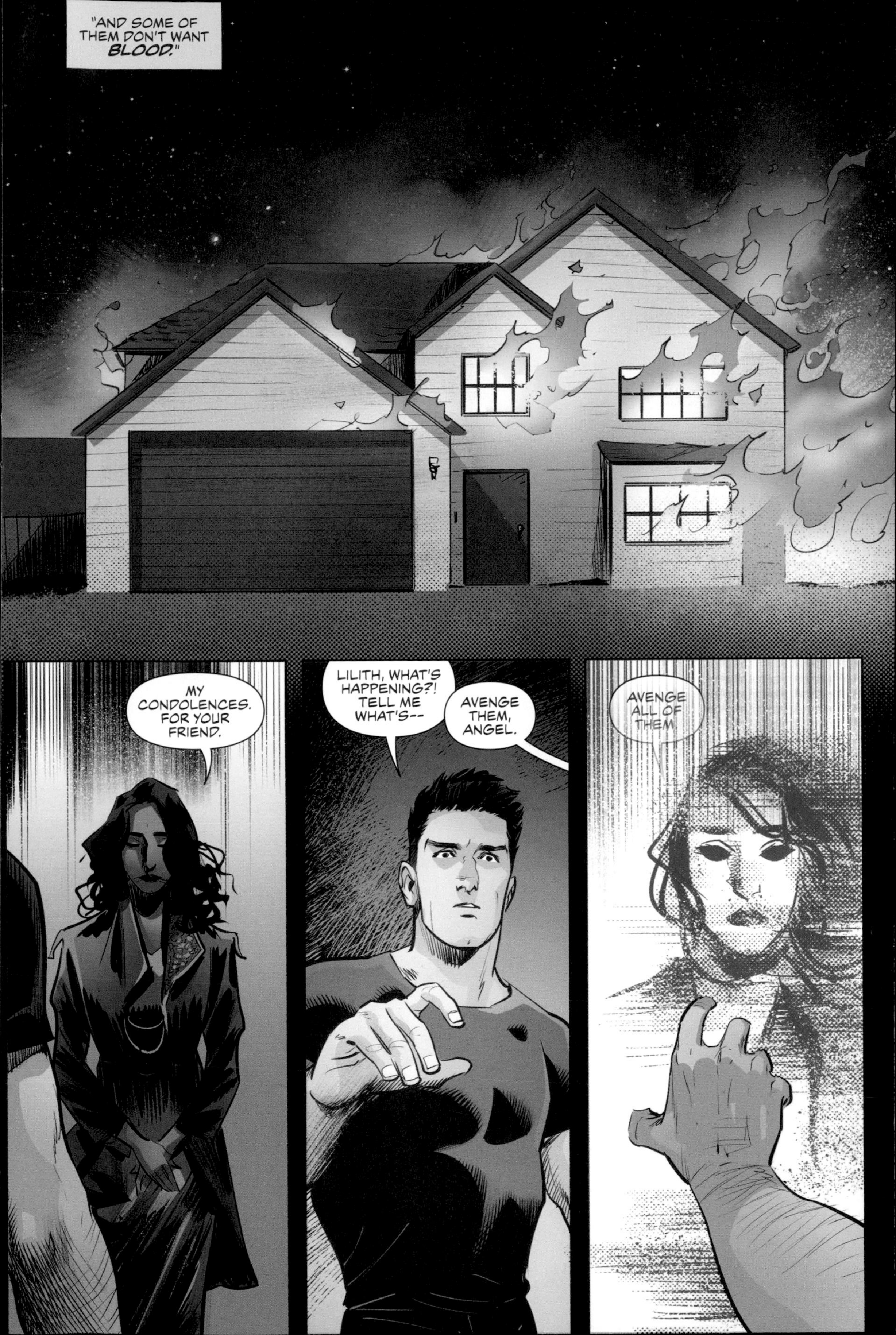
"AND SOME OF THEM DON'T WANT BLOOD."
MY CONDOLENCES. FOR YOUR FRIEND.
LILITH, WHAT'S HAPPENING?! TELL ME WHAT'S--
AVENGE THEM, ANGEL.
AVENGE ALL OF THEM.

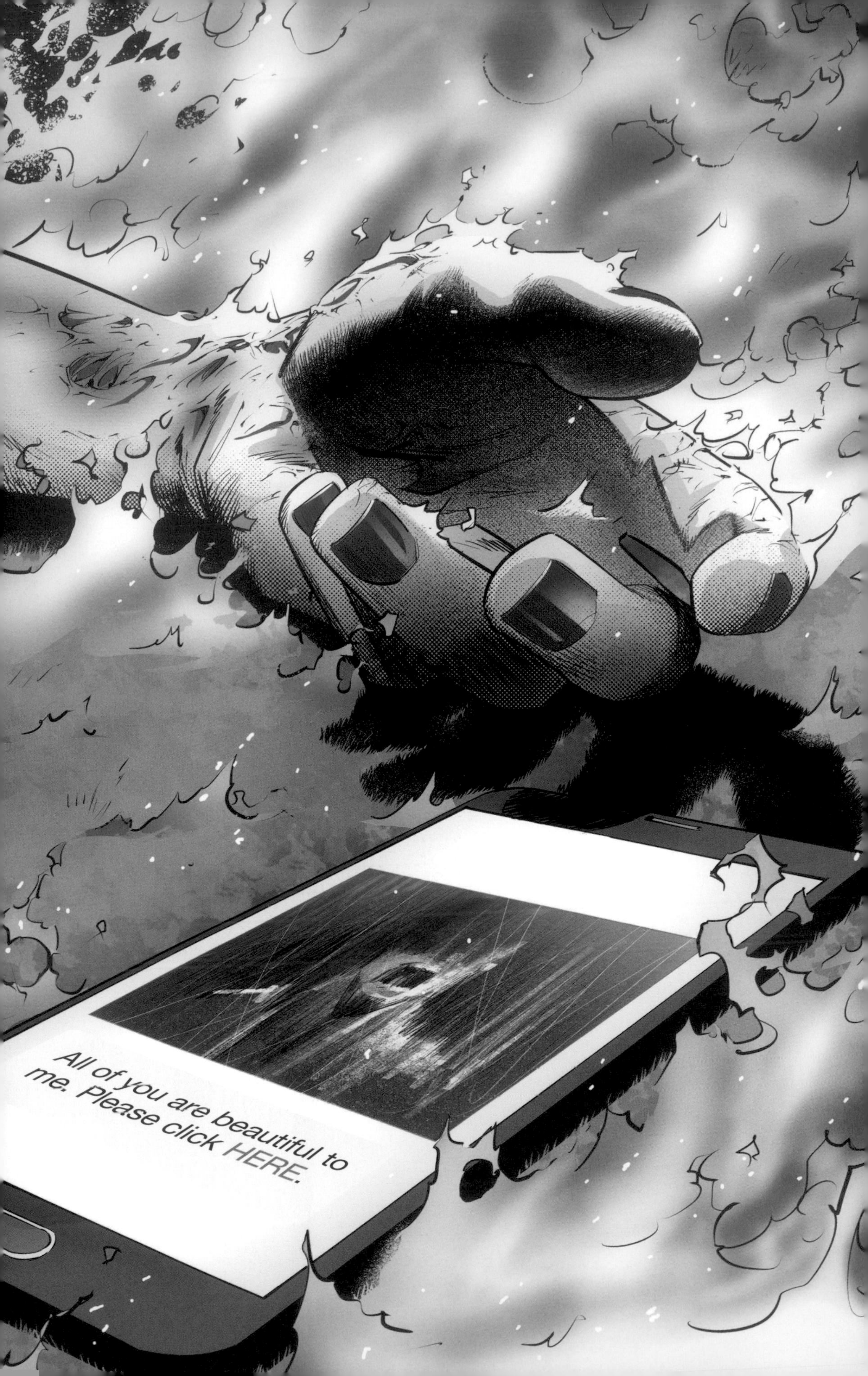
All of you are beautiful to me. Please click HERE.

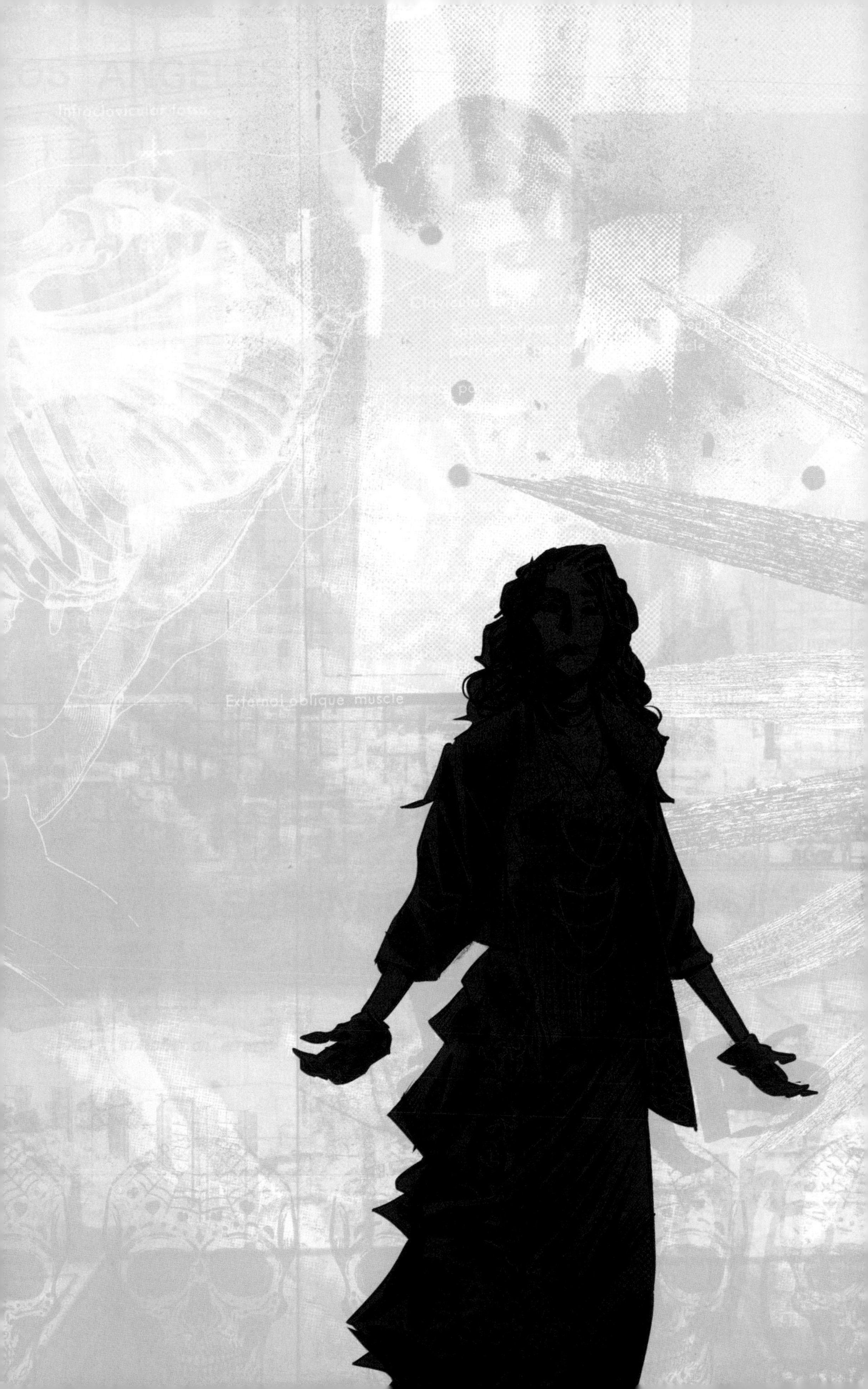
Infraclavicular fossa
External oblique muscle

CHAPTER TWO

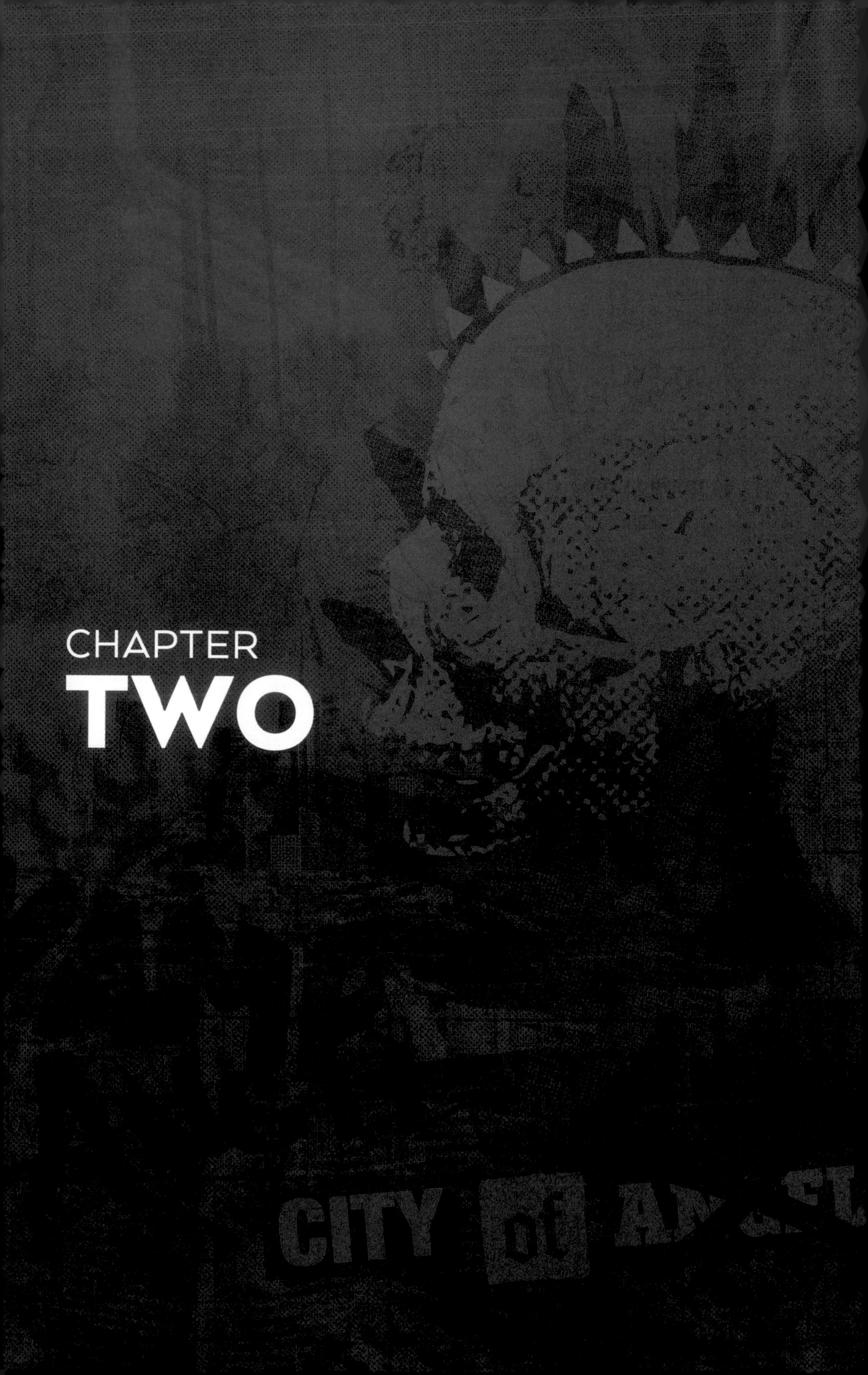
CITY of

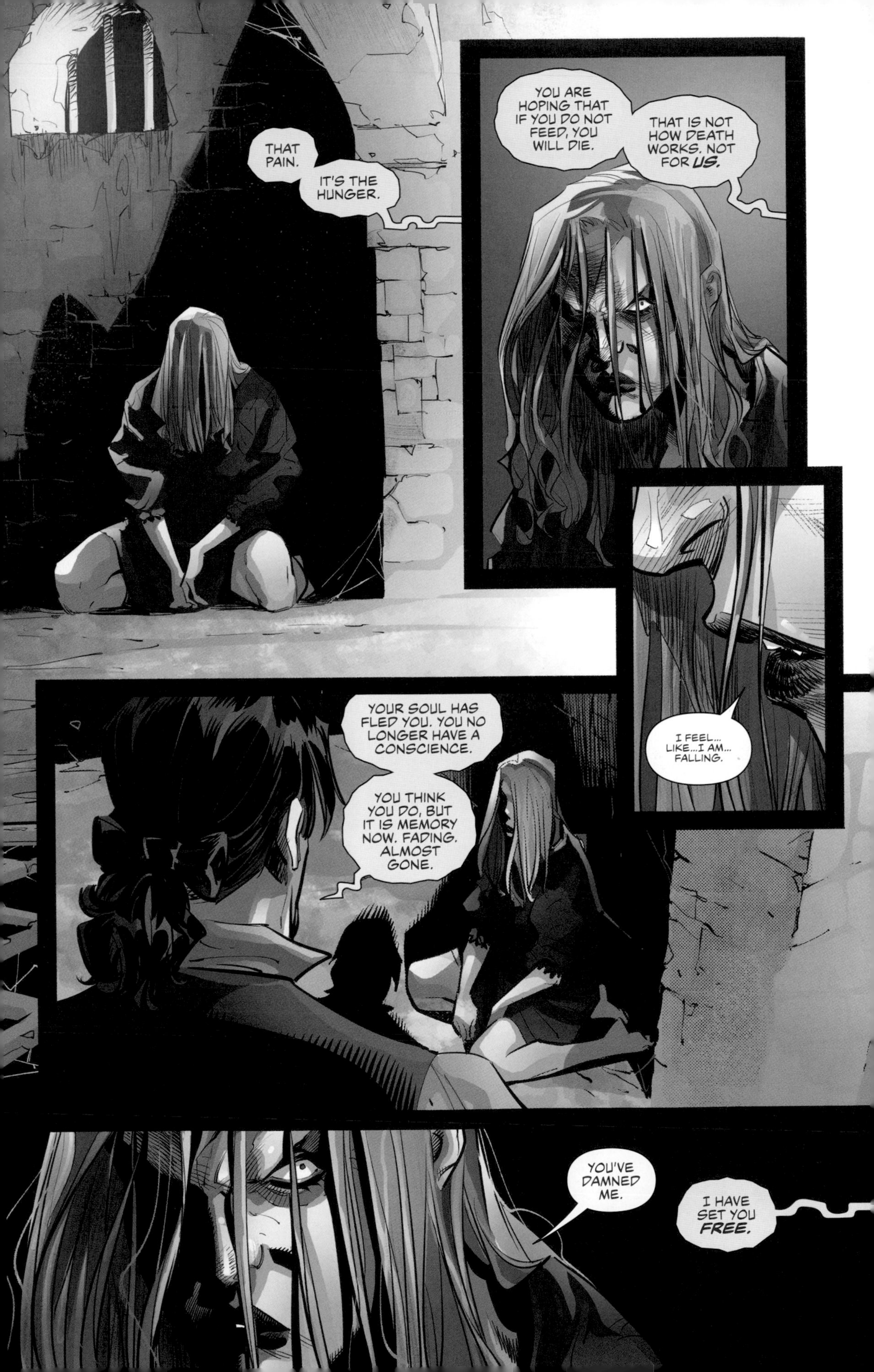
THAT PAIN.
IT'S THE HUNGER.
YOU ARE HOPING THAT IF YOU DO NOT FEED, YOU WILL DIE.
THAT IS NOT HOW DEATH WORKS. NOT FOR US.
I FEEL... LIKE...I AM... FALLING.
YOUR SOUL HAS FLED YOU. YOU NO LONGER HAVE A CONSCIENCE.
YOU THINK YOU DO, BUT IT IS MEMORY NOW. FADING. ALMOST GONE.
YOU'VE DAMNED ME.
I HAVE SET YOU FREE.

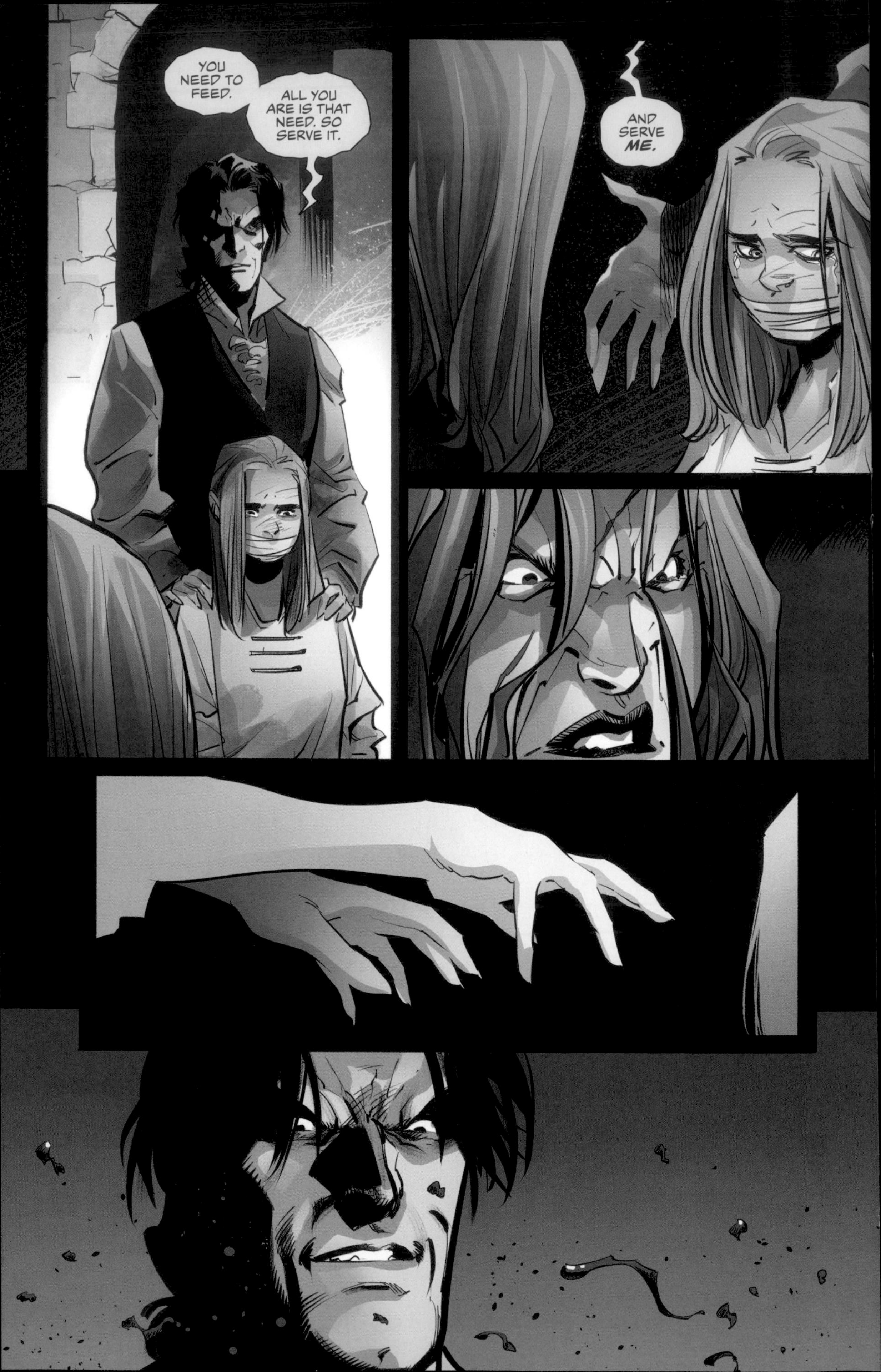
YOU NEED TO FEED.
ALL YOU ARE IS THAT NEED. SO SERVE IT.
AND SERVE ME.

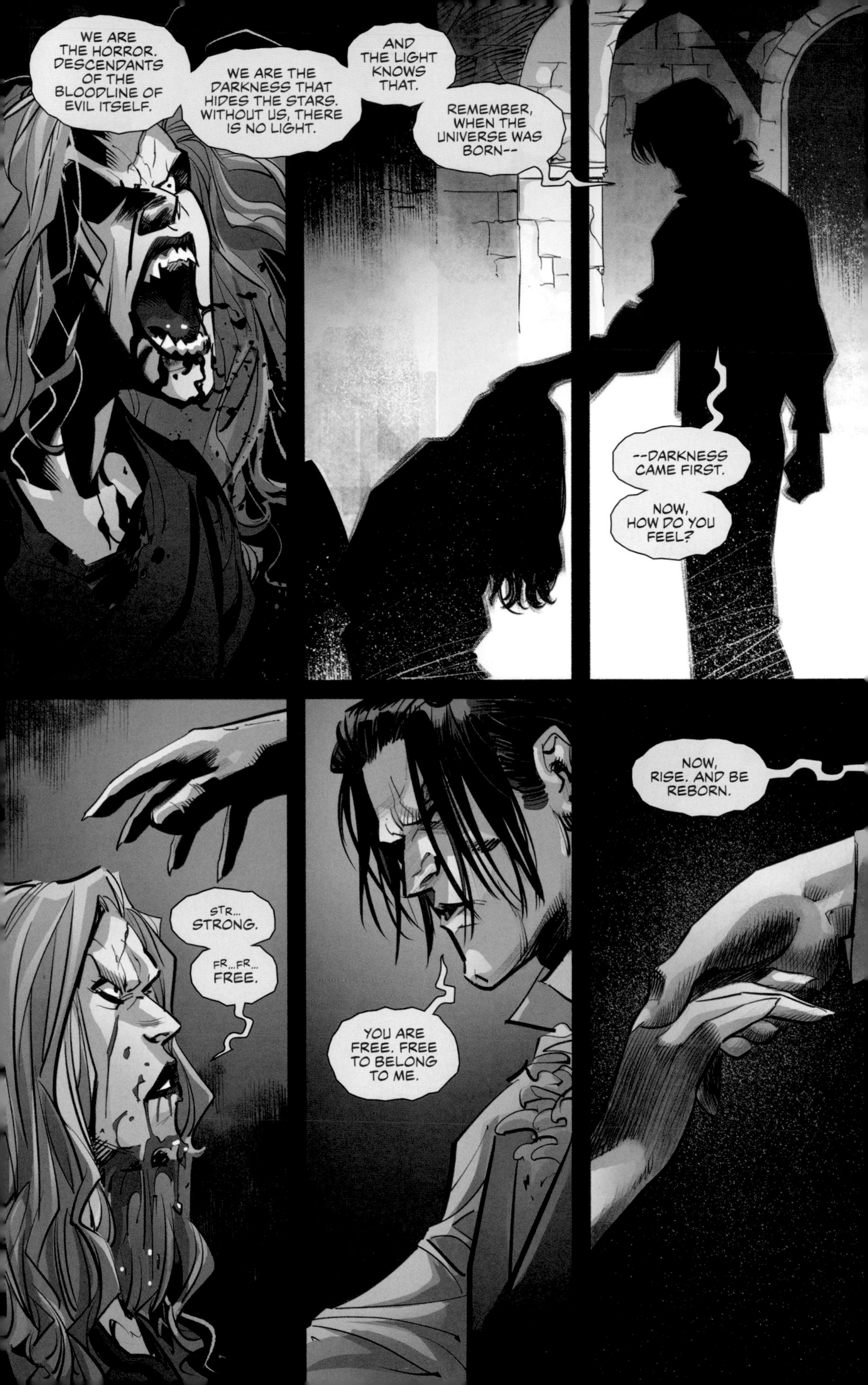
WE ARE THE HORROR. DESCENDANTS OF THE BLOODLINE OF EVIL ITSELF.
WE ARE THE DARKNESS THAT HIDES THE STARS. WITHOUT US, THERE IS NO LIGHT.
AND THE LIGHT KNOWS THAT.
REMEMBER, WHEN THE UNIVERSE WAS BORN--
--DARKNESS CAME FIRST.
NOW, HOW DO YOU FEEL?
STR... STRONG.
FR...FR... FREE.
YOU ARE FREE. FREE TO BELONG TO ME.
NOW, RISE. AND BE REBORN.

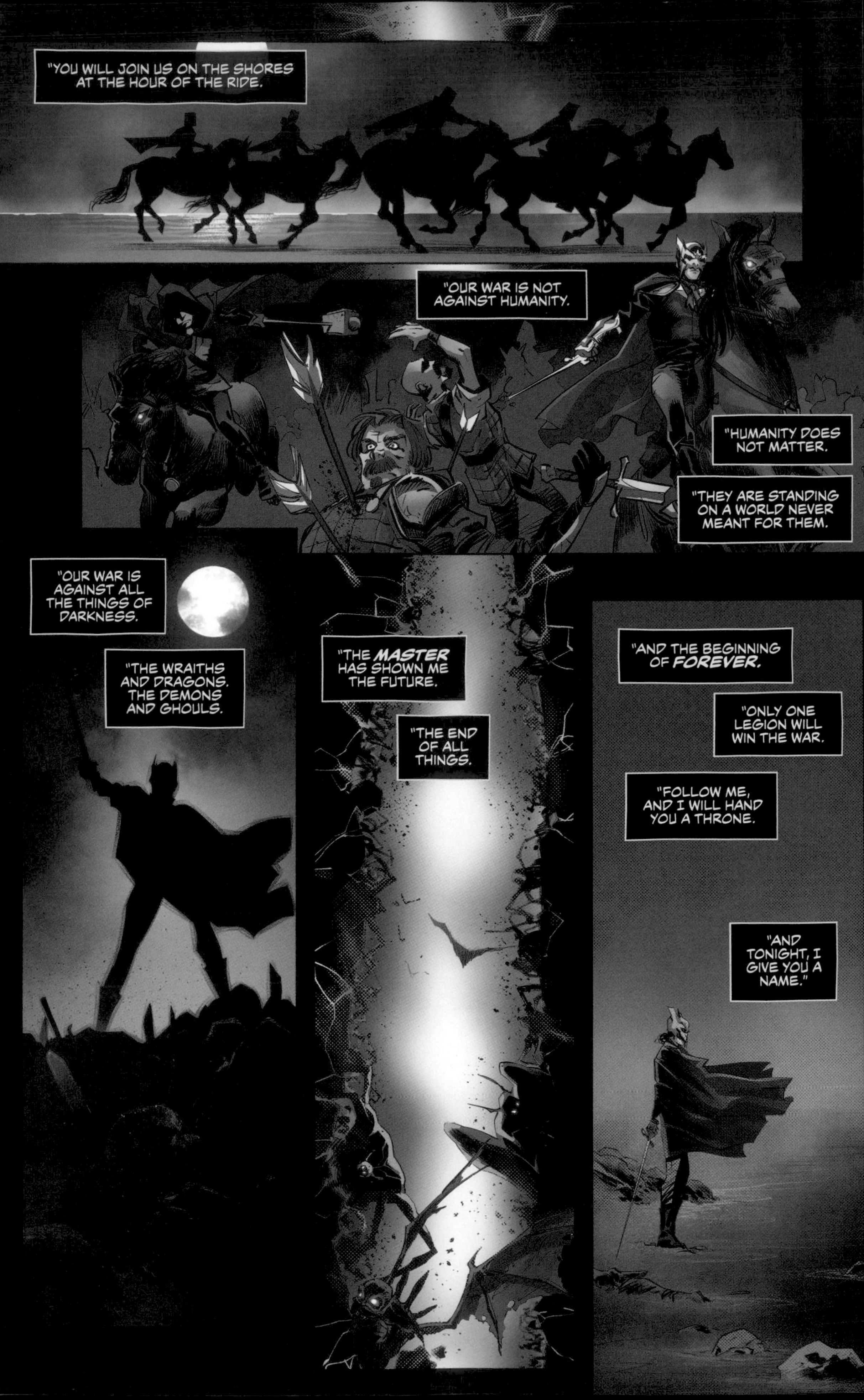
"YOU WILL JOIN US ON THE SHORES AT THE HOUR OF THE RIDE.
"OUR WAR IS NOT AGAINST HUMANITY.
"HUMANITY DOES NOT MATTER.
"THEY ARE STANDING ON A WORLD NEVER MEANT FOR THEM.
"OUR WAR IS AGAINST ALL THE THINGS OF DARKNESS.
"THE WRAITHS AND DRAGONS. THE DEMONS AND GHOULS.
"THE MASTER HAS SHOWN ME THE FUTURE.
"THE END OF ALL THINGS.
"AND THE BEGINNING OF FOREVER.
"ONLY ONE LEGION WILL WIN THE WAR.
"FOLLOW ME, AND I WILL HAND YOU A THRONE.
"AND TONIGHT, I GIVE YOU A NAME."

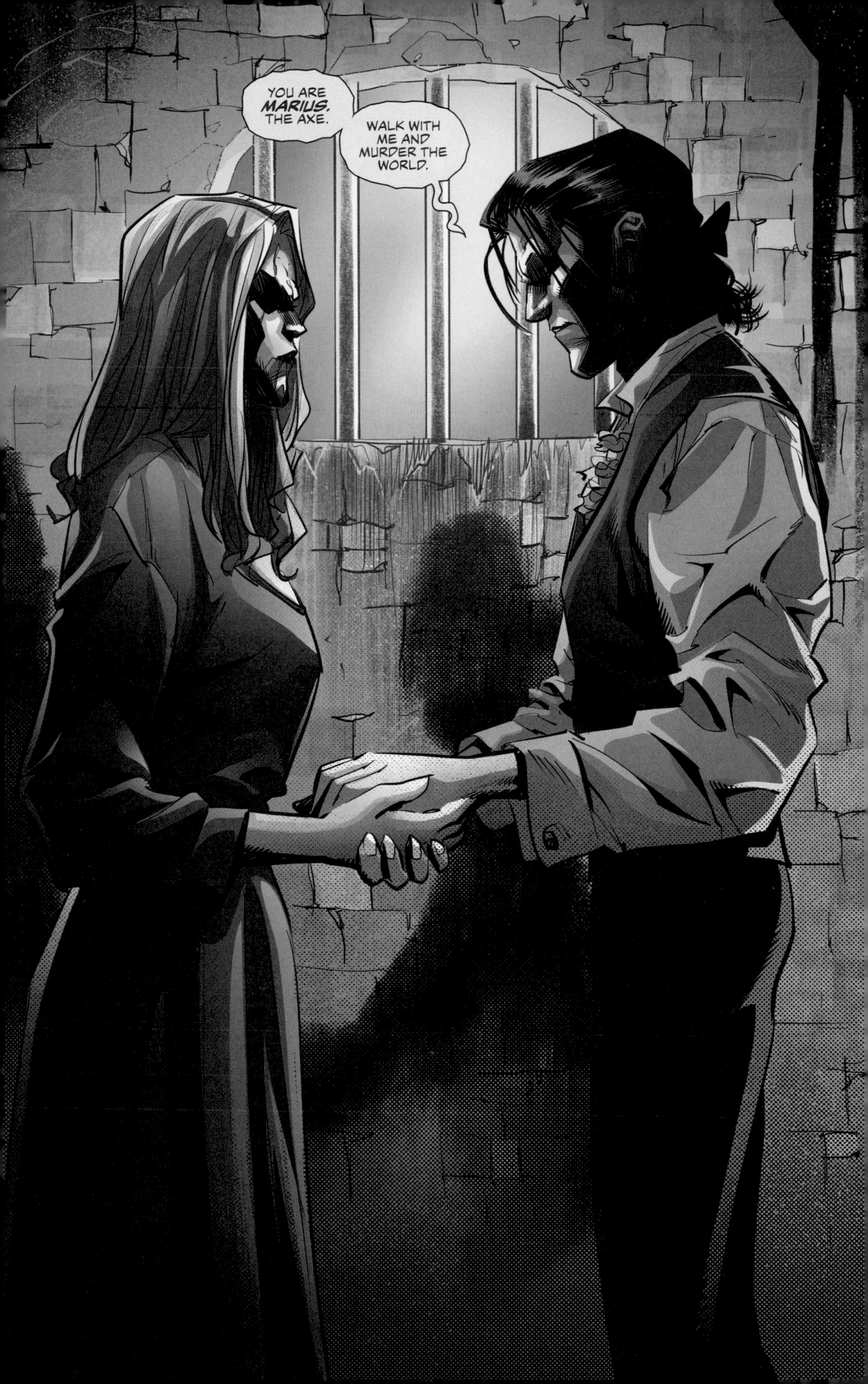
YOU ARE **MARIUS.** THE AXE.
WALK WITH ME AND MURDER THE WORLD.

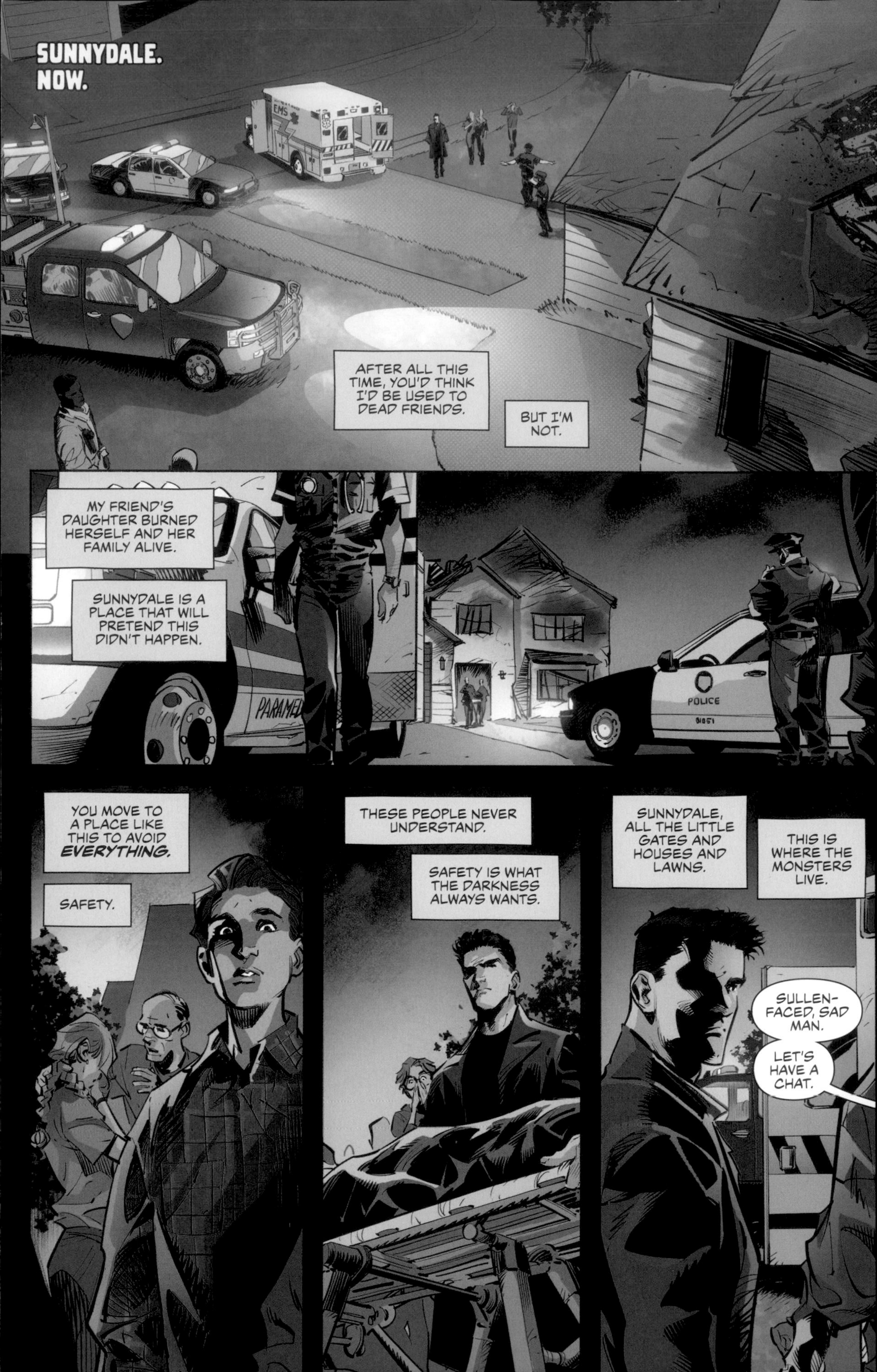
SUNNYDALE. NOW.
AFTER ALL THIS TIME, YOU'D THINK I'D BE USED TO DEAD FRIENDS.
BUT I'M NOT.
MY FRIEND'S DAUGHTER BURNED HERSELF AND HER FAMILY ALIVE.
SUNNYDALE IS A PLACE THAT WILL PRETEND THIS DIDN'T HAPPEN.
PARAMED
POLICE
YOU MOVE TO A PLACE LIKE THIS TO AVOID *EVERYTHING.*
SAFETY.
THESE PEOPLE NEVER UNDERSTAND.
SAFETY IS WHAT THE DARKNESS ALWAYS WANTS.
SUNNYDALE, ALL THE LITTLE GATES AND HOUSES AND LAWNS.
THIS IS WHERE THE MONSTERS LIVE.
SULLEN-FACED, SAD MAN.
LET'S HAVE A CHAT.

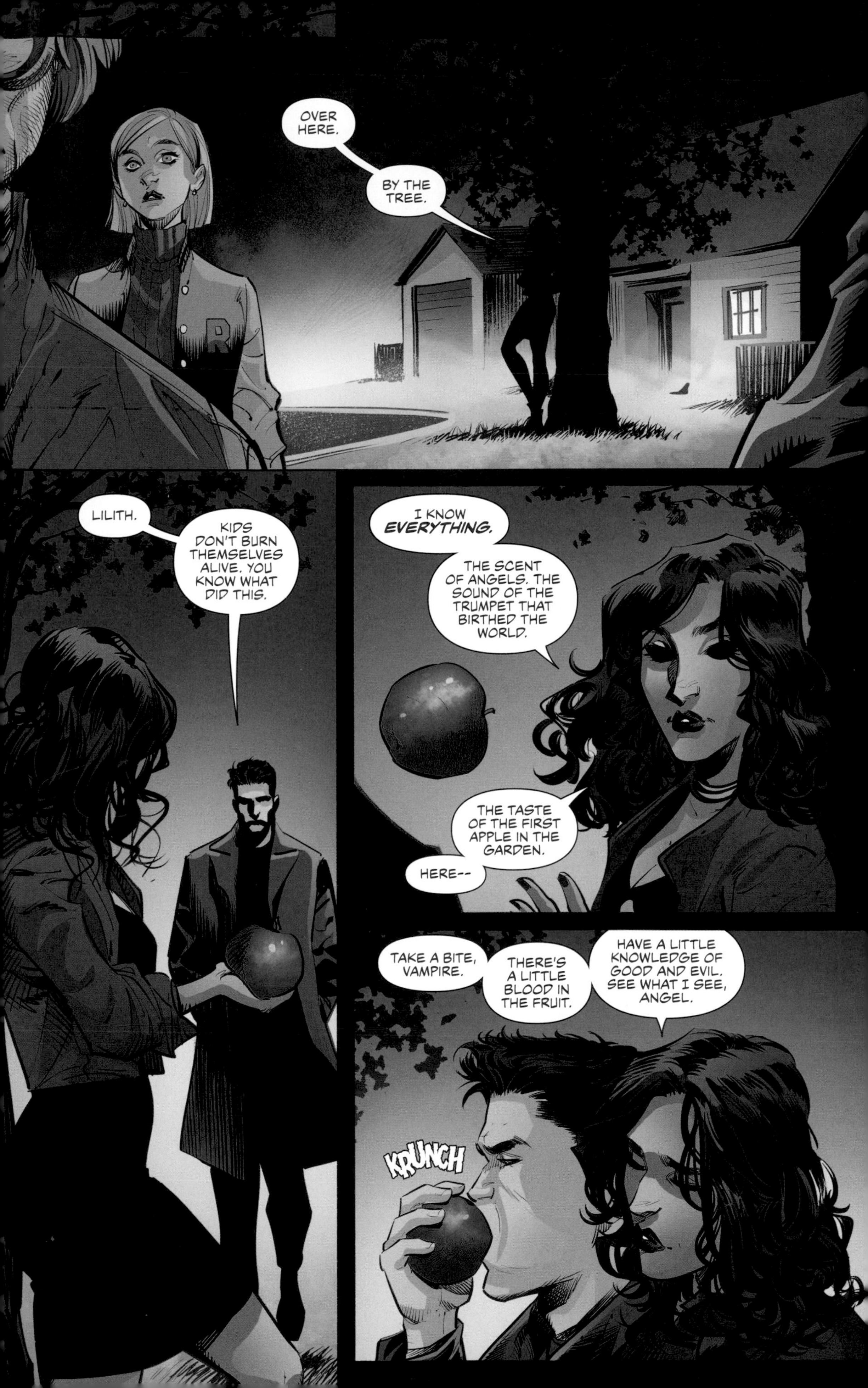
OVER HERE.
BY THE TREE.
LILITH.
KIDS DON'T BURN THEMSELVES ALIVE. YOU KNOW WHAT DID THIS.
I KNOW *EVERYTHING.*
THE SCENT OF ANGELS. THE SOUND OF THE TRUMPET THAT BIRTHED THE WORLD.
THE TASTE OF THE FIRST APPLE IN THE GARDEN.
HERE--
TAKE A BITE, VAMPIRE.
THERE'S A LITTLE BLOOD IN THE FRUIT.
HAVE A LITTLE KNOWLEDGE OF GOOD AND EVIL. SEE WHAT I SEE, ANGEL.
KRUNCH

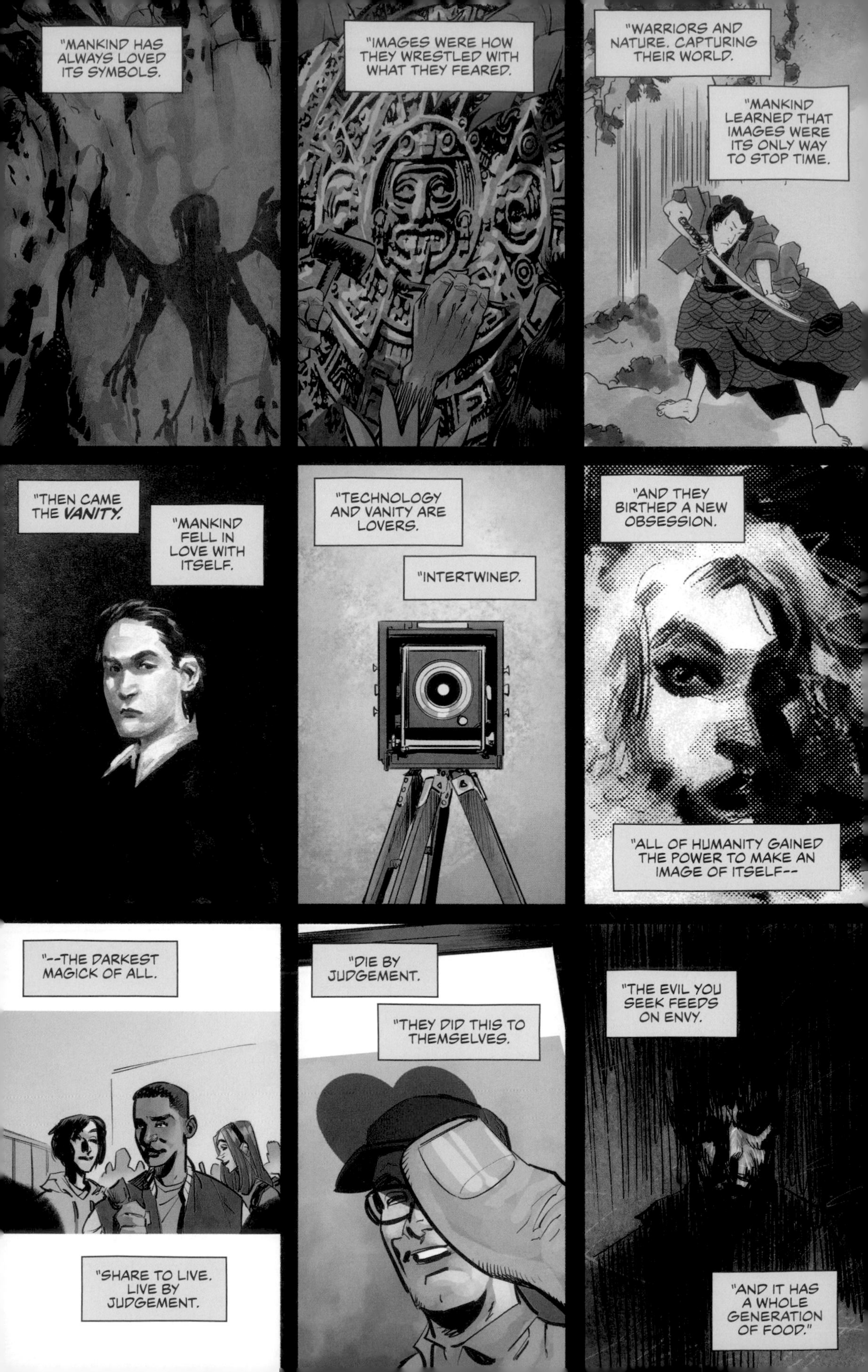
"MANKIND HAS ALWAYS LOVED ITS SYMBOLS.
"IMAGES WERE HOW THEY WRESTLED WITH WHAT THEY FEARED.
"WARRIORS AND NATURE. CAPTURING THEIR WORLD.
"MANKIND LEARNED THAT IMAGES WERE ITS ONLY WAY TO STOP TIME.
"THEN CAME THE *VANITY.*
"MANKIND FELL IN LOVE WITH ITSELF.
"TECHNOLOGY AND VANITY ARE LOVERS.
"INTERTWINED.
"AND THEY BIRTHED A NEW OBSESSION.
"ALL OF HUMANITY GAINED THE POWER TO MAKE AN IMAGE OF ITSELF--
"--THE DARKEST MAGICK OF ALL.
"SHARE TO LIVE. LIVE BY JUDGEMENT.
"DIE BY JUDGEMENT.
"THEY DID THIS TO THEMSELVES.
"THE EVIL YOU SEEK FEEDS ON ENVY.
"AND IT HAS A WHOLE GENERATION OF FOOD."

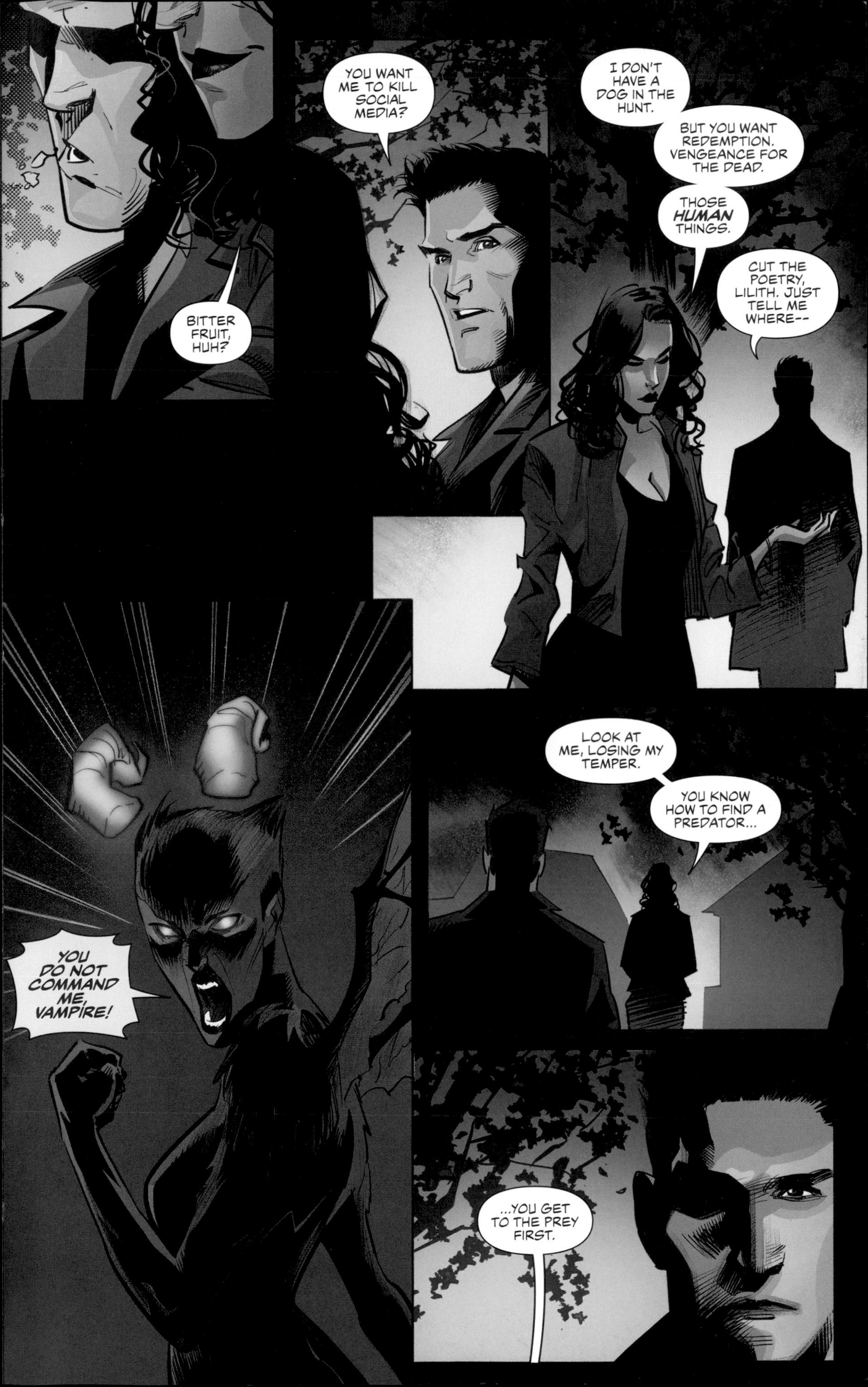
BITTER FRUIT, HUH?
YOU WANT ME TO KILL SOCIAL MEDIA?
I DON'T HAVE A DOG IN THE HUNT.
BUT YOU WANT REDEMPTION. VENGEANCE FOR THE DEAD.
THOSE *HUMAN* THINGS.
CUT THE POETRY, LILITH. JUST TELL ME WHERE--
YOU DO NOT COMMAND ME, VAMPIRE!
LOOK AT ME, LOSING MY TEMPER.
YOU KNOW HOW TO FIND A PREDATOR...
...YOU GET TO THE PREY FIRST.

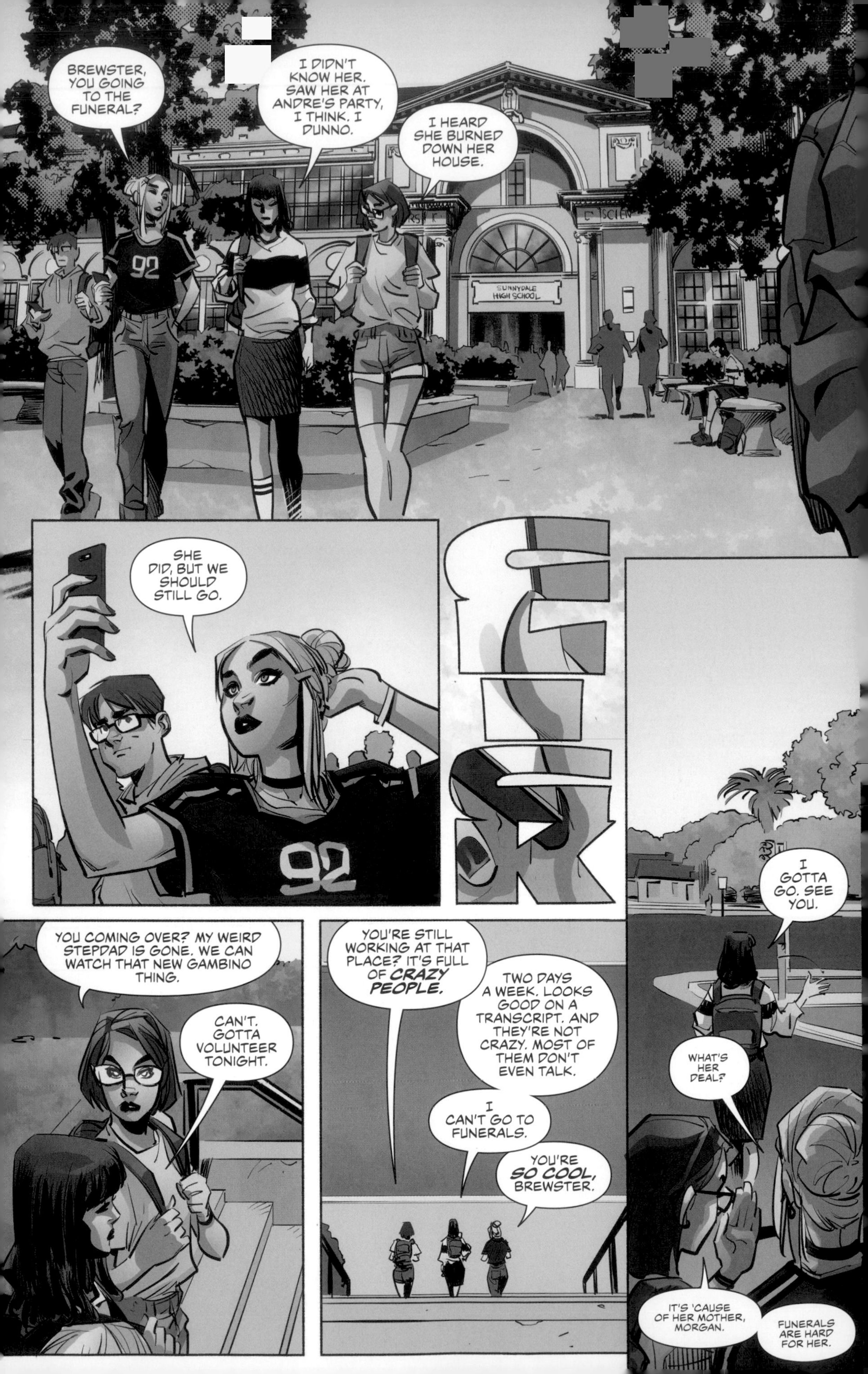
BREWSTER, YOU GOING TO THE FUNERAL?
I DIDN'T KNOW HER. SAW HER AT ANDRE'S PARTY, I THINK. I DUNNO.
I HEARD SHE BURNED DOWN HER HOUSE.
SUNNYDALE HIGH SCHOOL
SHE DID, BUT WE SHOULD STILL GO.
I GOTTA GO. SEE YOU.
YOU COMING OVER? MY WEIRD STEPDAD IS GONE. WE CAN WATCH THAT NEW GAMBINO THING.
CAN'T. GOTTA VOLUNTEER TONIGHT.
YOU'RE STILL WORKING AT THAT PLACE? IT'S FULL OF *CRAZY PEOPLE.*
TWO DAYS A WEEK. LOOKS GOOD ON A TRANSCRIPT. AND THEY'RE NOT CRAZY. MOST OF THEM DON'T EVEN TALK.
I CAN'T GO TO FUNERALS.
YOU'RE *SO COOL,* BREWSTER.
WHAT'S HER DEAL?
IT'S 'CAUSE OF HER MOTHER, MORGAN.
FUNERALS ARE HARD FOR HER.

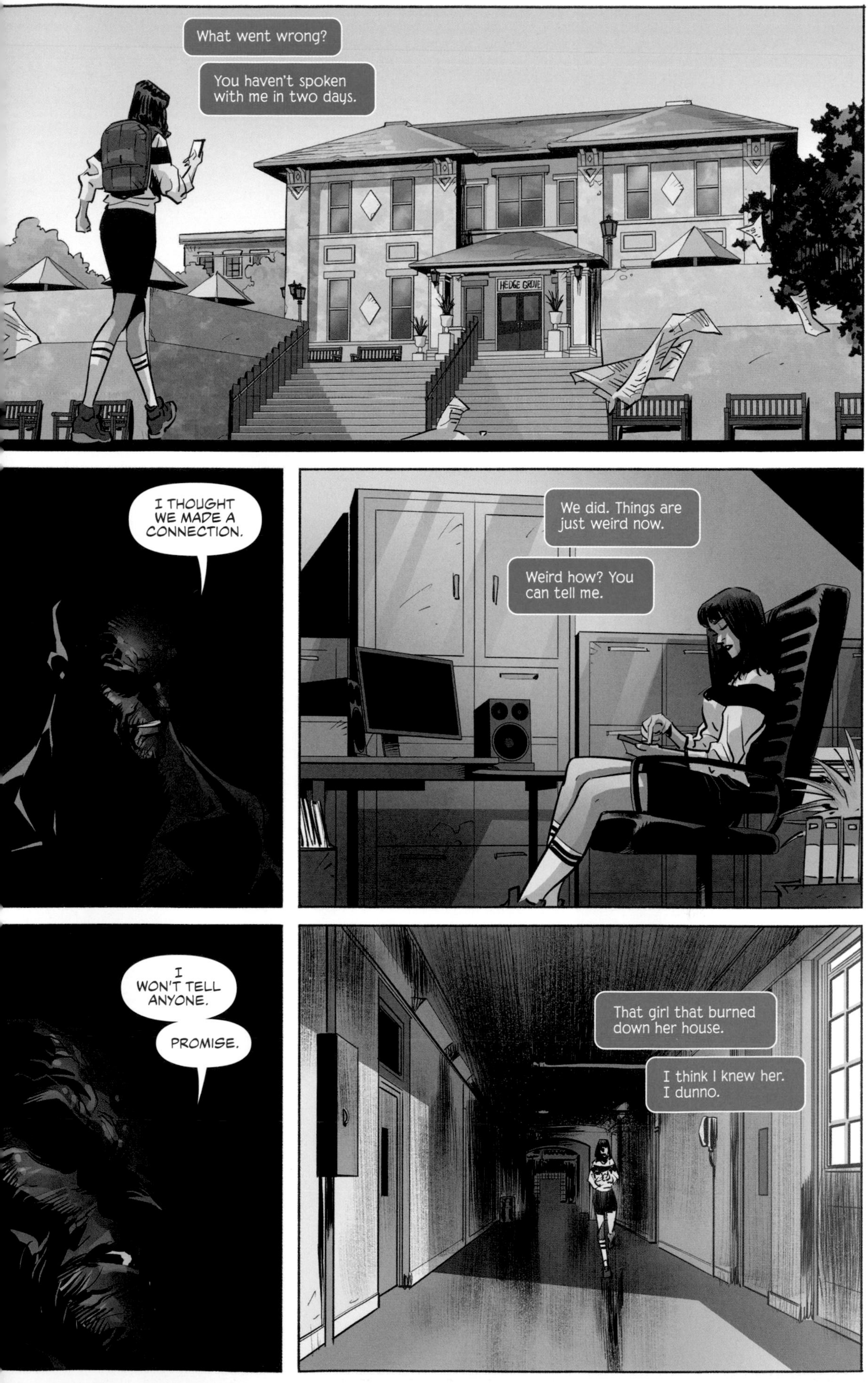
What went wrong?
You haven't spoken with me in two days.
HEDGE GROVE
I THOUGHT WE MADE A CONNECTION.
We did. Things are just weird now.
Weird how? You can tell me.
I WON'T TELL ANYONE.
PROMISE.
That girl that burned down her house.
I think I knew her. I dunno.

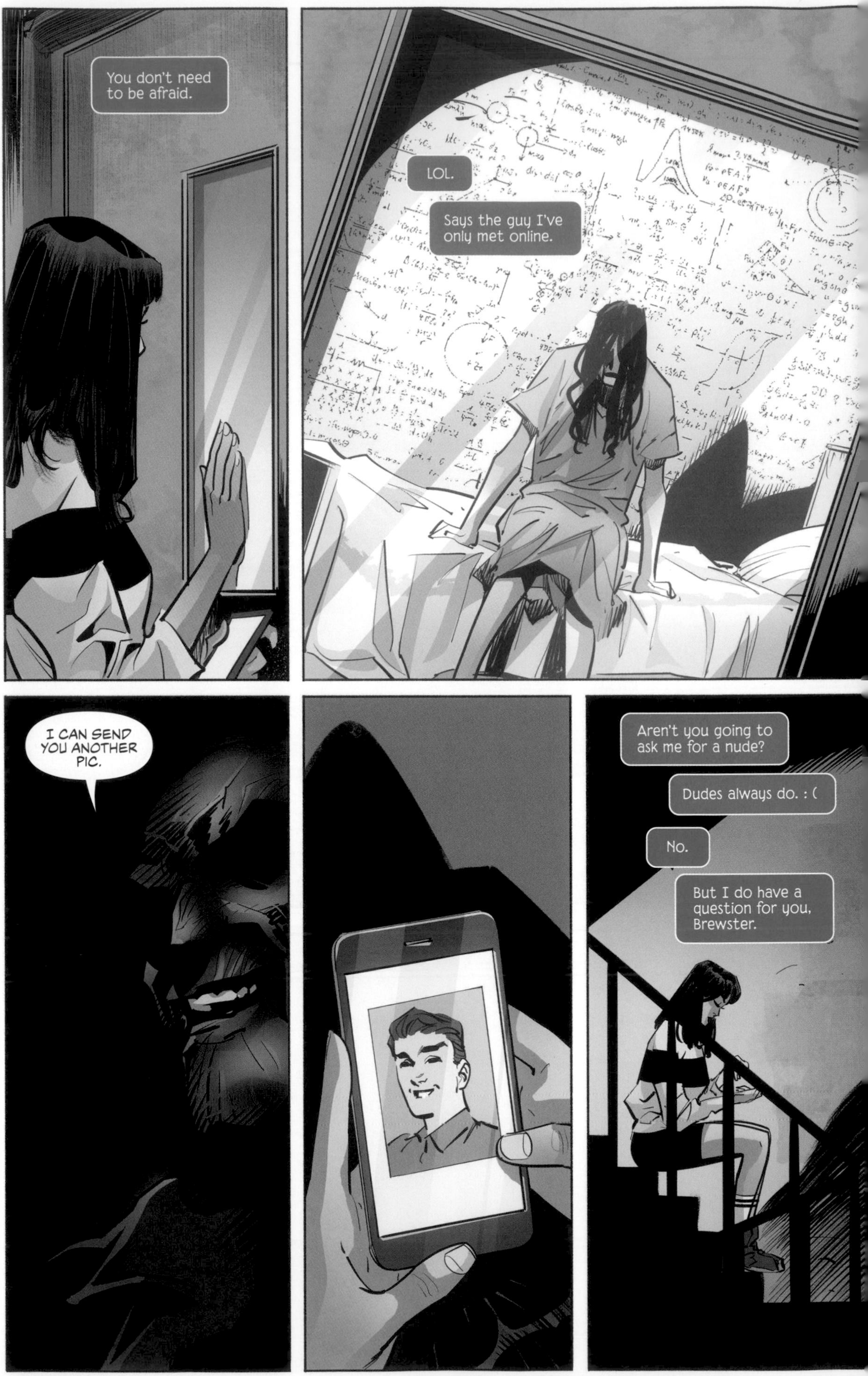
You don't need
to be afraid.
LOL.
Says the guy I've
only met online.
I CAN SEND
YOU ANOTHER
PIC.
Aren't you going to
ask me for a nude?
Dudes always do. : (
No.
But I do have a
question for you,
Brewster.

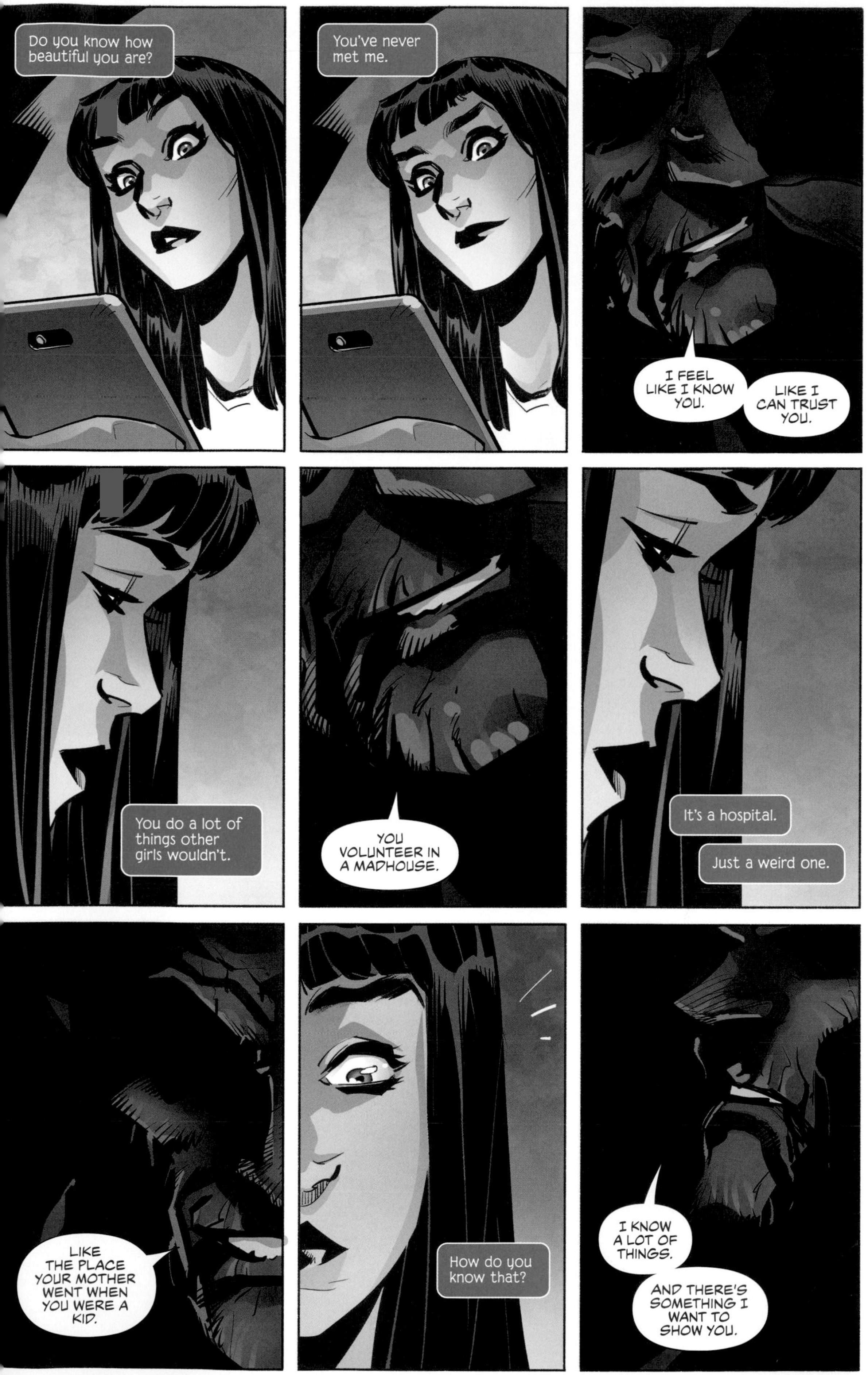
Do you know how beautiful you are?
You've never met me.
I FEEL LIKE I KNOW YOU.
LIKE I CAN TRUST YOU.
You do a lot of things other girls wouldn't.
YOU VOLUNTEER IN A MADHOUSE.
It's a hospital.
Just a weird one.
LIKE THE PLACE YOUR MOTHER WENT WHEN YOU WERE A KID.
How do you know that?
I KNOW A LOT OF THINGS.
AND THERE'S SOMETHING I WANT TO SHOW YOU.

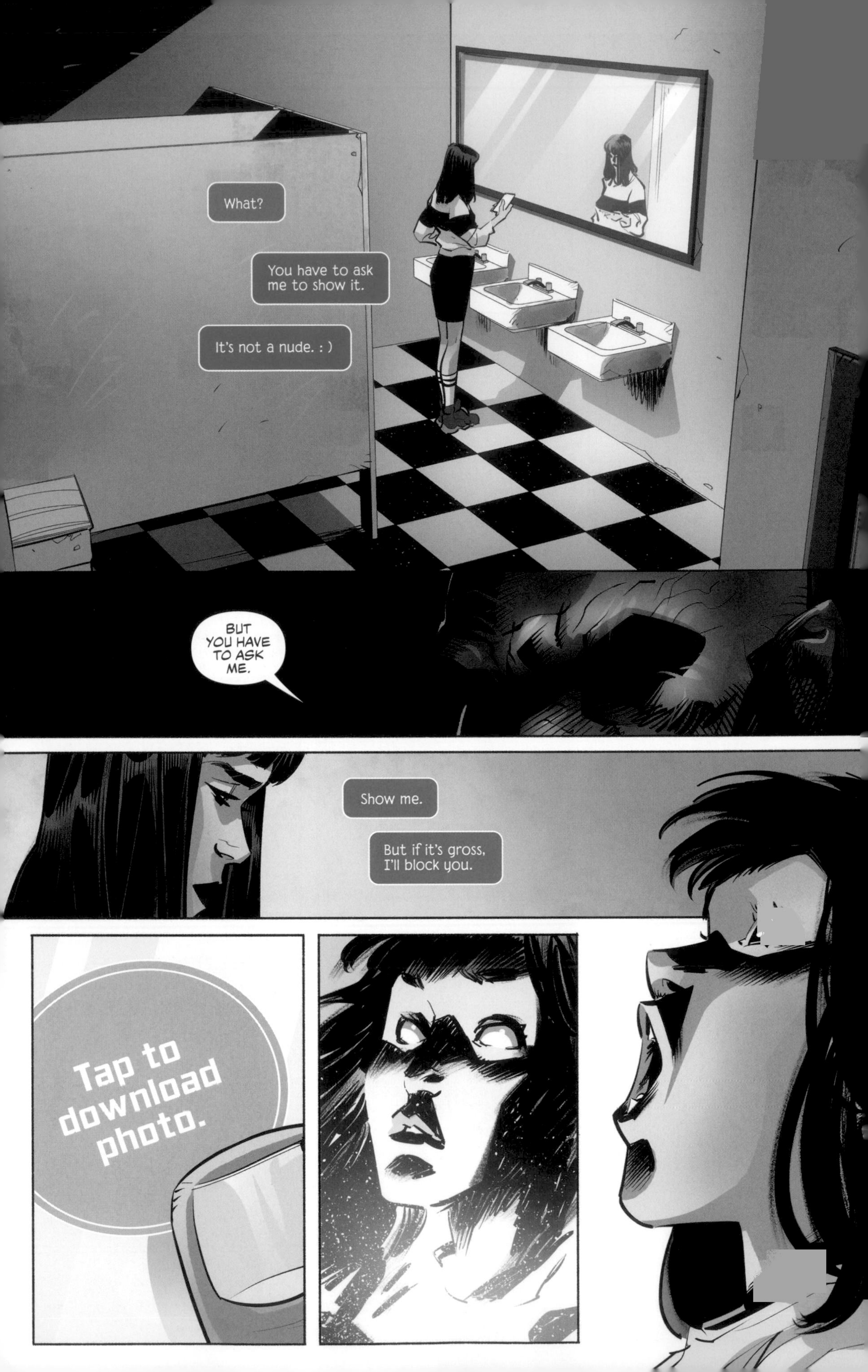
What?
You have to ask me to show it.
It's not a nude. :)
BUT YOU HAVE TO ASK ME.
Show me.
But if it's gross, I'll block you.
Tap to download photo.

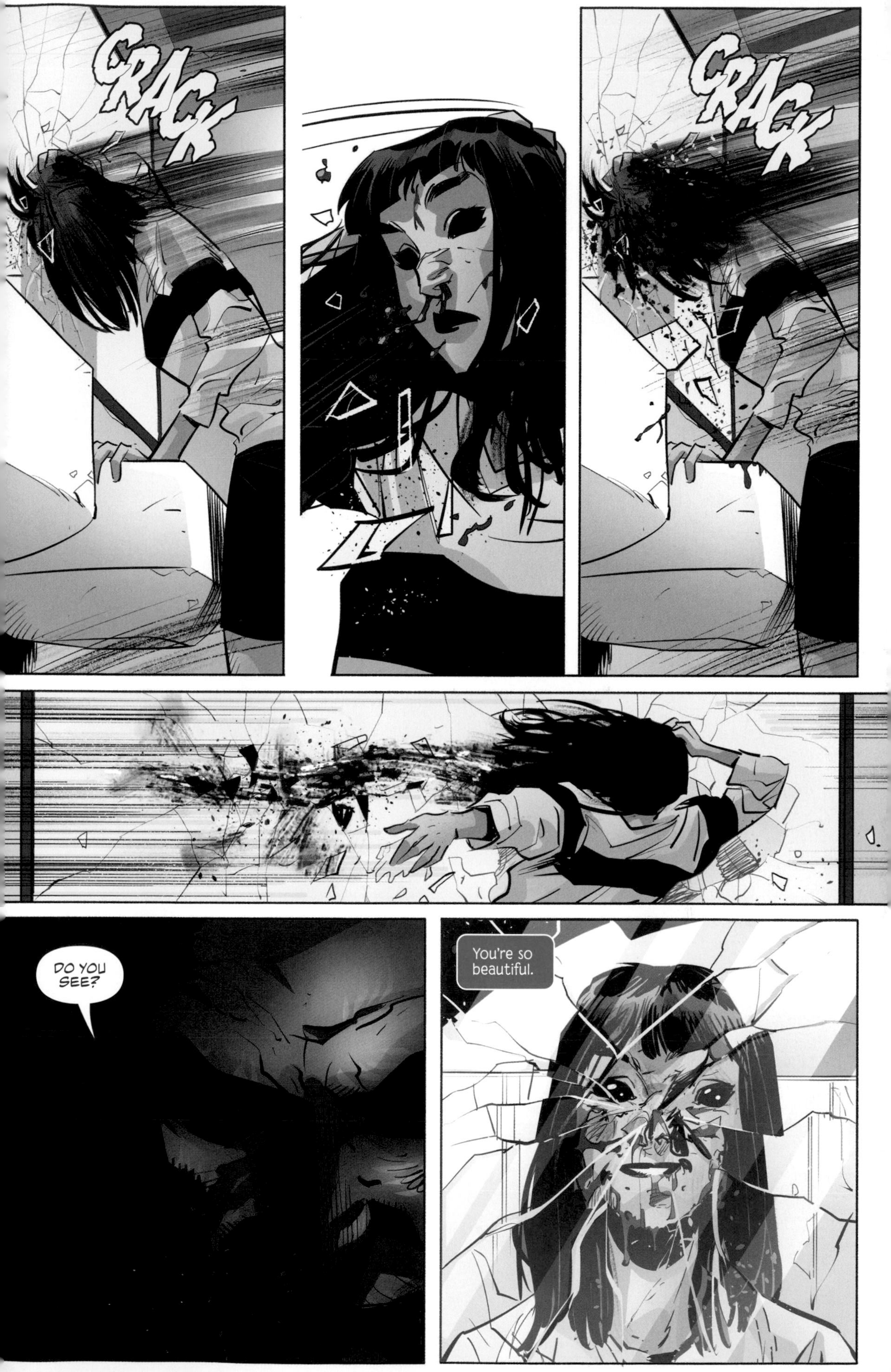
CRACK
CRACK
DO YOU SEE?
You're so beautiful.

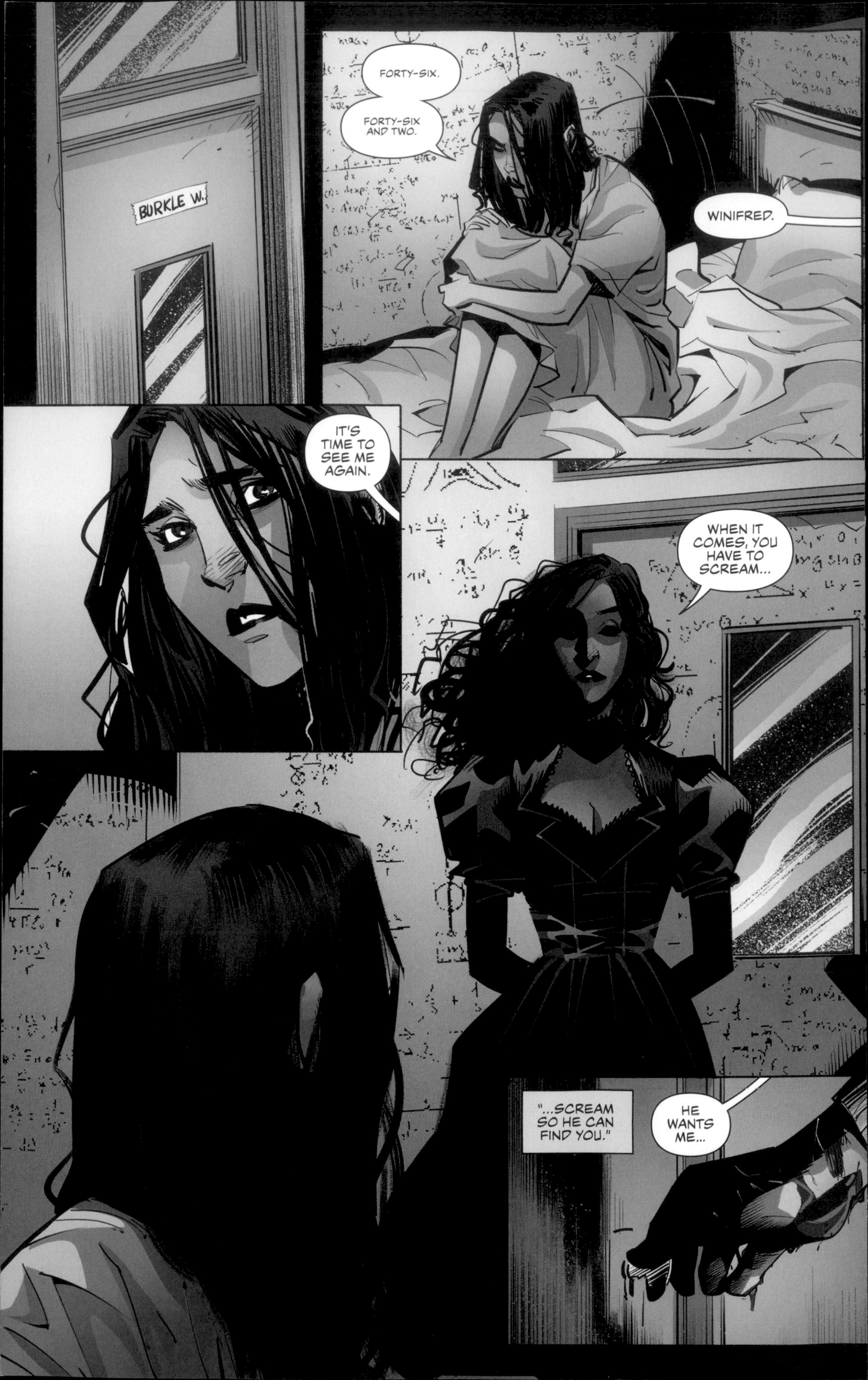
BURKLE W.
FORTY-SIX.
FORTY-SIX AND TWO.
WINIFRED.
IT'S TIME TO SEE ME AGAIN.
WHEN IT COMES, YOU HAVE TO SCREAM...
"...SCREAM SO HE CAN FIND YOU."
HE WANTS ME...

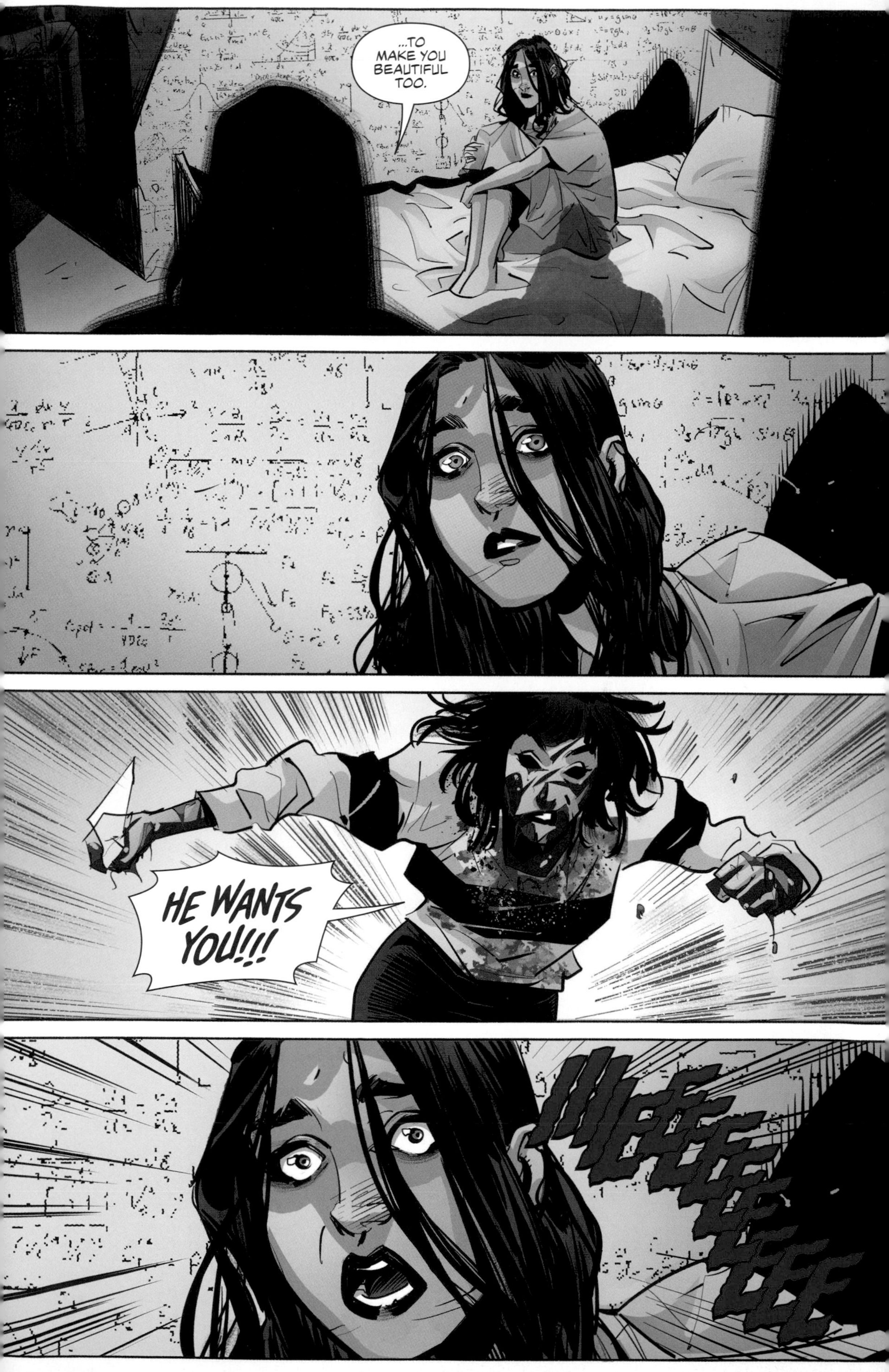
...TO MAKE YOU BEAUTIFUL TOO.
HE WANTS YOU!!!

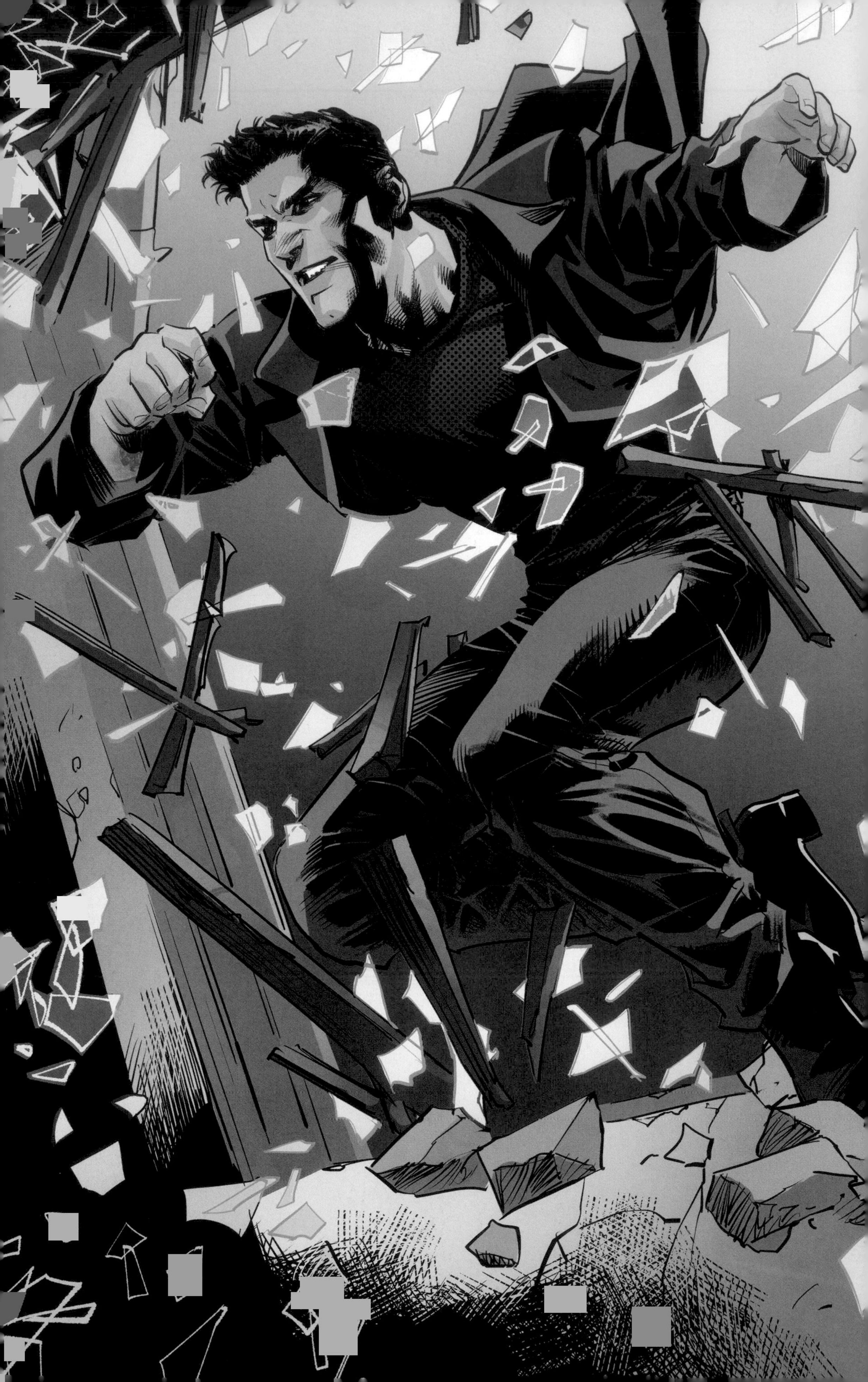

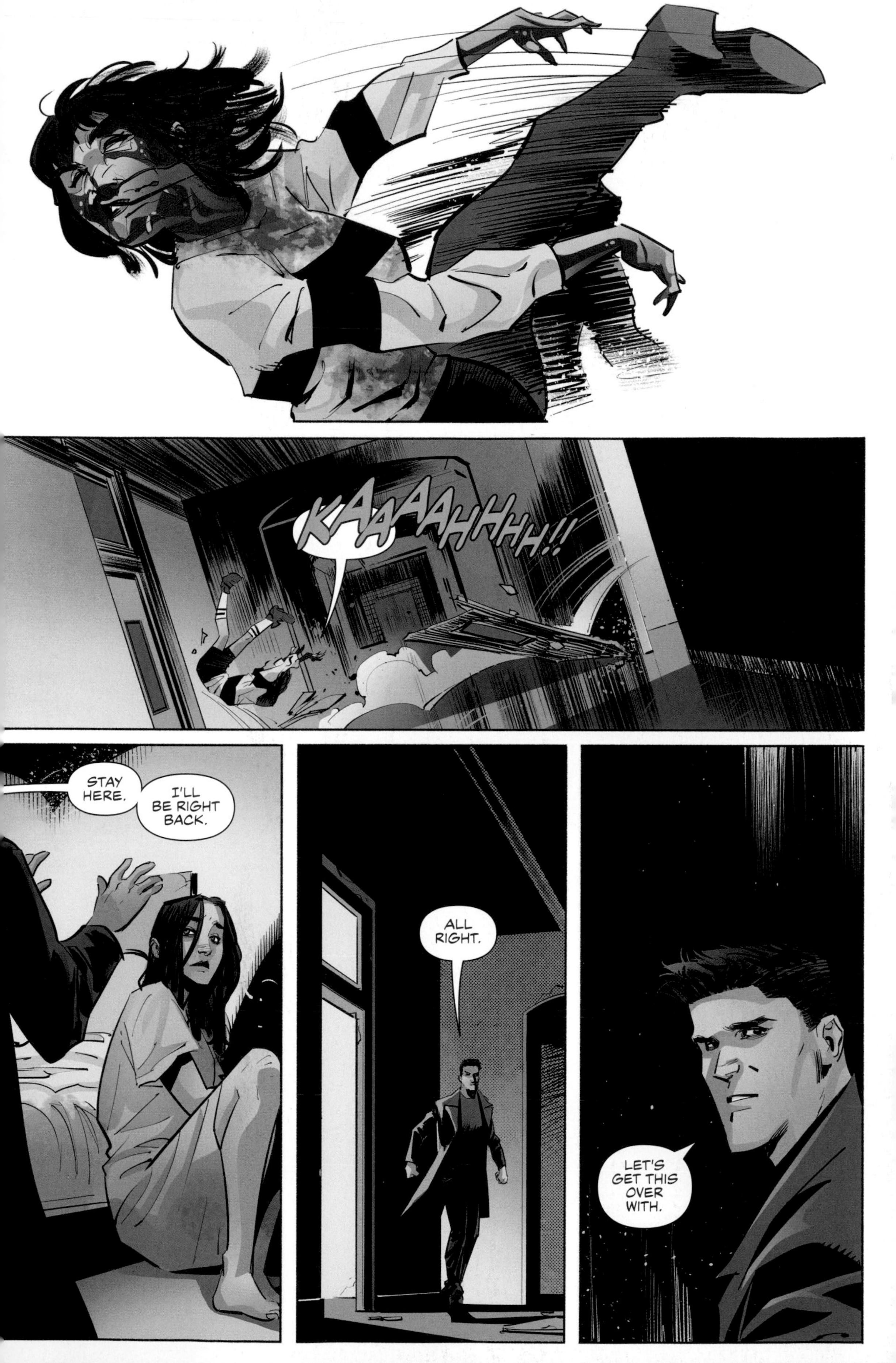
KAAAAHHHH!!
STAY HERE.
I'LL BE RIGHT BACK.
ALL RIGHT.
LET'S GET THIS OVER WITH.

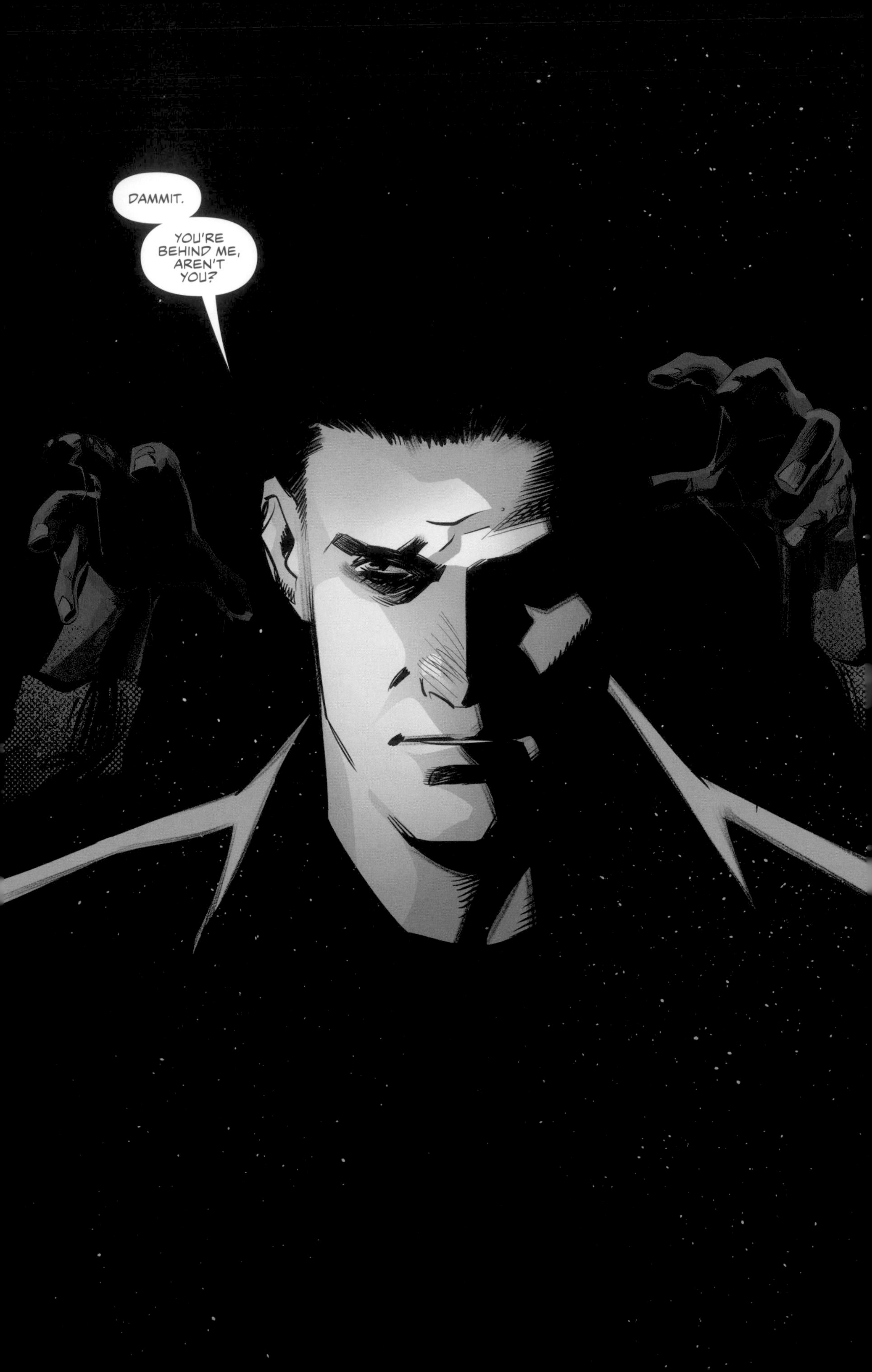
DAMMIT.
YOU'RE BEHIND ME, AREN'T YOU?

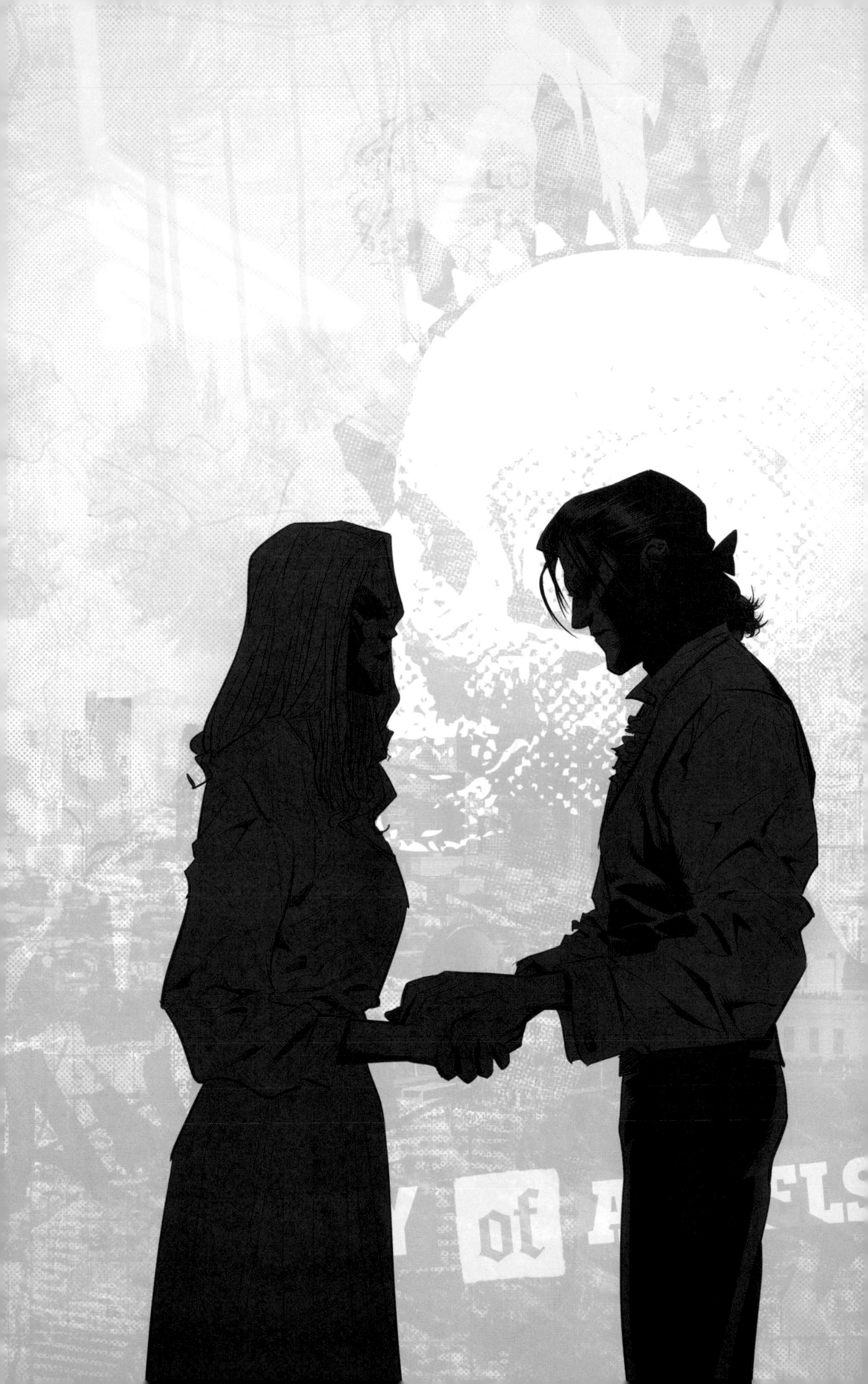
of

CHAPTER
THREE

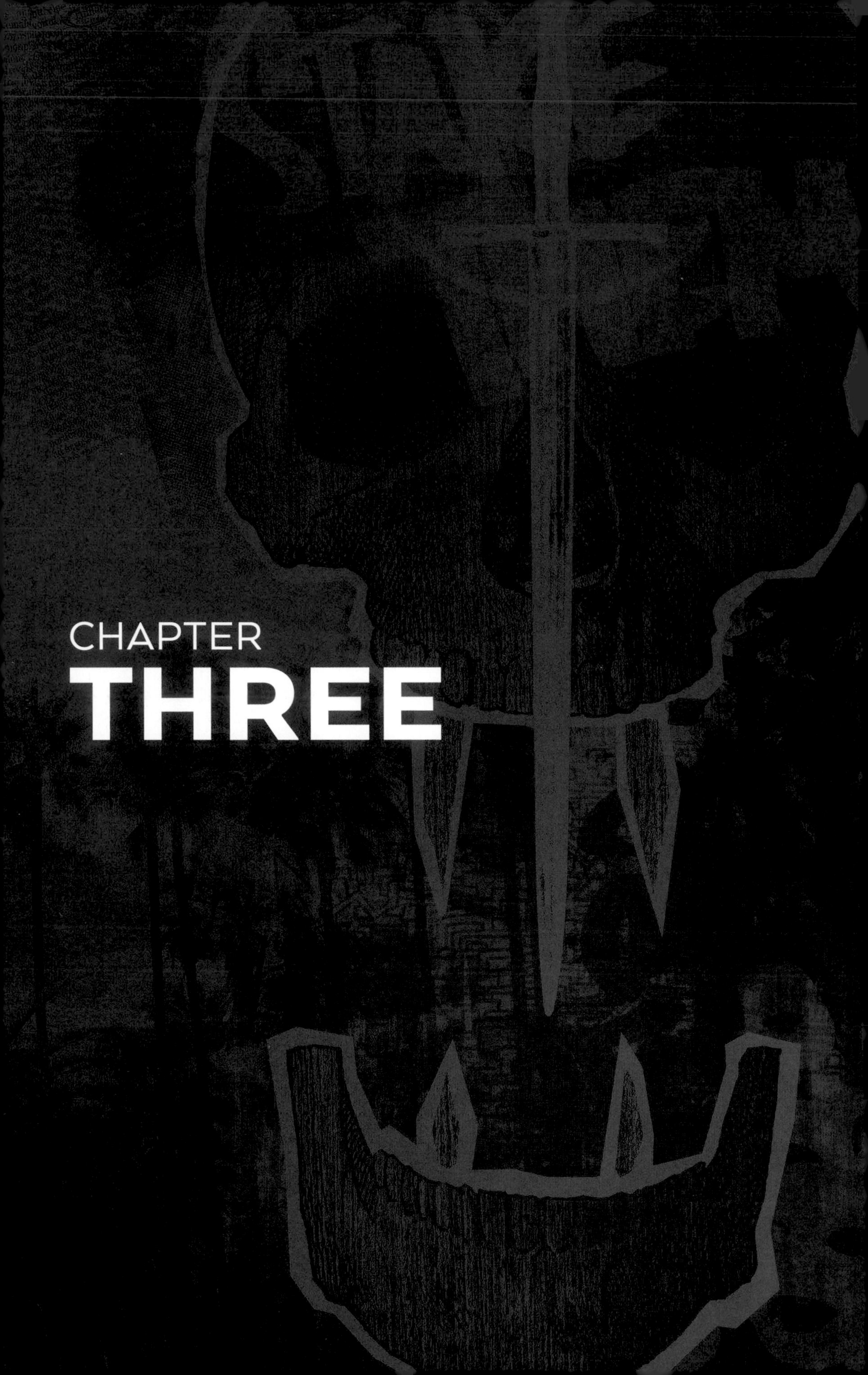

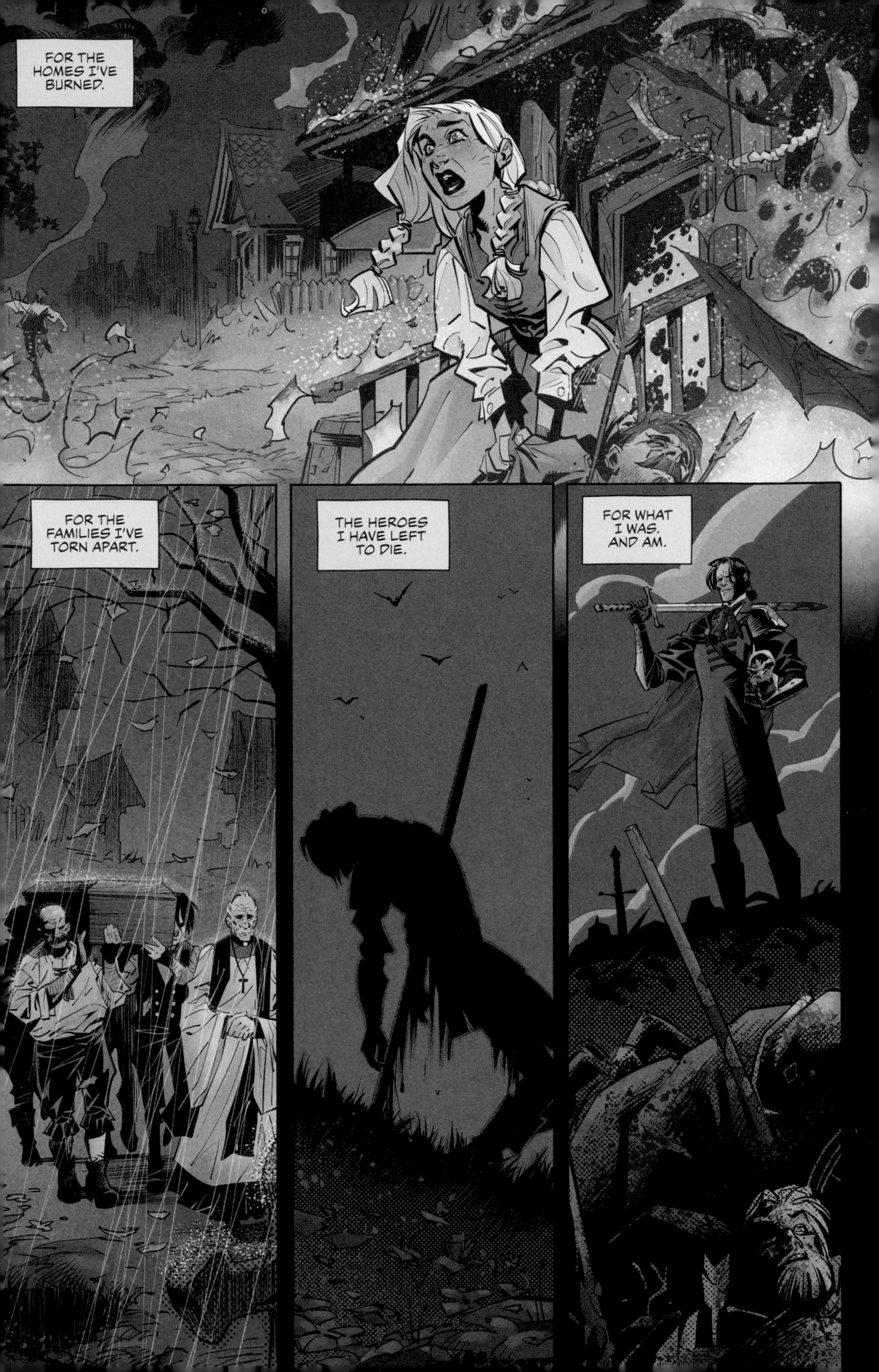
FOR THE HOMES I'VE BURNED.
FOR THE FAMILIES I'VE TORN APART.
THE HEROES I HAVE LEFT TO DIE.
FOR WHAT I WAS. AND AM.

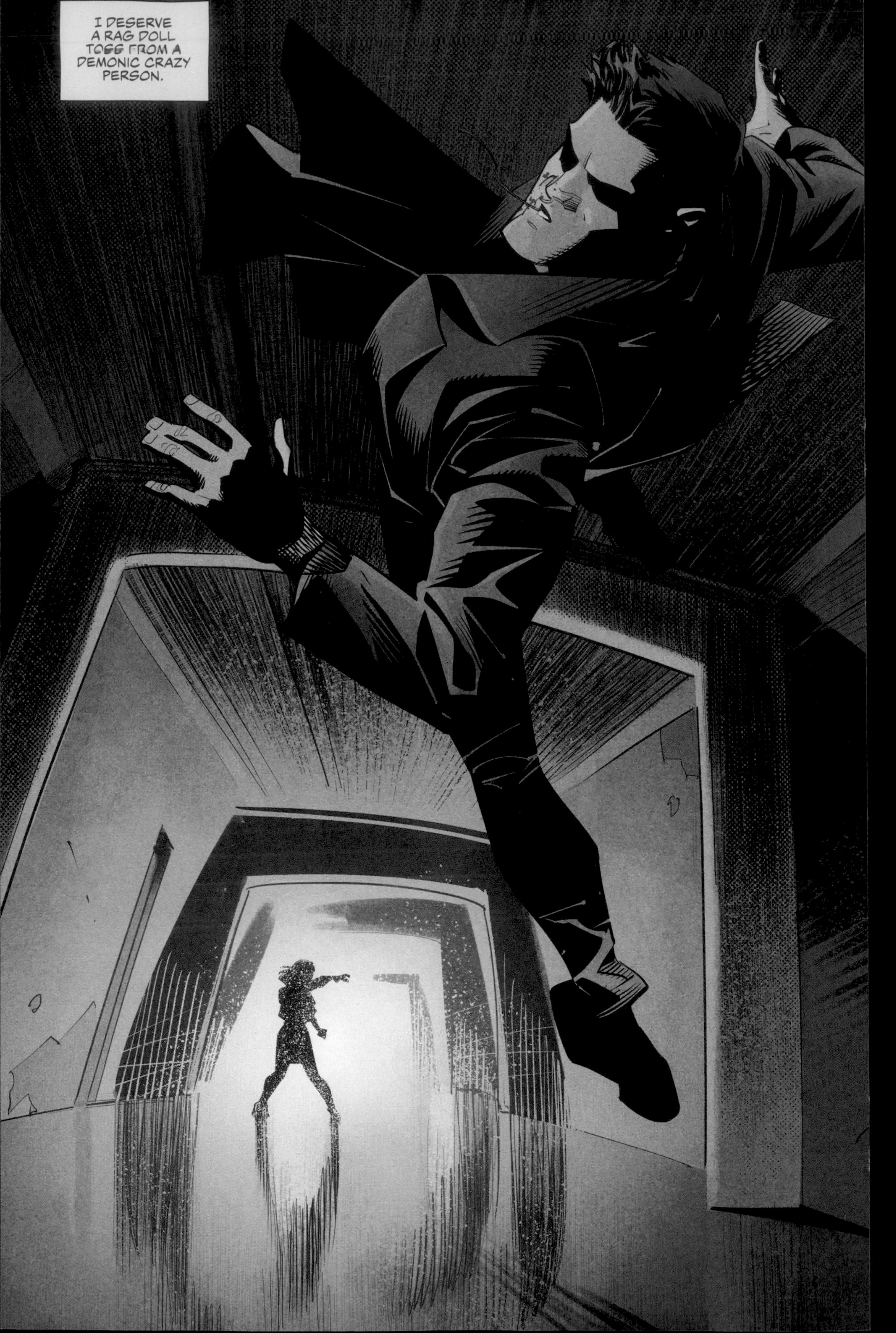
I DESERVE A RAG DOLL TOSS FROM A DEMONIC CRAZY PERSON.

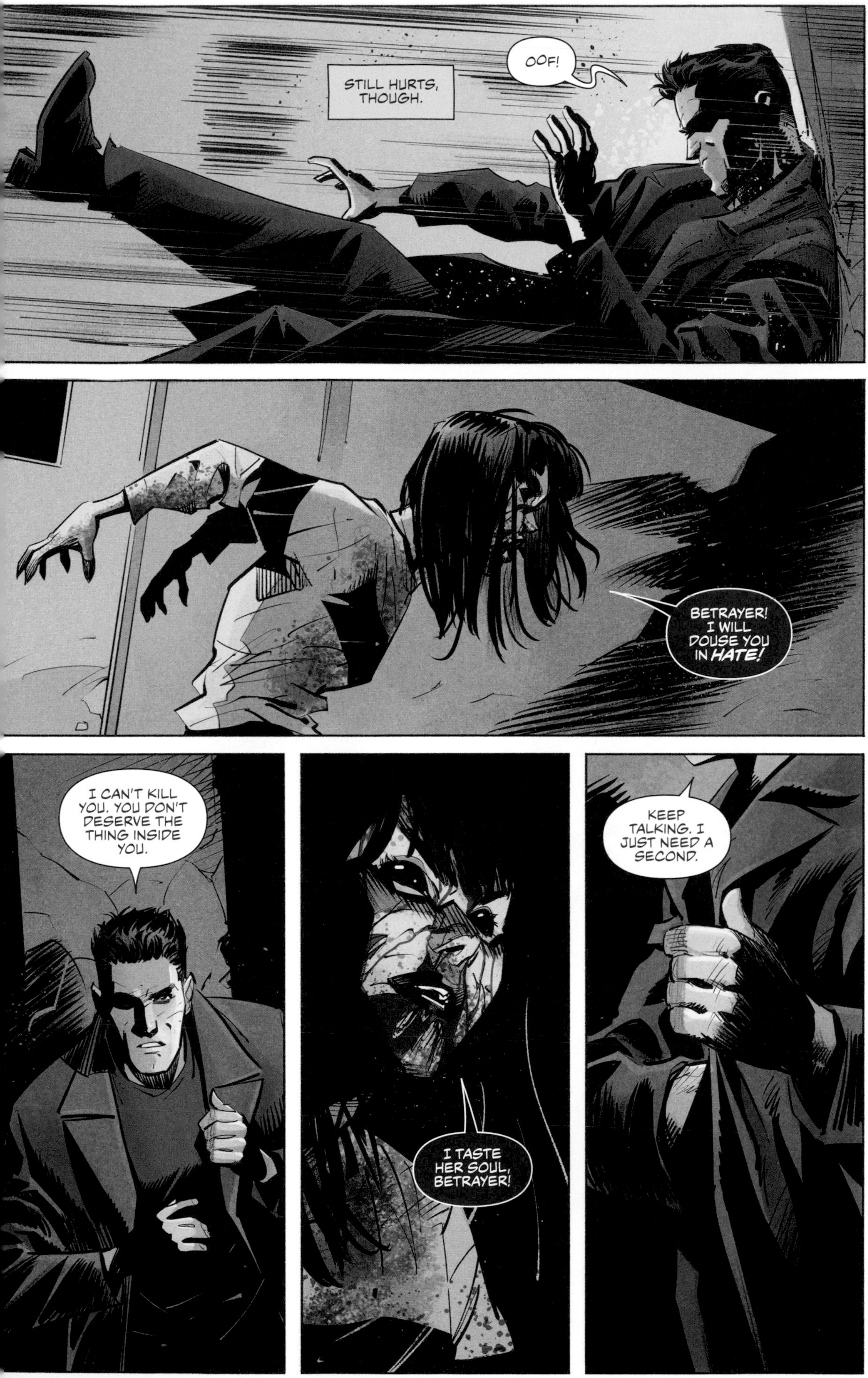
STILL HURTS, THOUGH.
OOF!
BETRAYER! I WILL DOUSE YOU IN *HATE!*
I CAN'T KILL YOU. YOU DON'T DESERVE THE THING INSIDE YOU.
I TASTE HER SOUL, BETRAYER!
KEEP TALKING. I JUST NEED A SECOND.

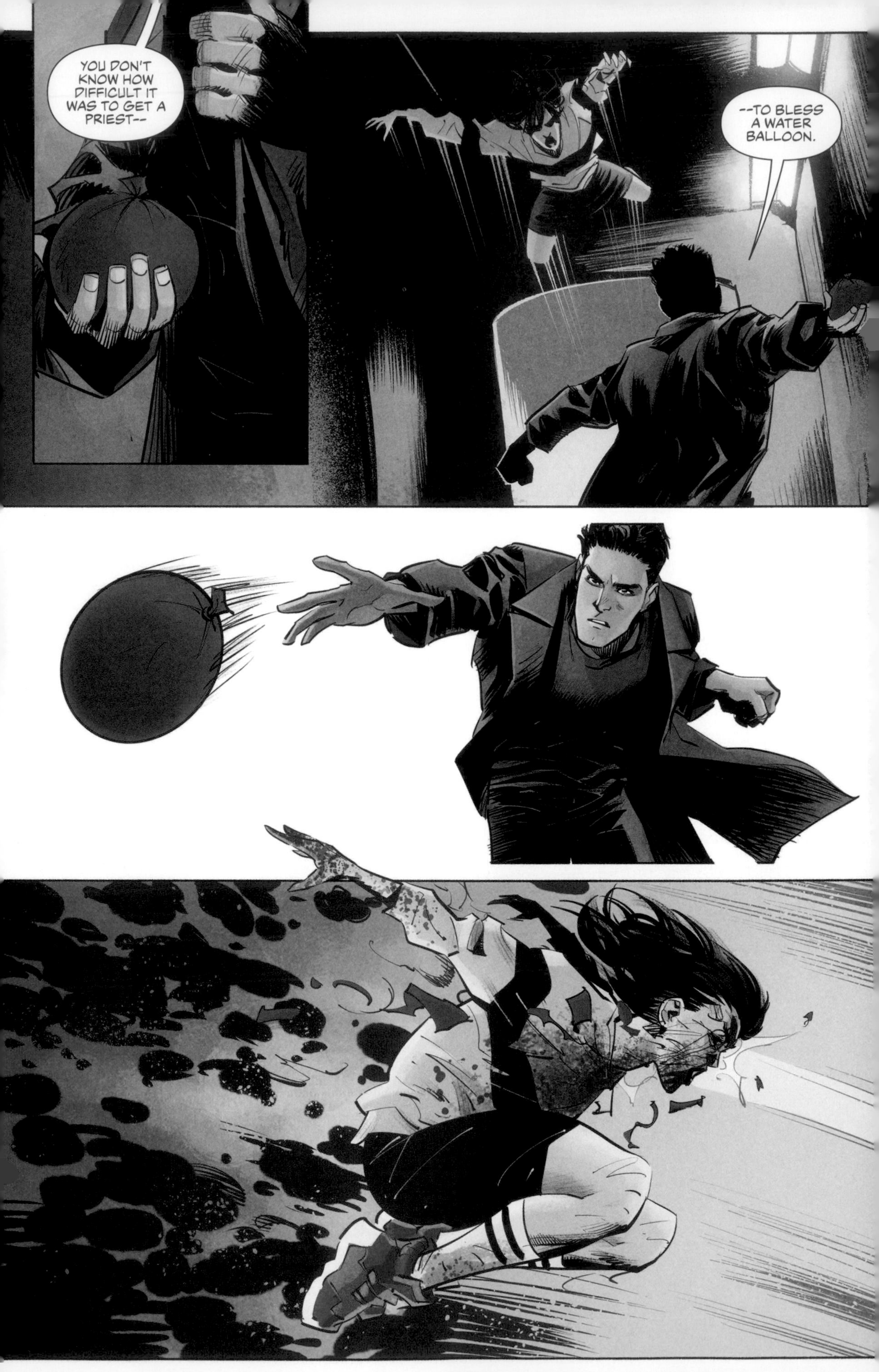
YOU DON'T KNOW HOW DIFFICULT IT WAS TO GET A PRIEST--
--TO BLESS A WATER BALLOON.

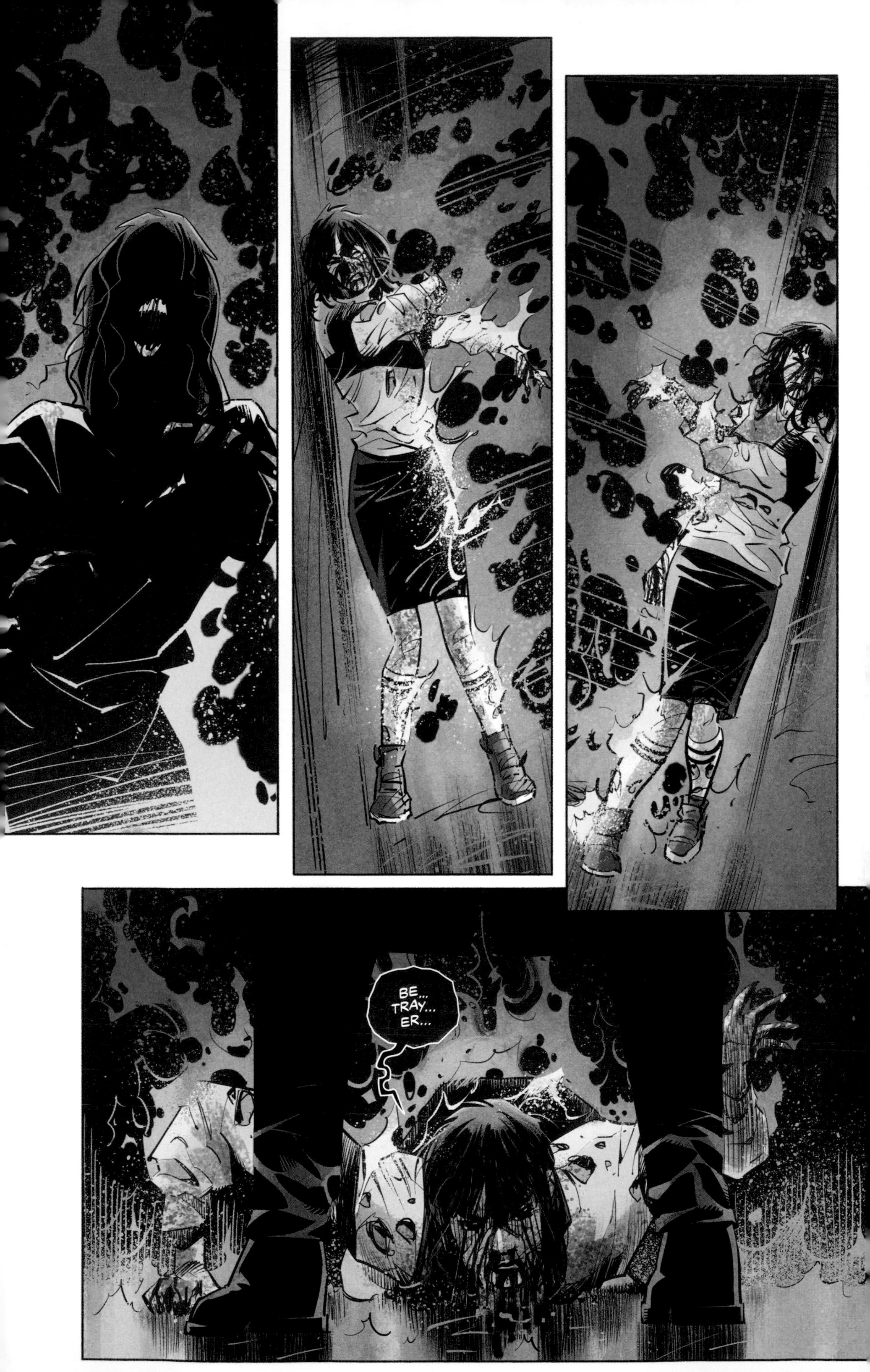
BE... TRAY... ER...

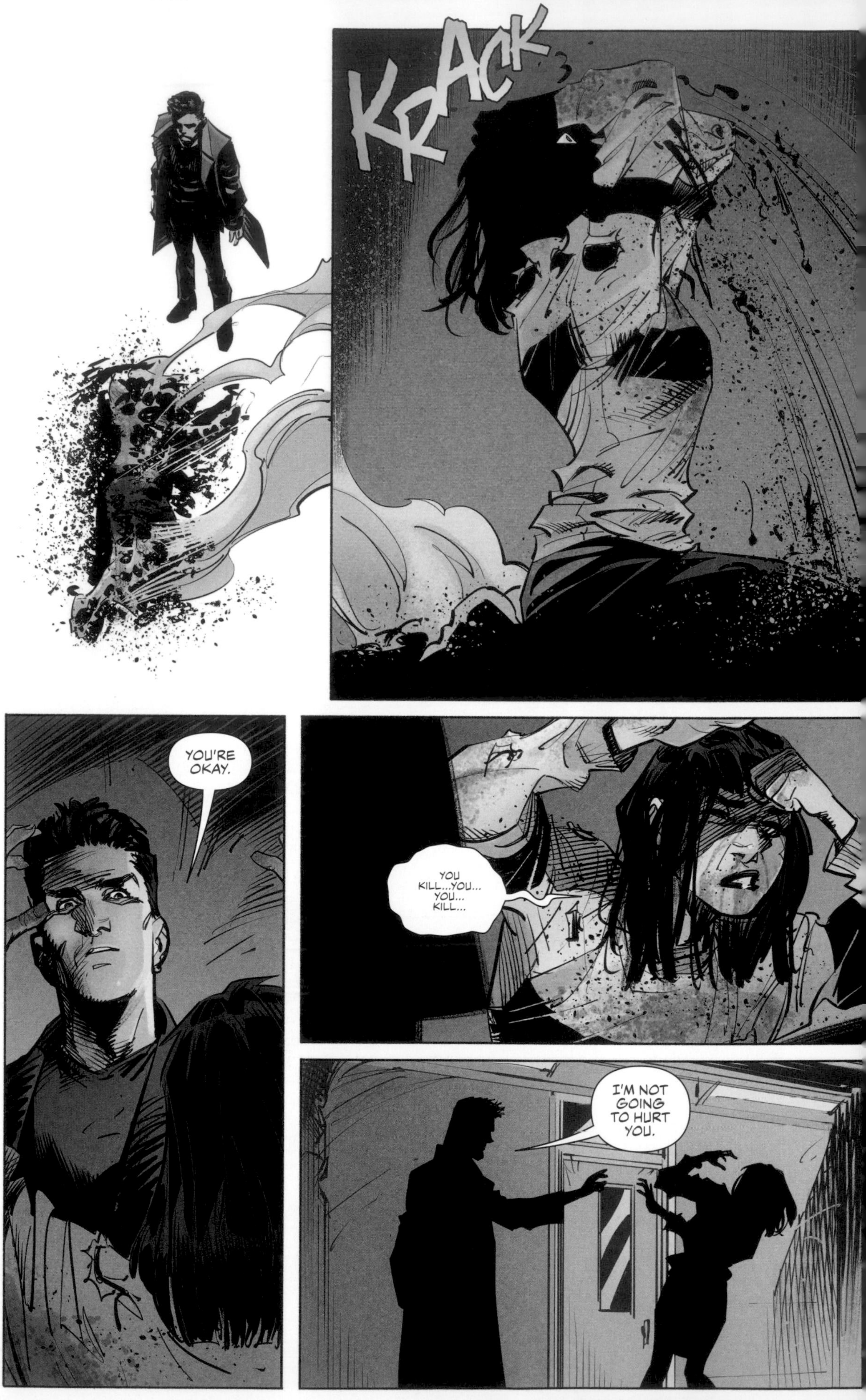
KRACK
YOU'RE OKAY.
YOU KILL...YOU... YOU... KILL...
I'M NOT GOING TO HURT YOU.

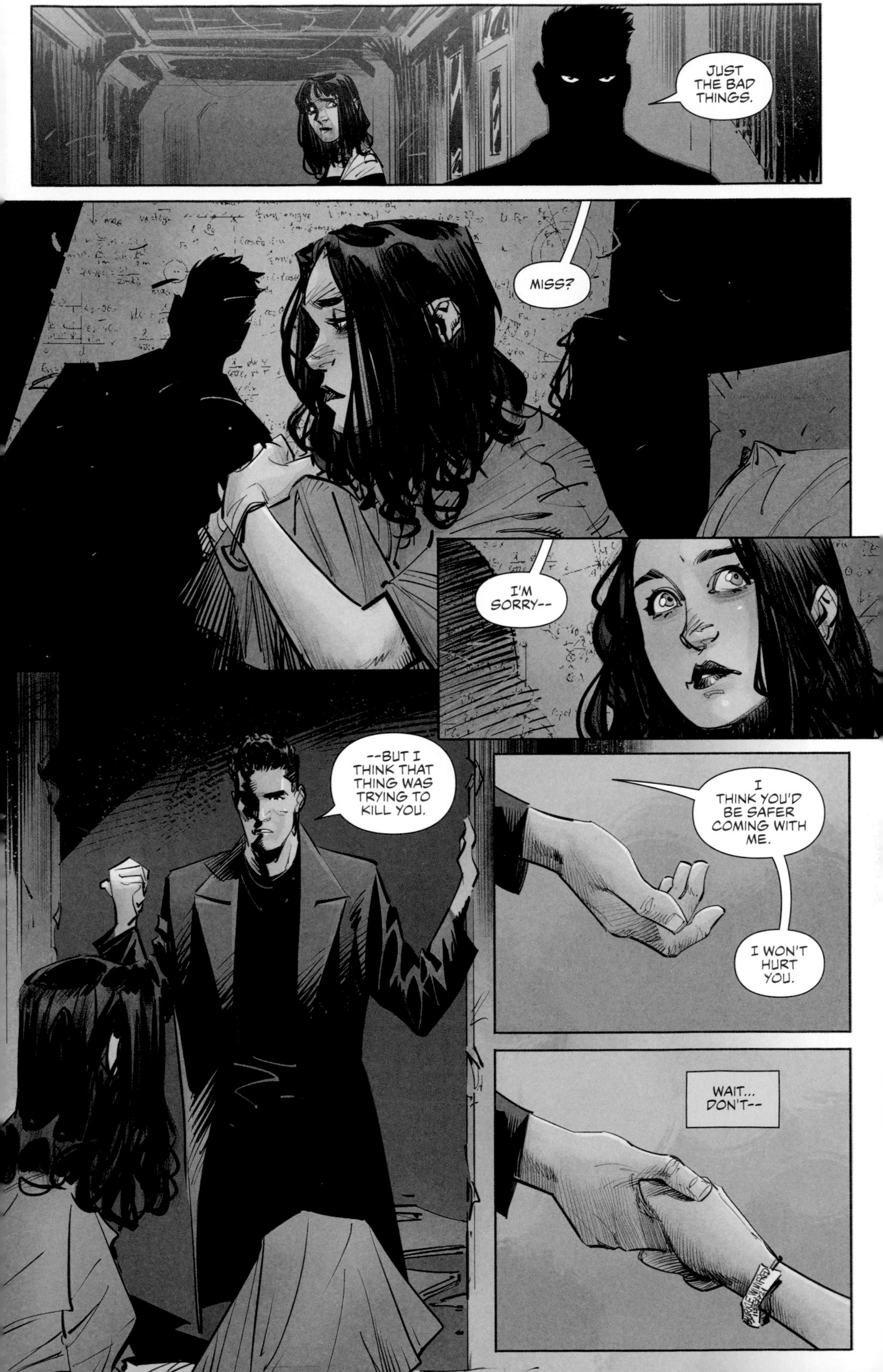
JUST THE BAD THINGS.
MISS?
I'M SORRY--
--BUT I THINK THAT THING WAS TRYING TO KILL YOU.
I THINK YOU'D BE SAFER COMING WITH ME.
I WON'T HURT YOU.
WAIT... DON'T--

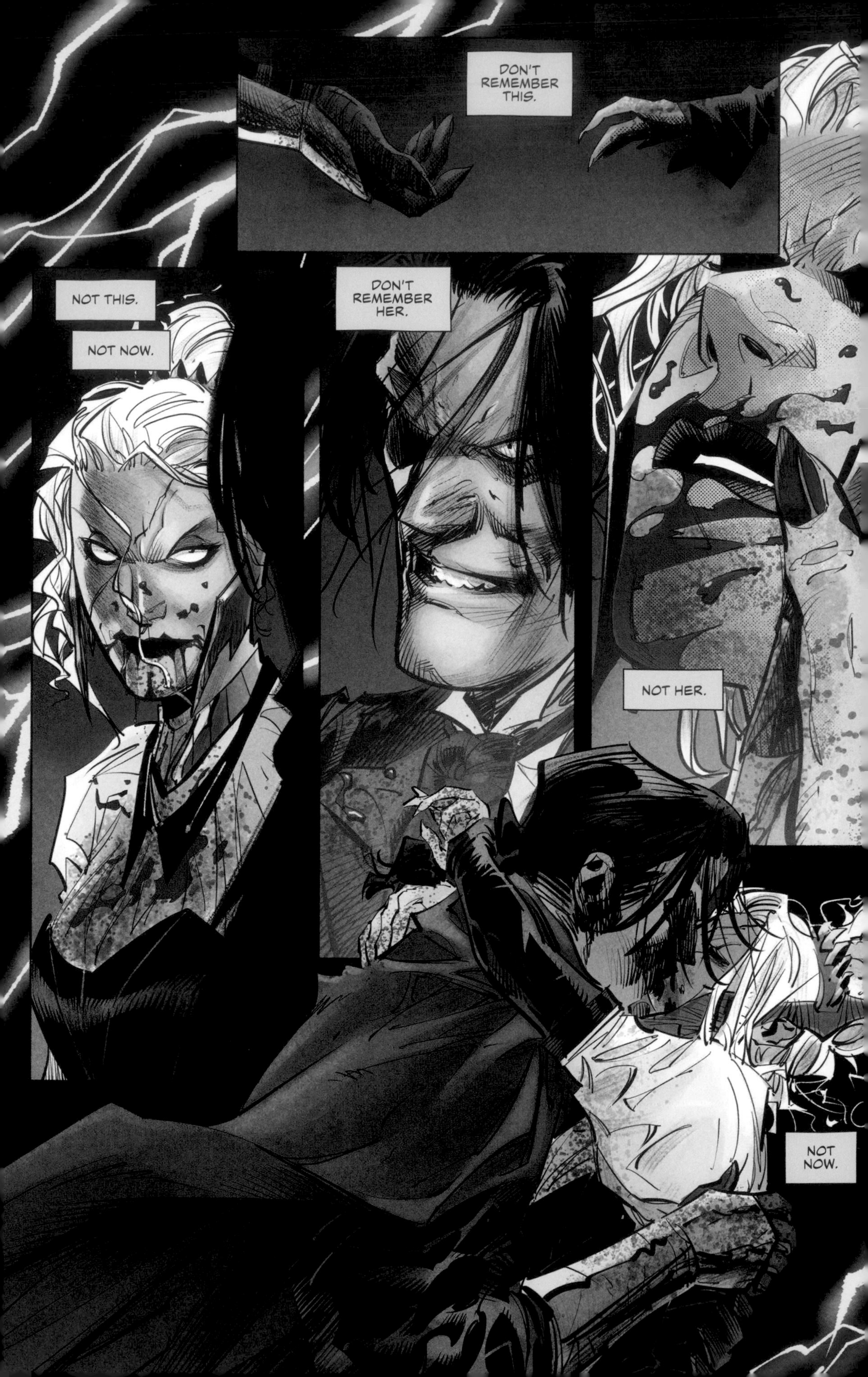
DON'T REMEMBER THIS.
NOT THIS.
NOT NOW.
DON'T REMEMBER HER.
NOT HER.
NOT NOW.

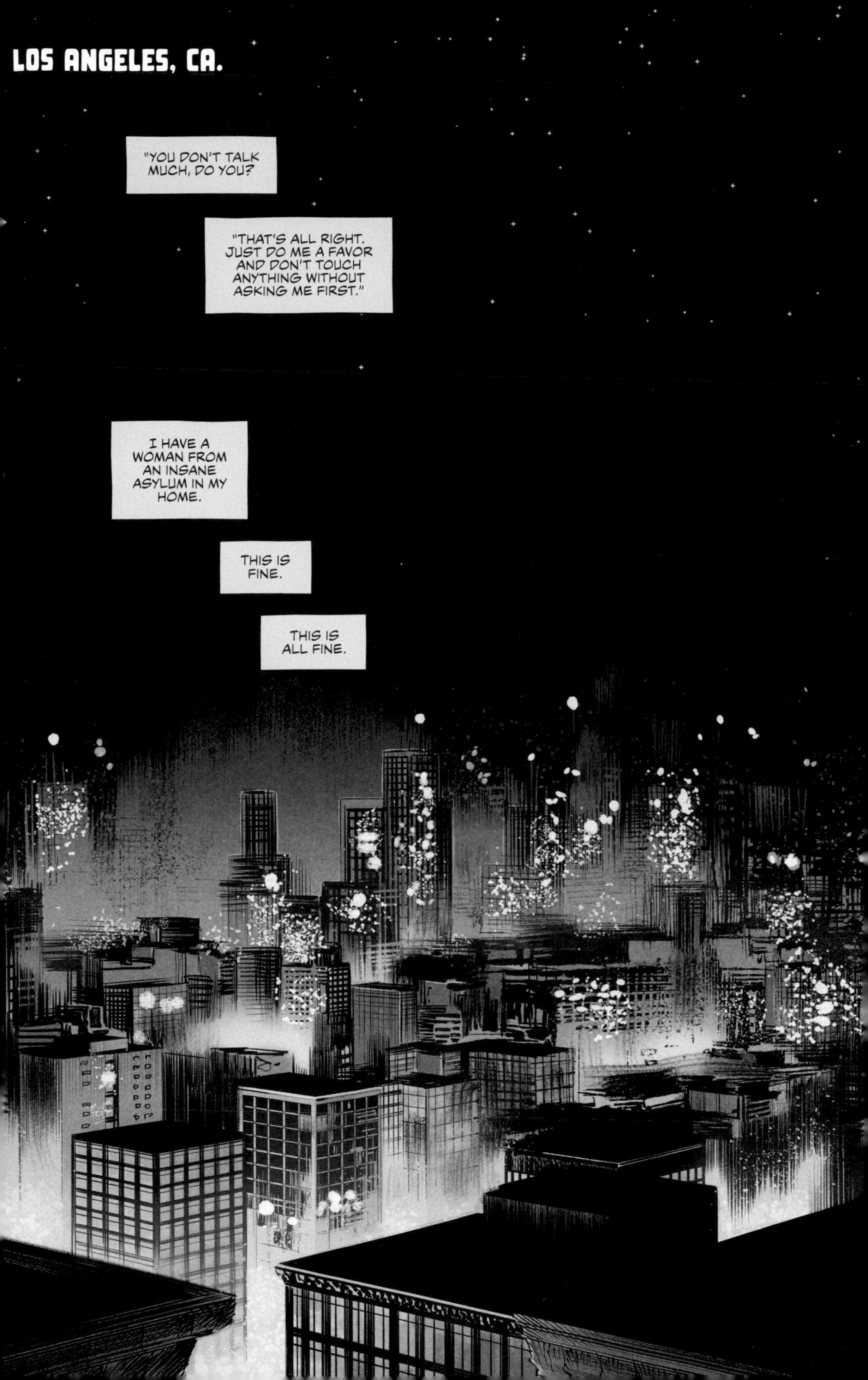
LOS ANGELES, CA.
"YOU DON'T TALK MUCH, DO YOU?
"THAT'S ALL RIGHT. JUST DO ME A FAVOR AND DON'T TOUCH ANYTHING WITHOUT ASKING ME FIRST."
I HAVE A WOMAN FROM AN INSANE ASYLUM IN MY HOME.
THIS IS FINE.
THIS IS ALL FINE.

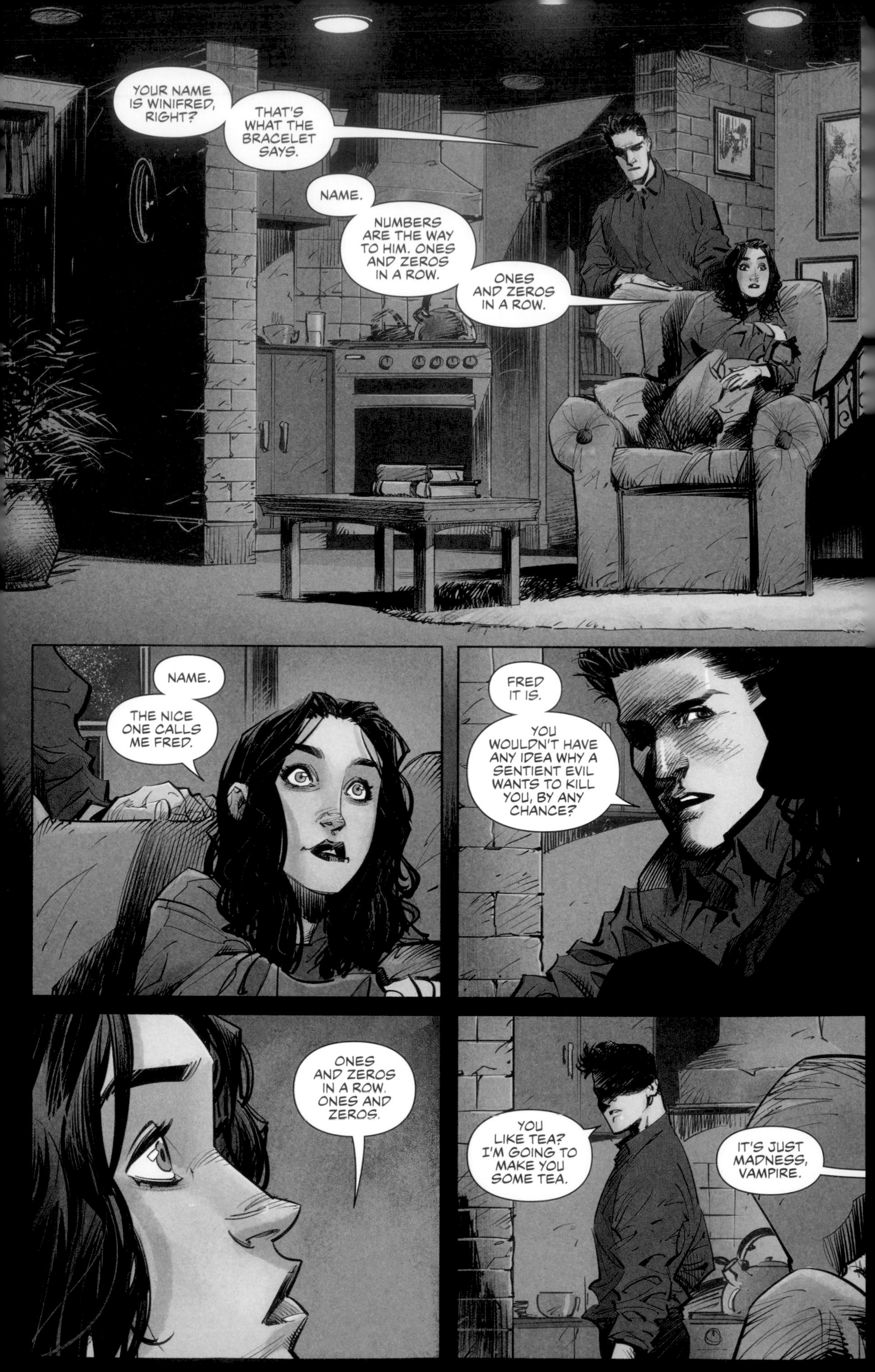
YOUR NAME IS WINIFRED, RIGHT?
THAT'S WHAT THE BRACELET SAYS.
NAME.
NUMBERS ARE THE WAY TO HIM. ONES AND ZEROS IN A ROW.
ONES AND ZEROS IN A ROW.
NAME.
THE NICE ONE CALLS ME FRED.
FRED IT IS.
YOU WOULDN'T HAVE ANY IDEA WHY A SENTIENT EVIL WANTS TO KILL YOU, BY ANY CHANCE?
ONES AND ZEROS IN A ROW. ONES AND ZEROS.
YOU LIKE TEA? I'M GOING TO MAKE YOU SOME TEA.
IT'S JUST MADNESS, VAMPIRE.

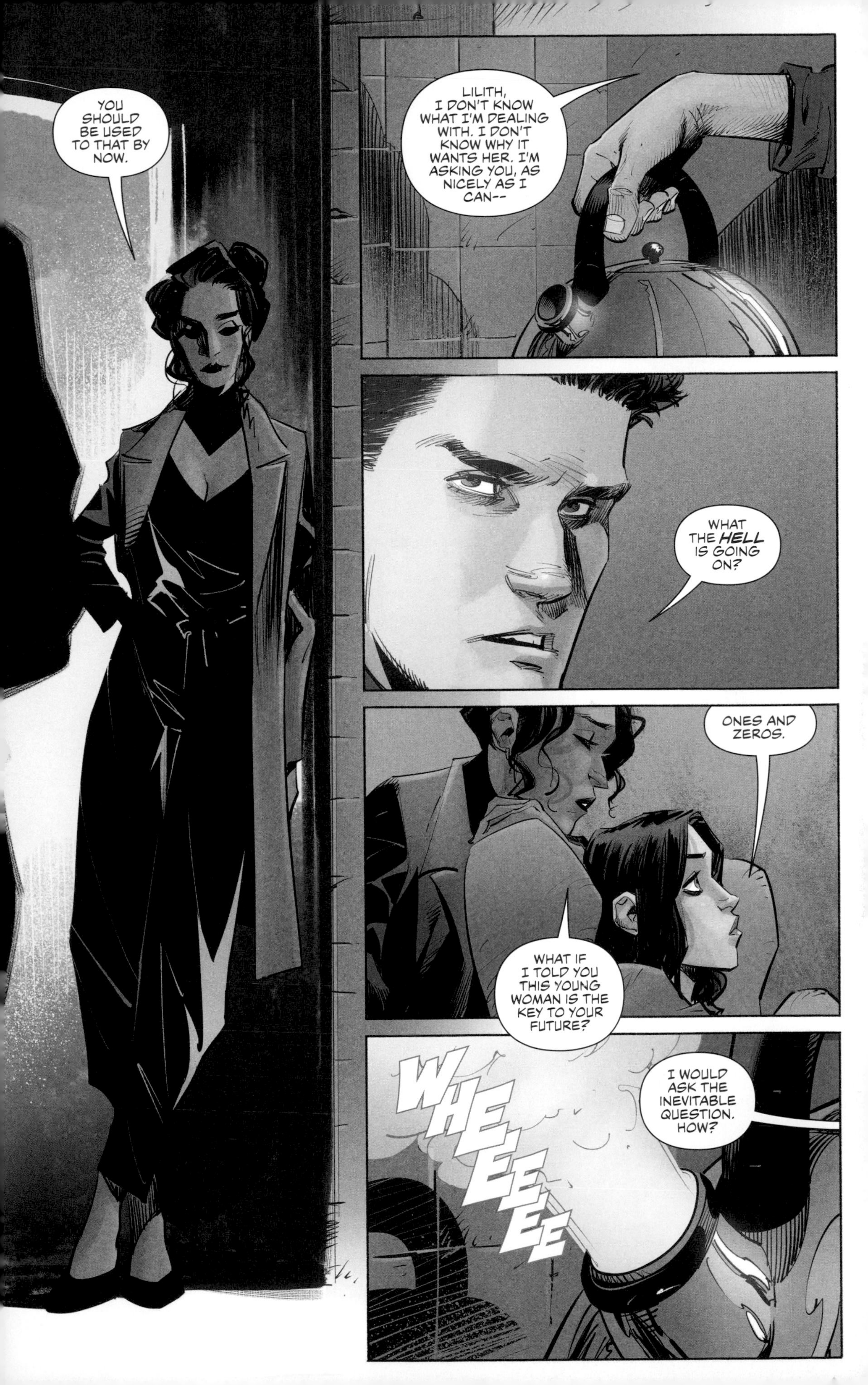
YOU SHOULD BE USED TO THAT BY NOW.
LILITH, I DON'T KNOW WHAT I'M DEALING WITH. I DON'T KNOW WHY IT WANTS HER. I'M ASKING YOU, AS NICELY AS I CAN--
WHAT THE *HELL* IS GOING ON?
ONES AND ZEROS.
WHAT IF I TOLD YOU THIS YOUNG WOMAN IS THE KEY TO YOUR FUTURE?
WHEEEEEE
I WOULD ASK THE INEVITABLE QUESTION. HOW?

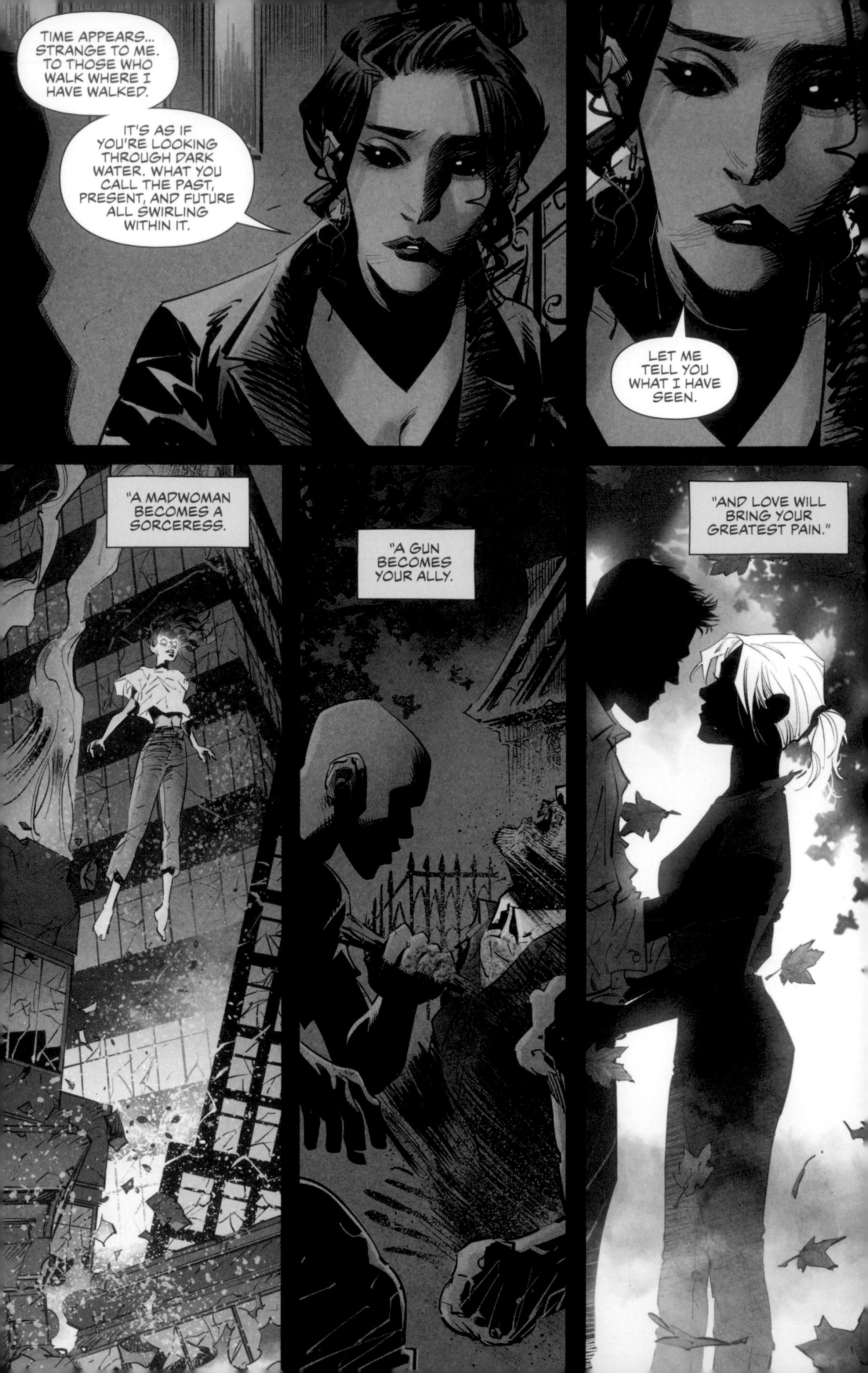
TIME APPEARS... STRANGE TO ME. TO THOSE WHO WALK WHERE I HAVE WALKED.
IT'S AS IF YOU'RE LOOKING THROUGH DARK WATER. WHAT YOU CALL THE PAST, PRESENT, AND FUTURE ALL SWIRLING WITHIN IT.
LET ME TELL YOU WHAT I HAVE SEEN.
"A MADWOMAN BECOMES A SORCERESS.
"A GUN BECOMES YOUR ALLY.
"AND LOVE WILL BRING YOUR GREATEST PAIN."

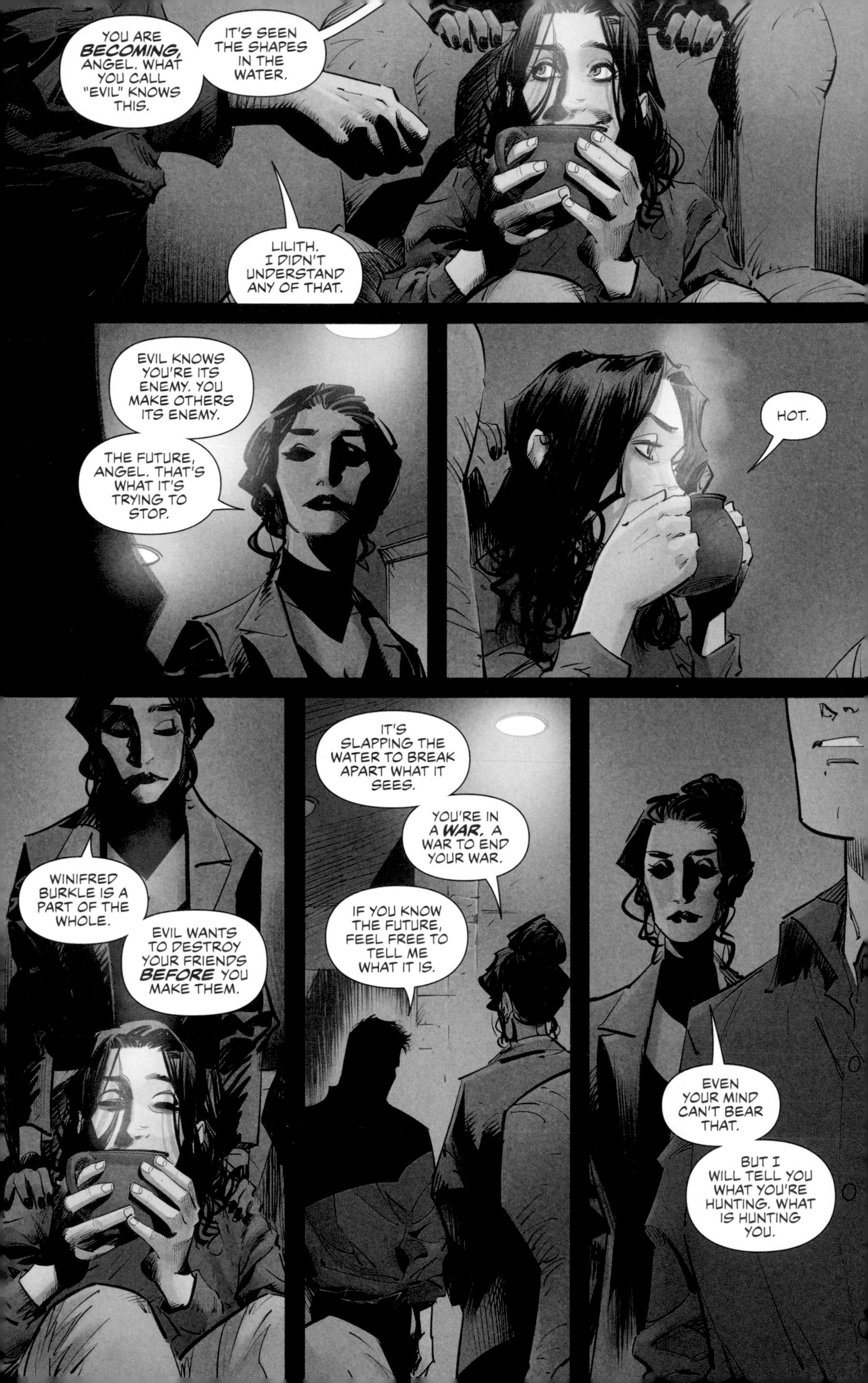
YOU ARE BECOMING, ANGEL. WHAT YOU CALL "EVIL" KNOWS THIS.
IT'S SEEN THE SHAPES IN THE WATER.
LILITH. I DIDN'T UNDERSTAND ANY OF THAT.
EVIL KNOWS YOU'RE ITS ENEMY. YOU MAKE OTHERS ITS ENEMY.
THE FUTURE, ANGEL. THAT'S WHAT IT'S TRYING TO STOP.
HOT.
WINIFRED BURKLE IS A PART OF THE WHOLE.
EVIL WANTS TO DESTROY YOUR FRIENDS BEFORE YOU MAKE THEM.
IT'S SLAPPING THE WATER TO BREAK APART WHAT IT SEES.
YOU'RE IN A WAR. A WAR TO END YOUR WAR.
IF YOU KNOW THE FUTURE, FEEL FREE TO TELL ME WHAT IT IS.
EVEN YOUR MIND CAN'T BEAR THAT.
BUT I WILL TELL YOU WHAT YOU'RE HUNTING. WHAT IS HUNTING YOU.

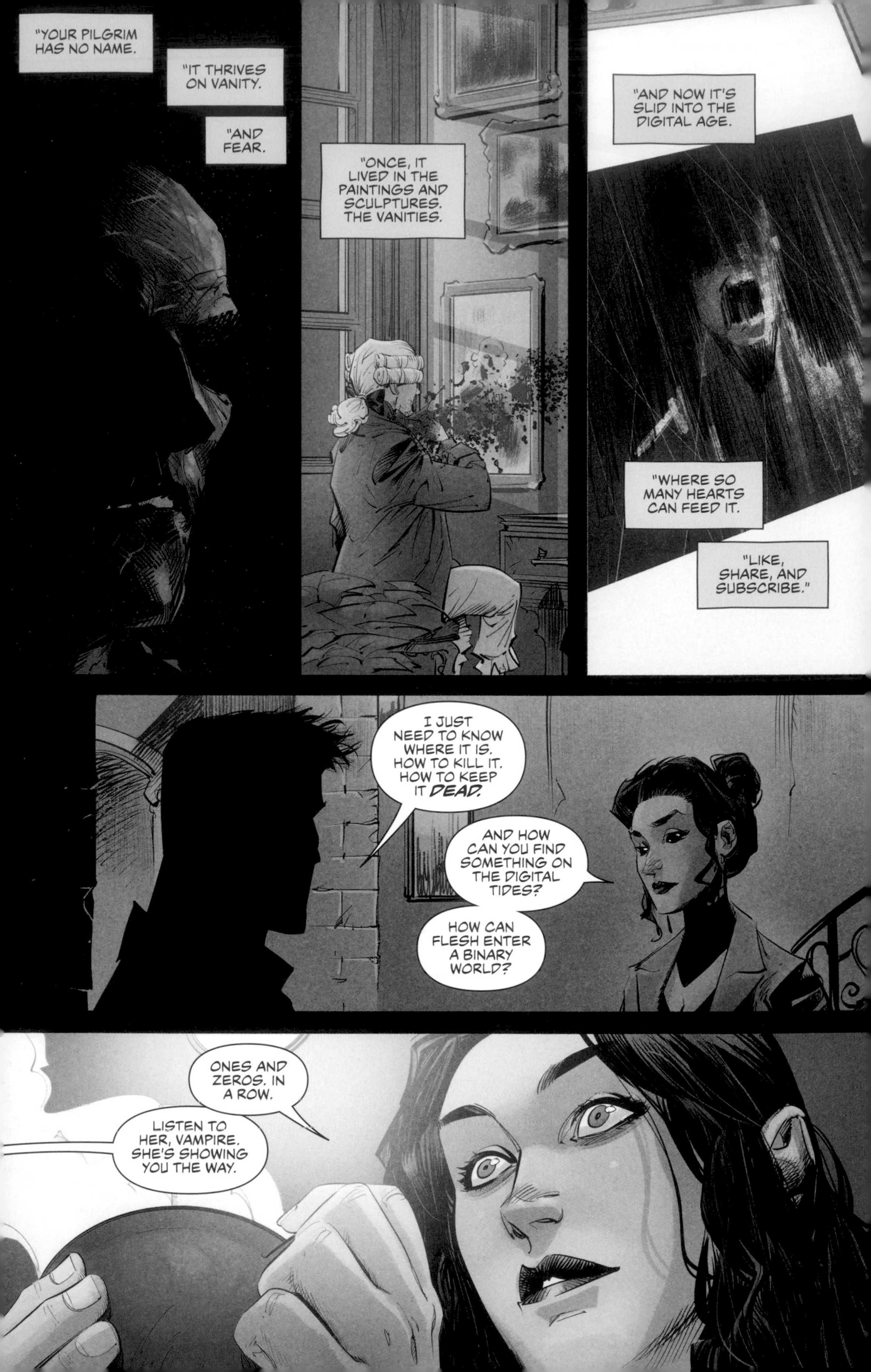
"YOUR PILGRIM HAS NO NAME.
"IT THRIVES ON VANITY.
"AND FEAR.
"ONCE, IT LIVED IN THE PAINTINGS AND SCULPTURES. THE VANITIES.
"AND NOW IT'S SLID INTO THE DIGITAL AGE.
"WHERE SO MANY HEARTS CAN FEED IT.
"LIKE, SHARE, AND SUBSCRIBE."
I JUST NEED TO KNOW WHERE IT IS. HOW TO KILL IT. HOW TO KEEP IT DEAD.
AND HOW CAN YOU FIND SOMETHING ON THE DIGITAL TIDES?
HOW CAN FLESH ENTER A BINARY WORLD?
ONES AND ZEROS. IN A ROW.
LISTEN TO HER, VAMPIRE. SHE'S SHOWING YOU THE WAY.

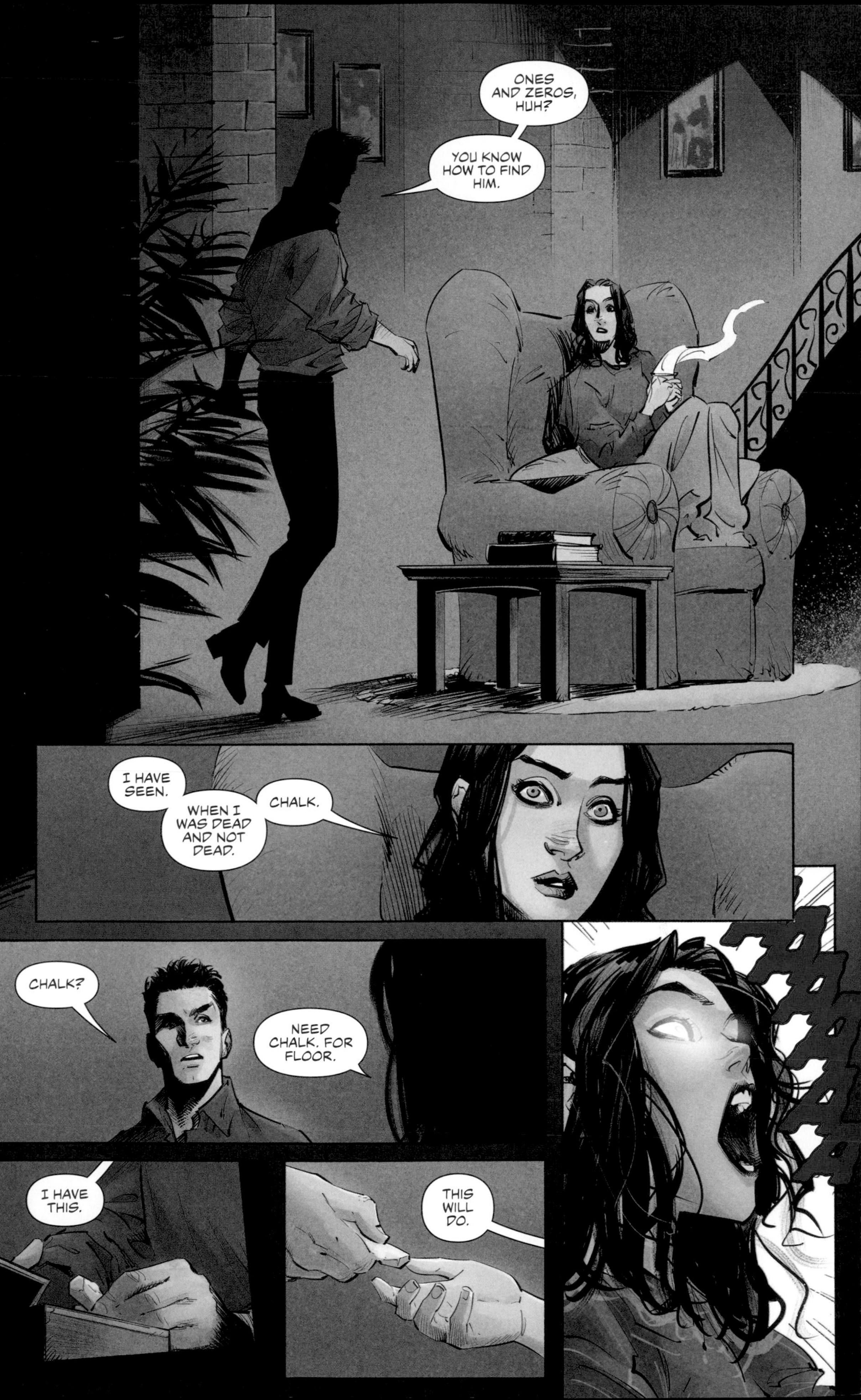
ONES AND ZEROS, HUH?
YOU KNOW HOW TO FIND HIM.
I HAVE SEEN.
WHEN I WAS DEAD AND NOT DEAD.
CHALK.
CHALK?
NEED CHALK. FOR FLOOR.
I HAVE THIS.
THIS WILL DO.

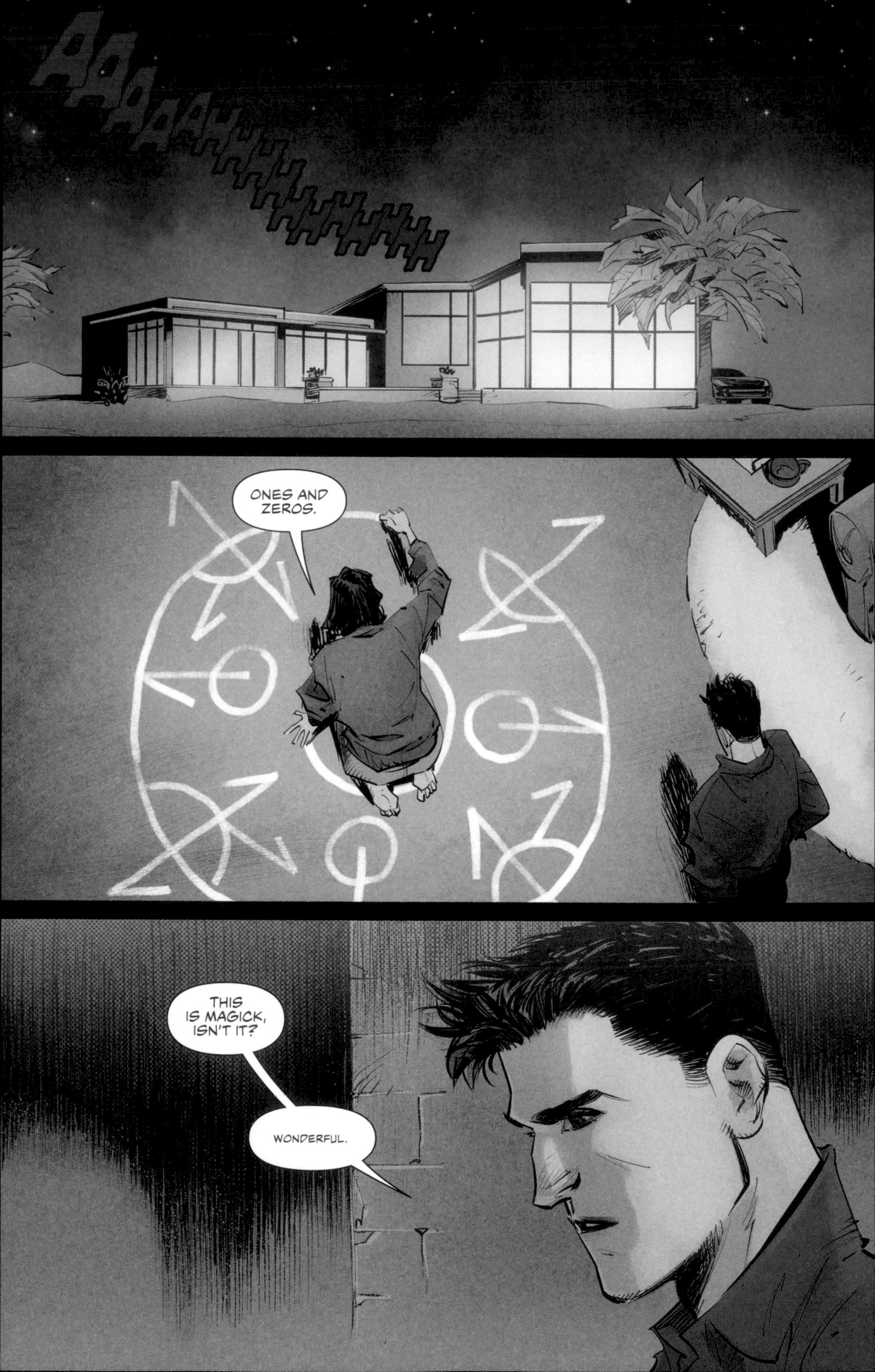
AAAAAAHHHHHHHHHH
ONES AND ZEROS.
THIS IS MAGICK, ISN'T IT?
WONDERFUL.

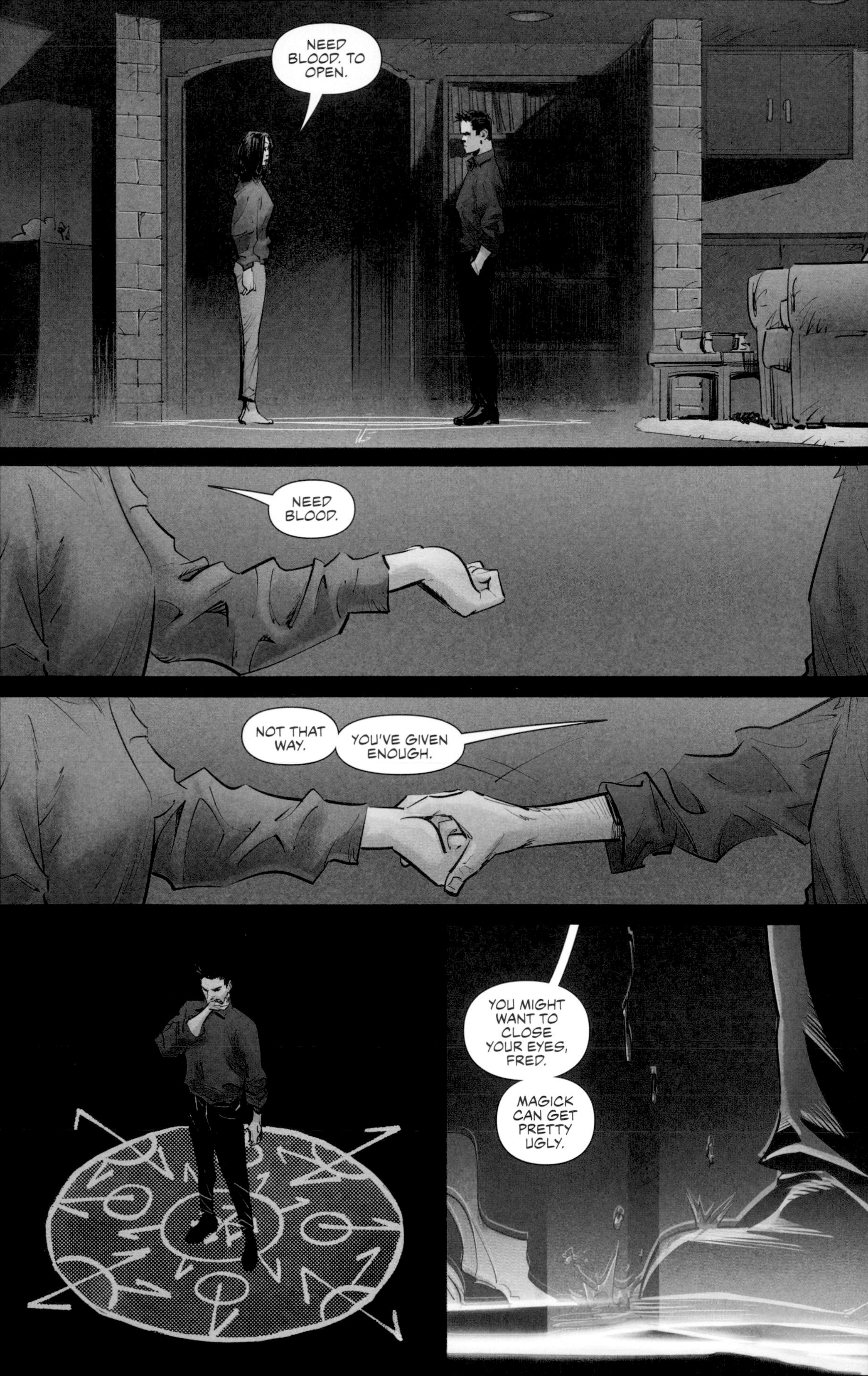
NEED BLOOD. TO OPEN.
NEED BLOOD.
NOT THAT WAY.
YOU'VE GIVEN ENOUGH.
YOU MIGHT WANT TO CLOSE YOUR EYES, FRED.
MAGICK CAN GET PRETTY UGLY.

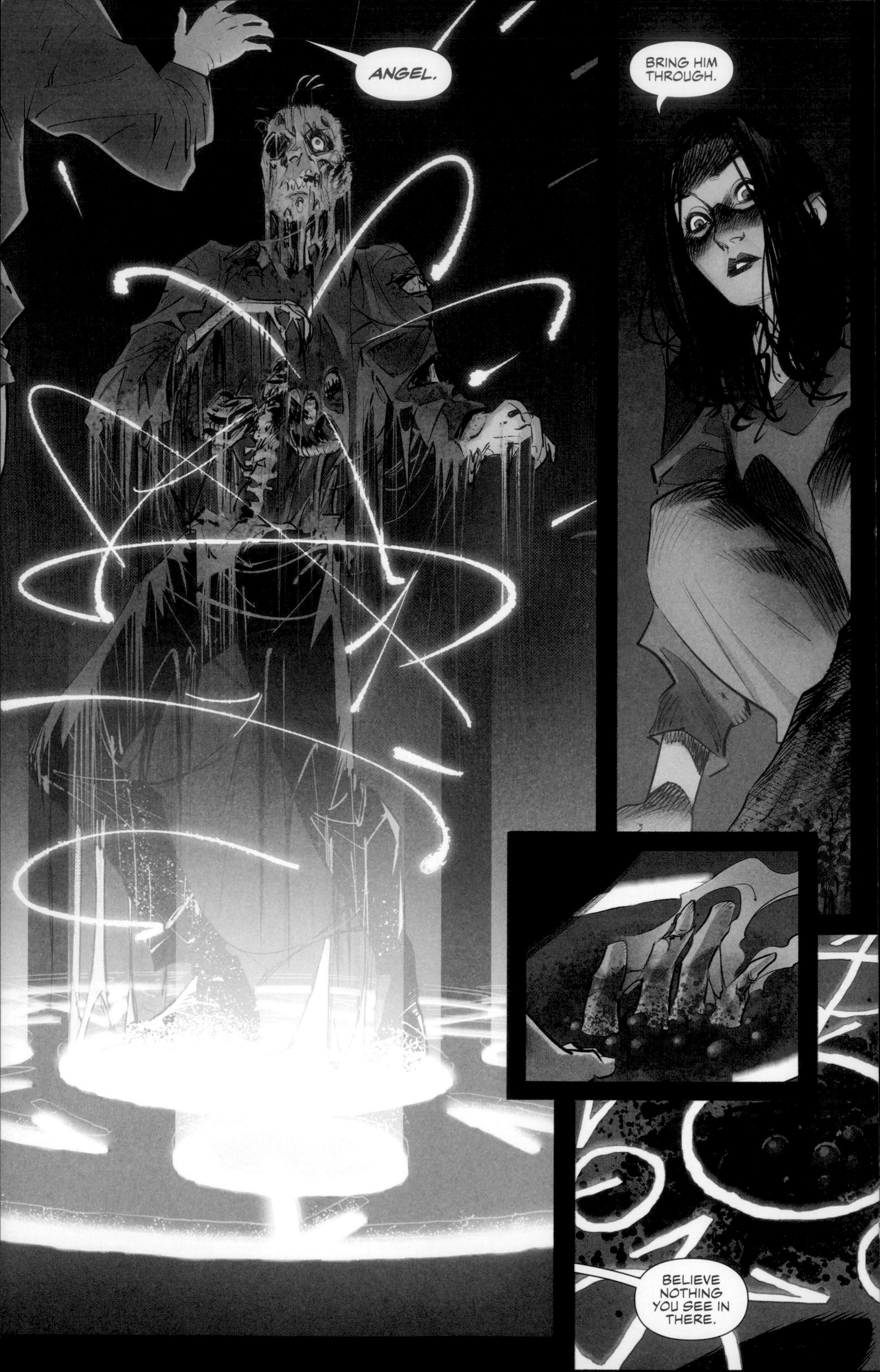
ANGEL.
BRING HIM THROUGH.
BELIEVE NOTHING YOU SEE IN THERE.

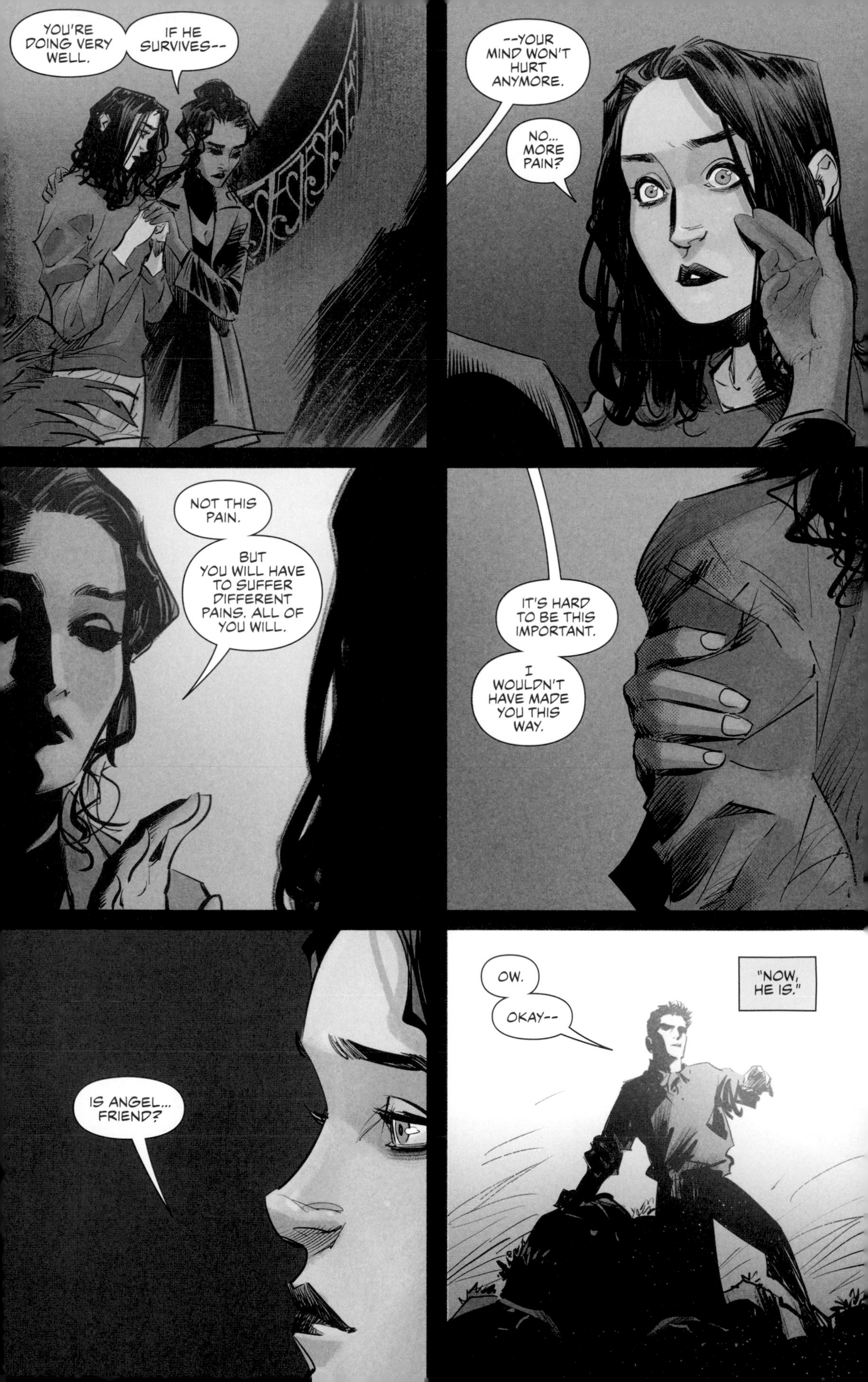
YOU'RE DOING VERY WELL.
IF HE SURVIVES--
--YOUR MIND WON'T HURT ANYMORE.
NO... MORE PAIN?
NOT THIS PAIN.
BUT YOU WILL HAVE TO SUFFER DIFFERENT PAINS. ALL OF YOU WILL.
IT'S HARD TO BE THIS IMPORTANT.
I WOULDN'T HAVE MADE YOU THIS WAY.
IS ANGEL... FRIEND?
"NOW, HE IS."
OW.
OKAY--

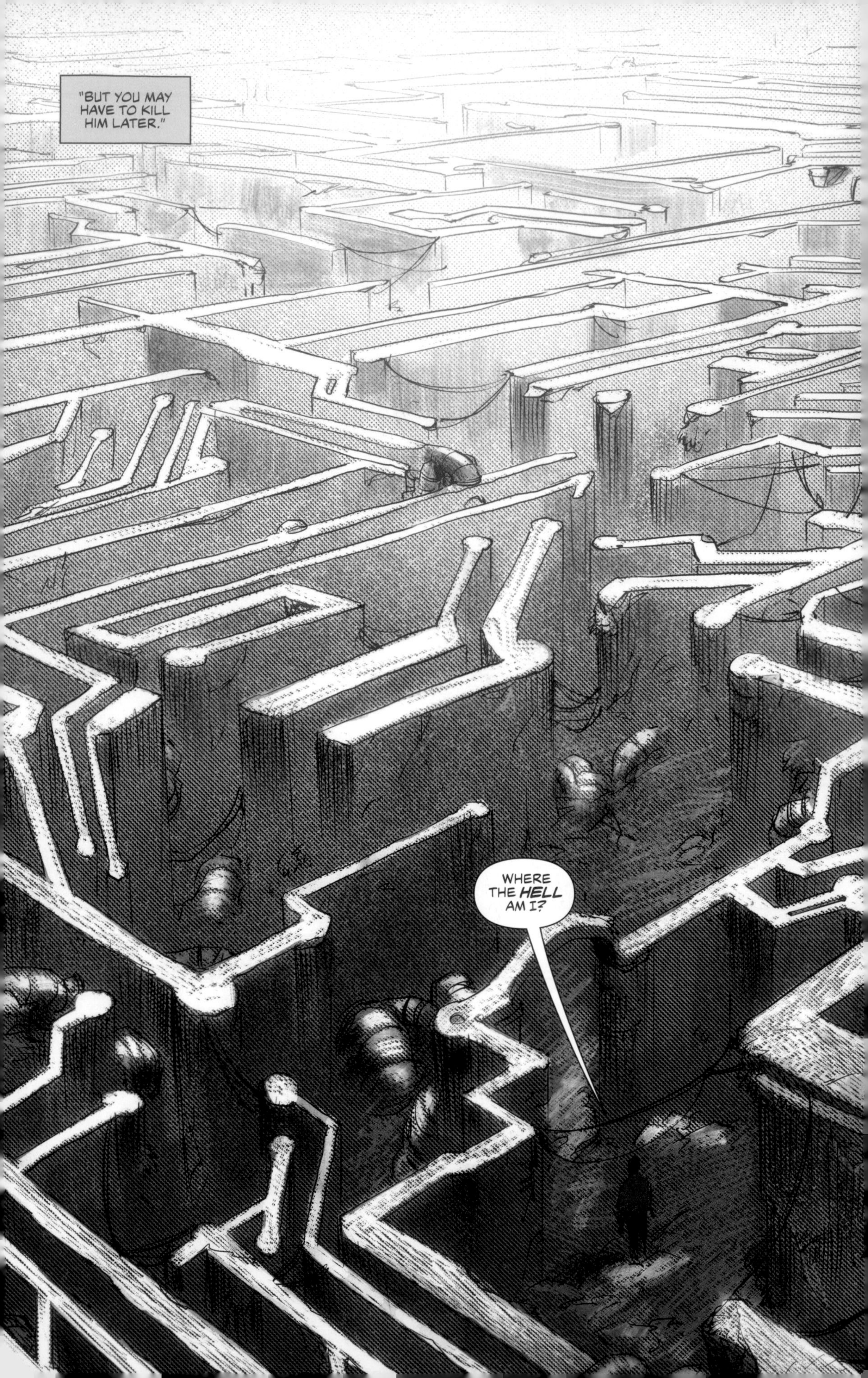
"BUT YOU MAY HAVE TO KILL HIM LATER."
WHERE THE HELL AM I?

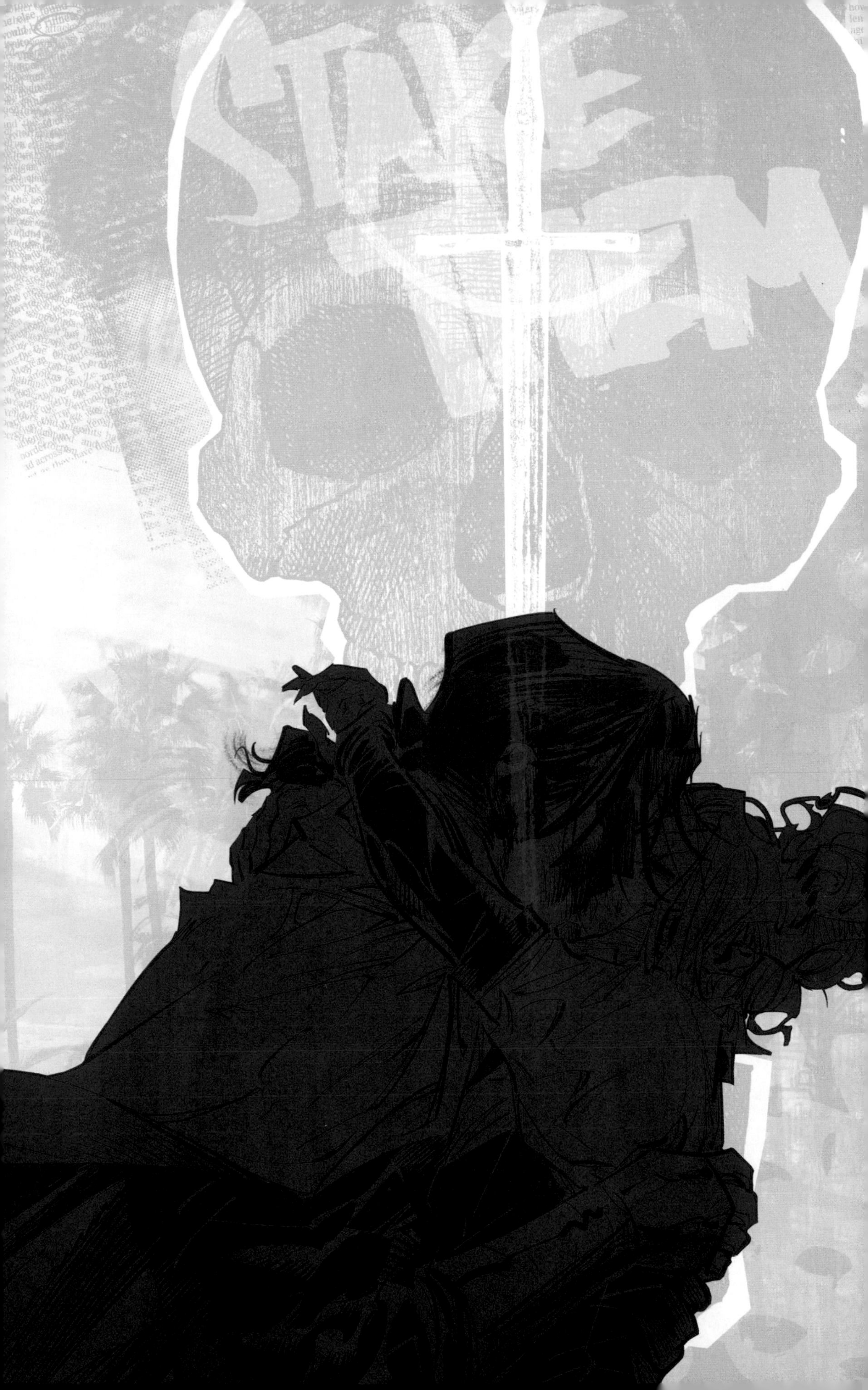

CHAPTER
FOUR

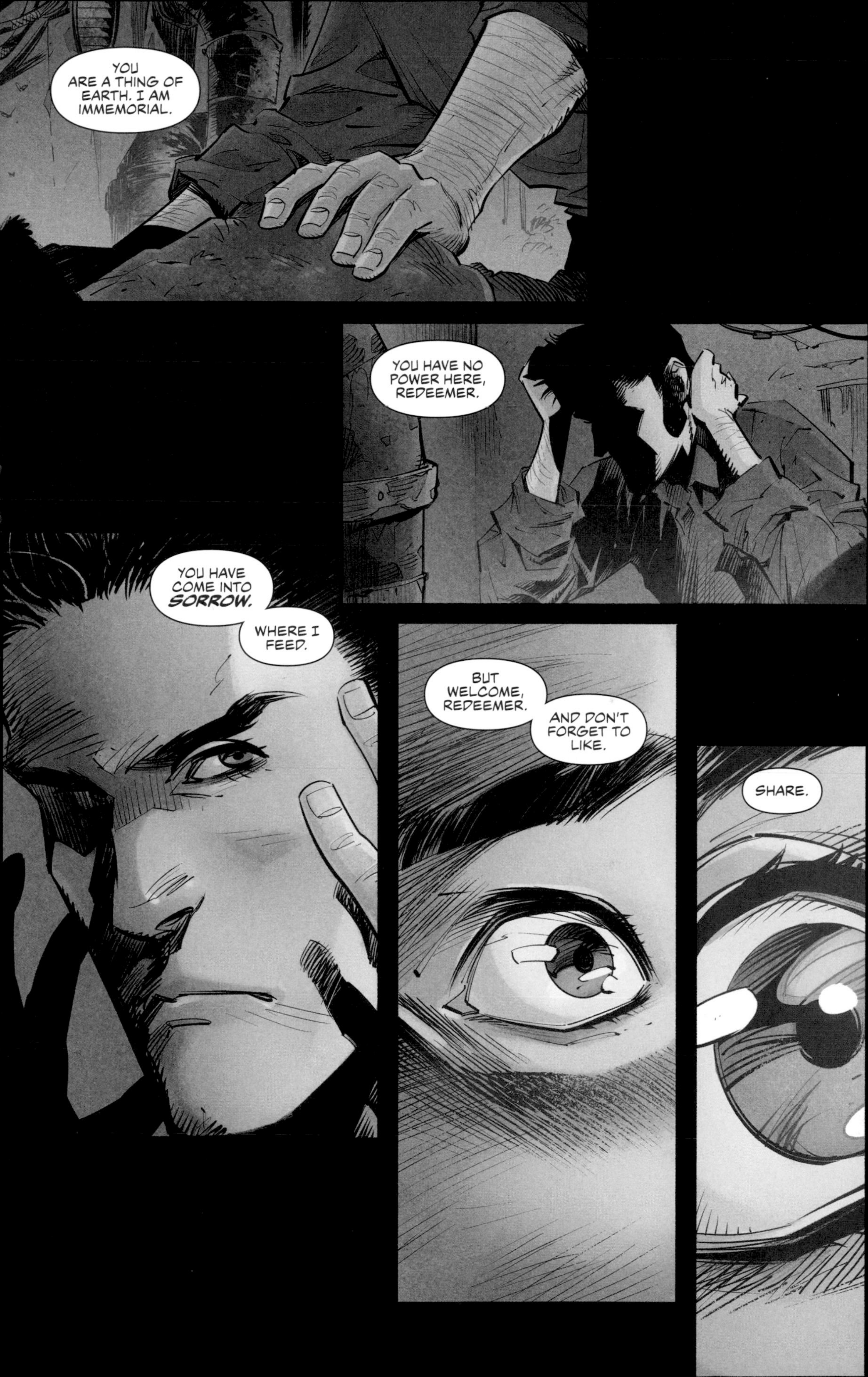
YOU ARE A THING OF EARTH. I AM IMMEMORIAL.
YOU HAVE NO POWER HERE, REDEEMER.
YOU HAVE COME INTO SORROW.
WHERE I FEED.
BUT WELCOME, REDEEMER.
AND DON'T FORGET TO LIKE.
SHARE.

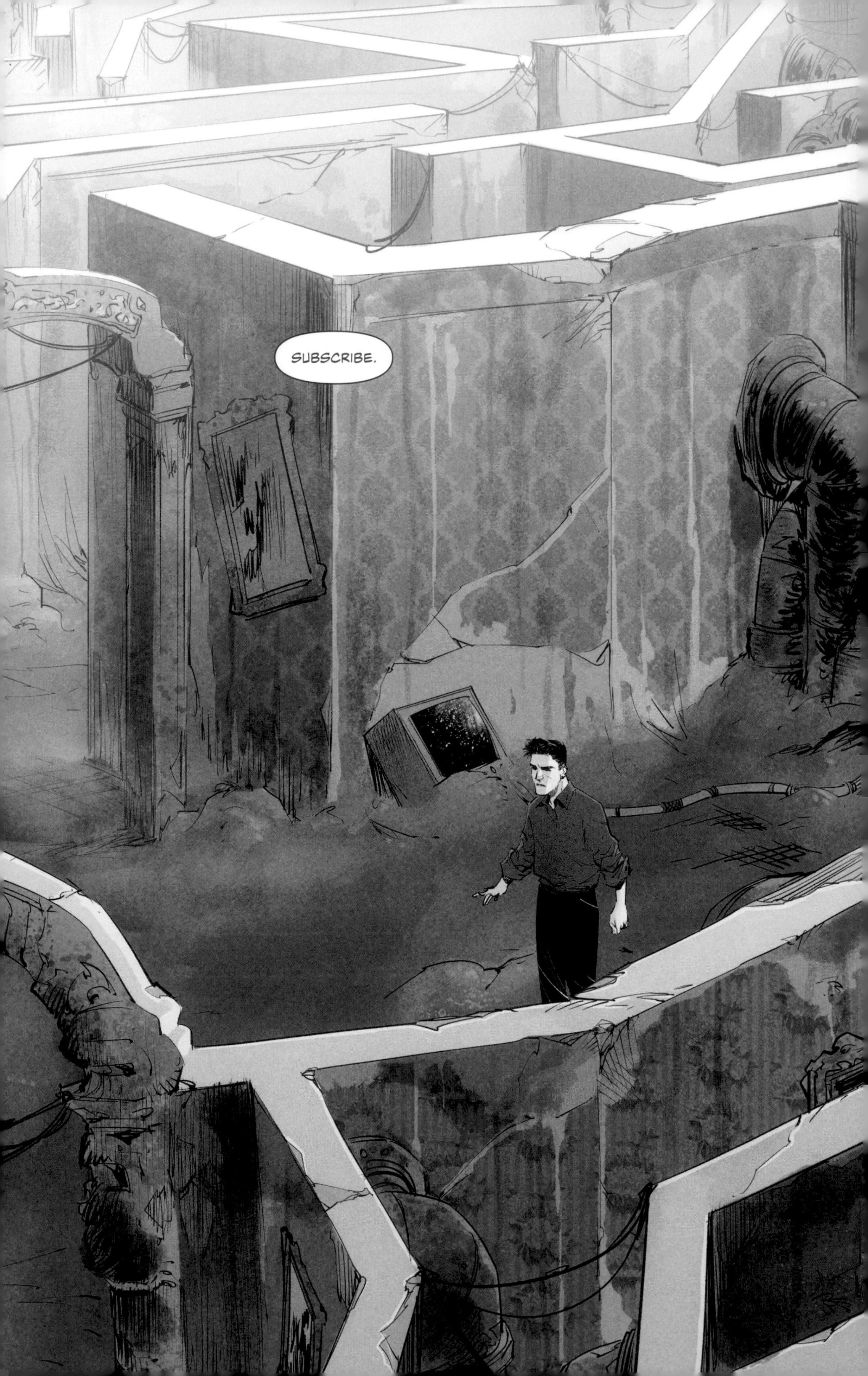
SUBSCRIBE.

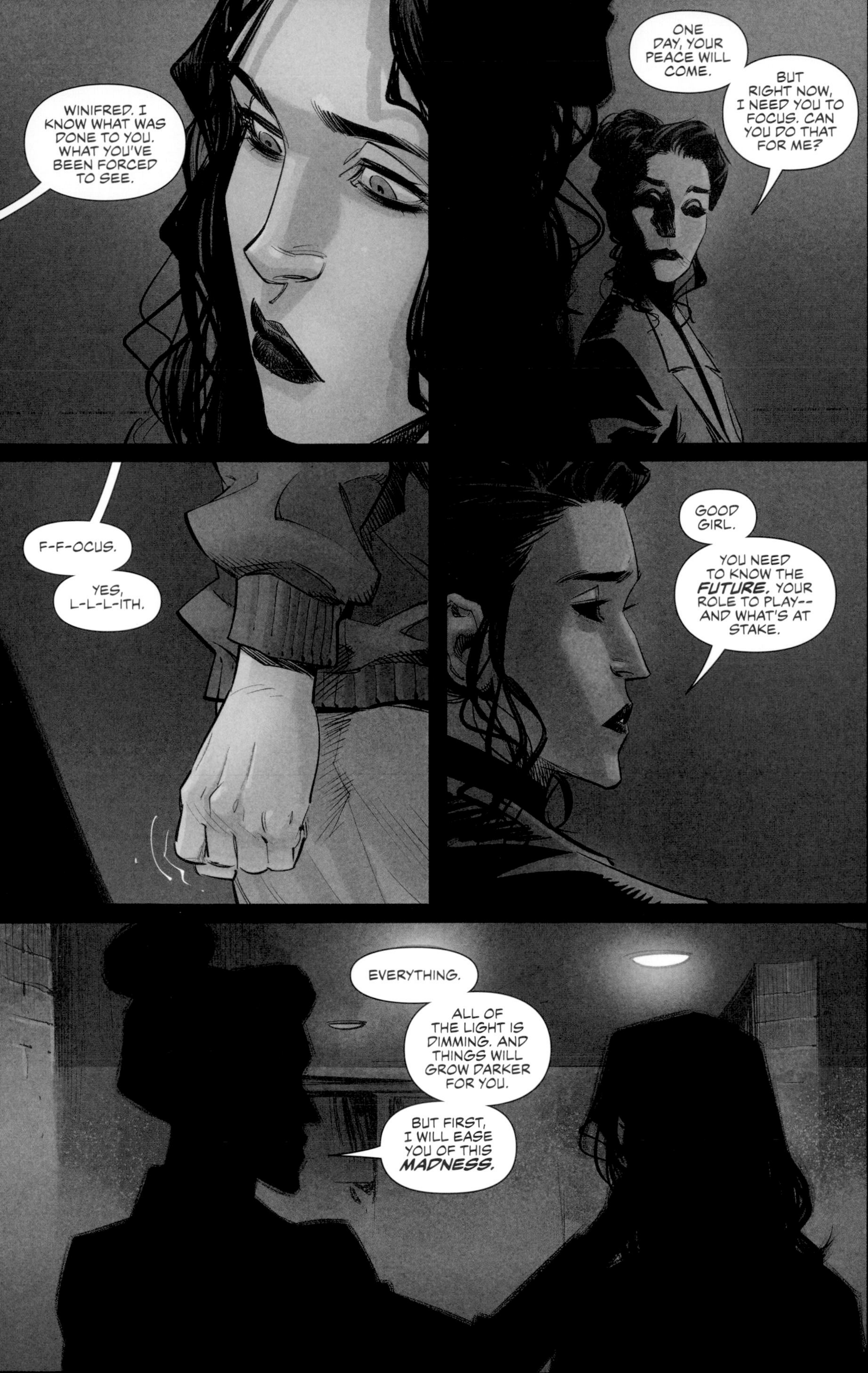
WINIFRED. I KNOW WHAT WAS DONE TO YOU. WHAT YOU'VE BEEN FORCED TO SEE.
ONE DAY, YOUR PEACE WILL COME.
BUT RIGHT NOW, I NEED YOU TO FOCUS. CAN YOU DO THAT FOR ME?
F-F-OCUS.
YES, L-L-L-ITH.
GOOD GIRL.
YOU NEED TO KNOW THE ***FUTURE.*** YOUR ROLE TO PLAY-- AND WHAT'S AT STAKE.
EVERYTHING.
ALL OF THE LIGHT IS DIMMING. AND THINGS WILL GROW DARKER FOR YOU.
BUT FIRST, I WILL EASE YOU OF THIS ***MADNESS.***

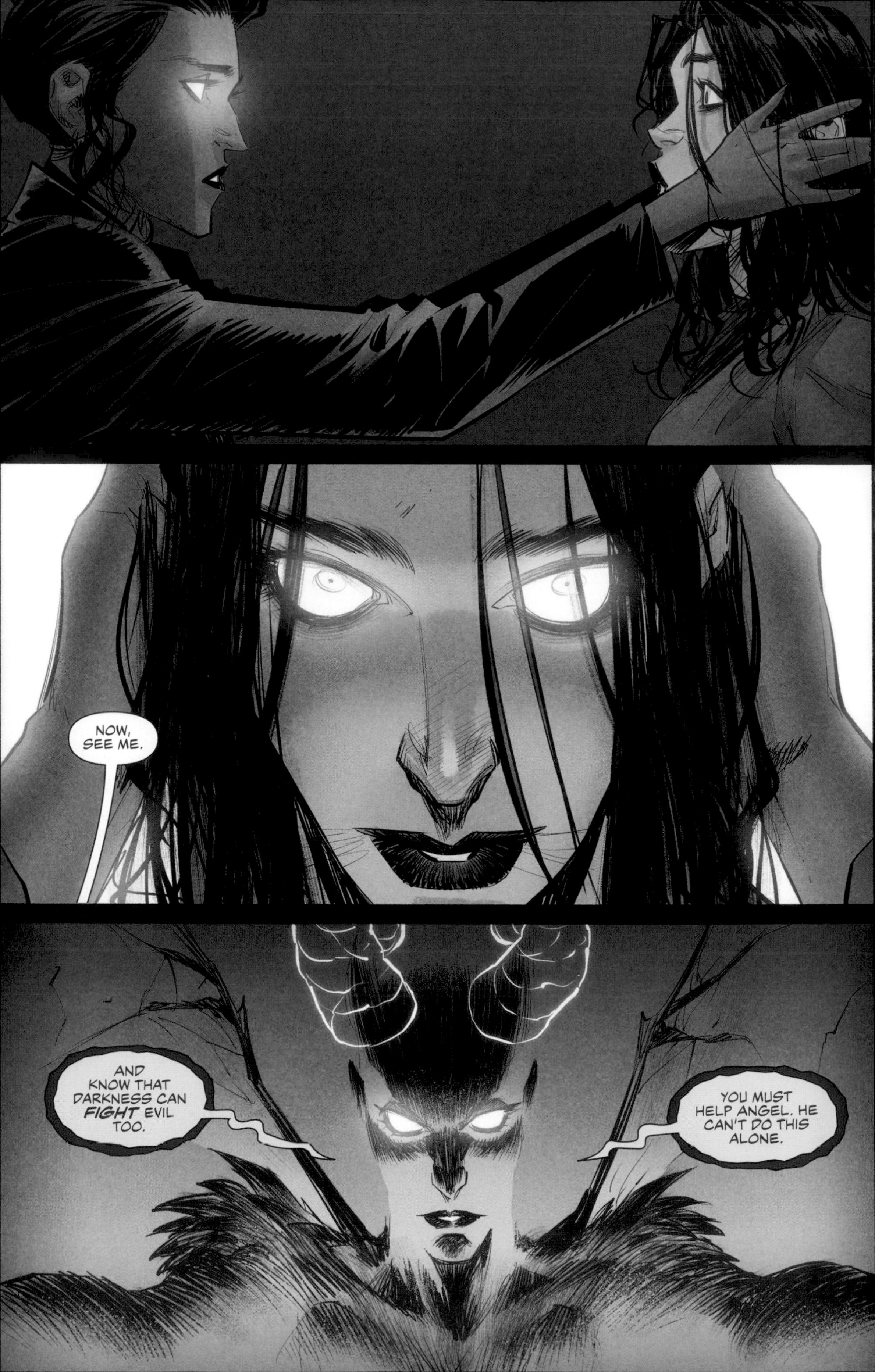
NOW, SEE ME.
AND KNOW THAT DARKNESS CAN FIGHT EVIL TOO.
YOU MUST HELP ANGEL. HE CAN'T DO THIS ALONE.

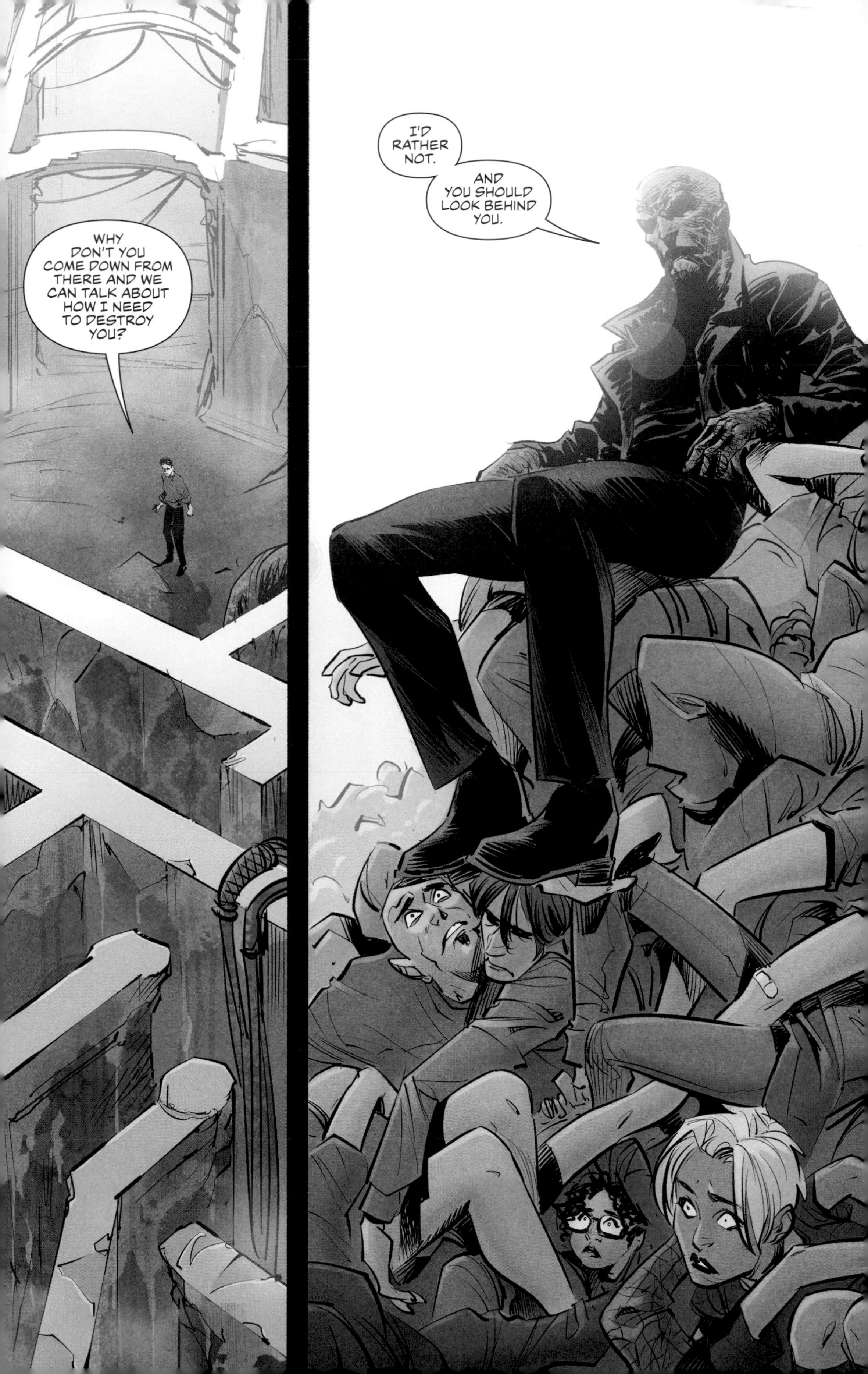
WHY DON'T YOU COME DOWN FROM THERE AND WE CAN TALK ABOUT HOW I NEED TO DESTROY YOU?
I'D RATHER NOT.
AND YOU SHOULD LOOK BEHIND YOU.

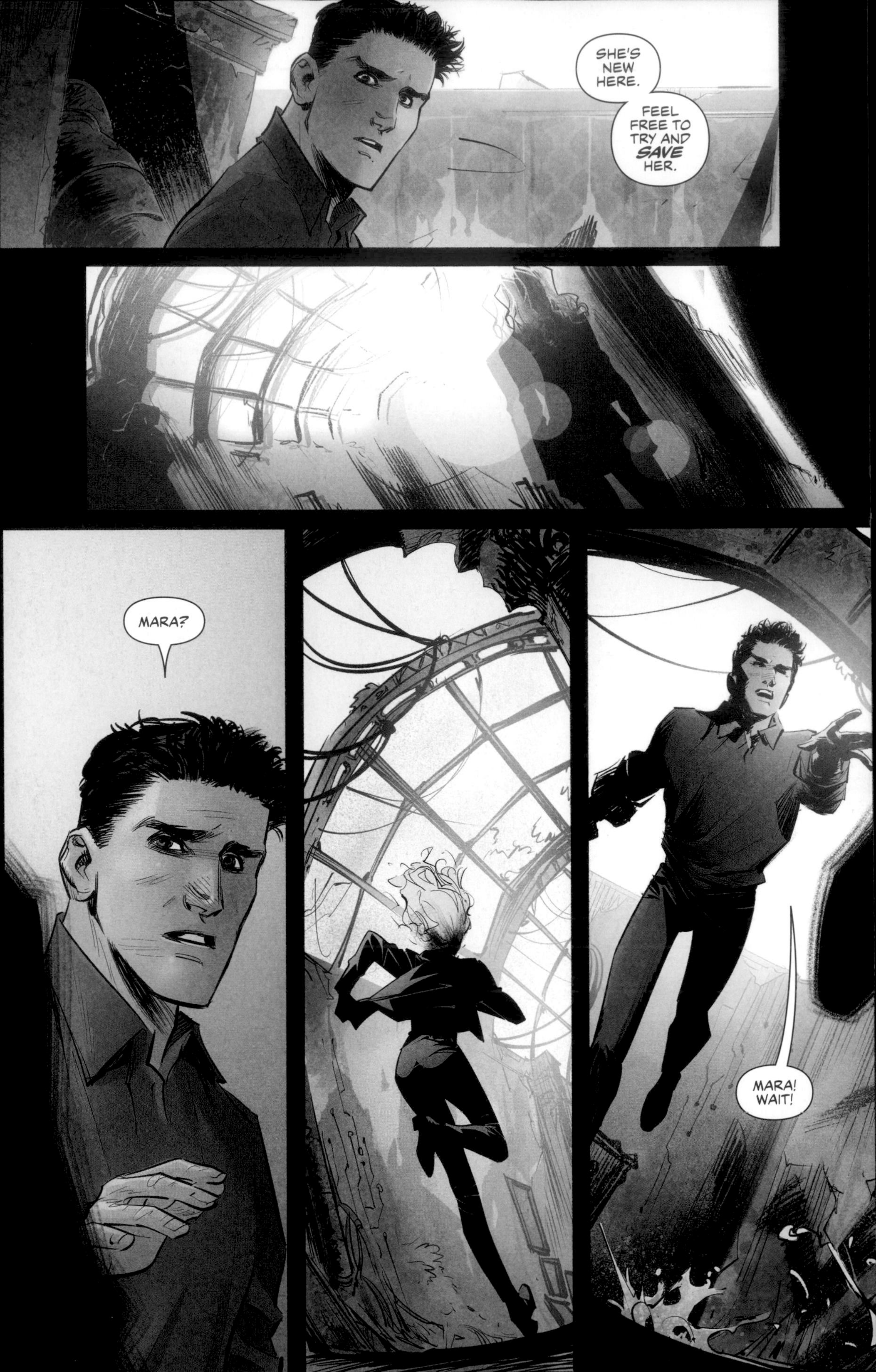
SHE'S NEW HERE.
FEEL FREE TO TRY AND *SAVE* HER.
MARA?
MARA! WAIT!

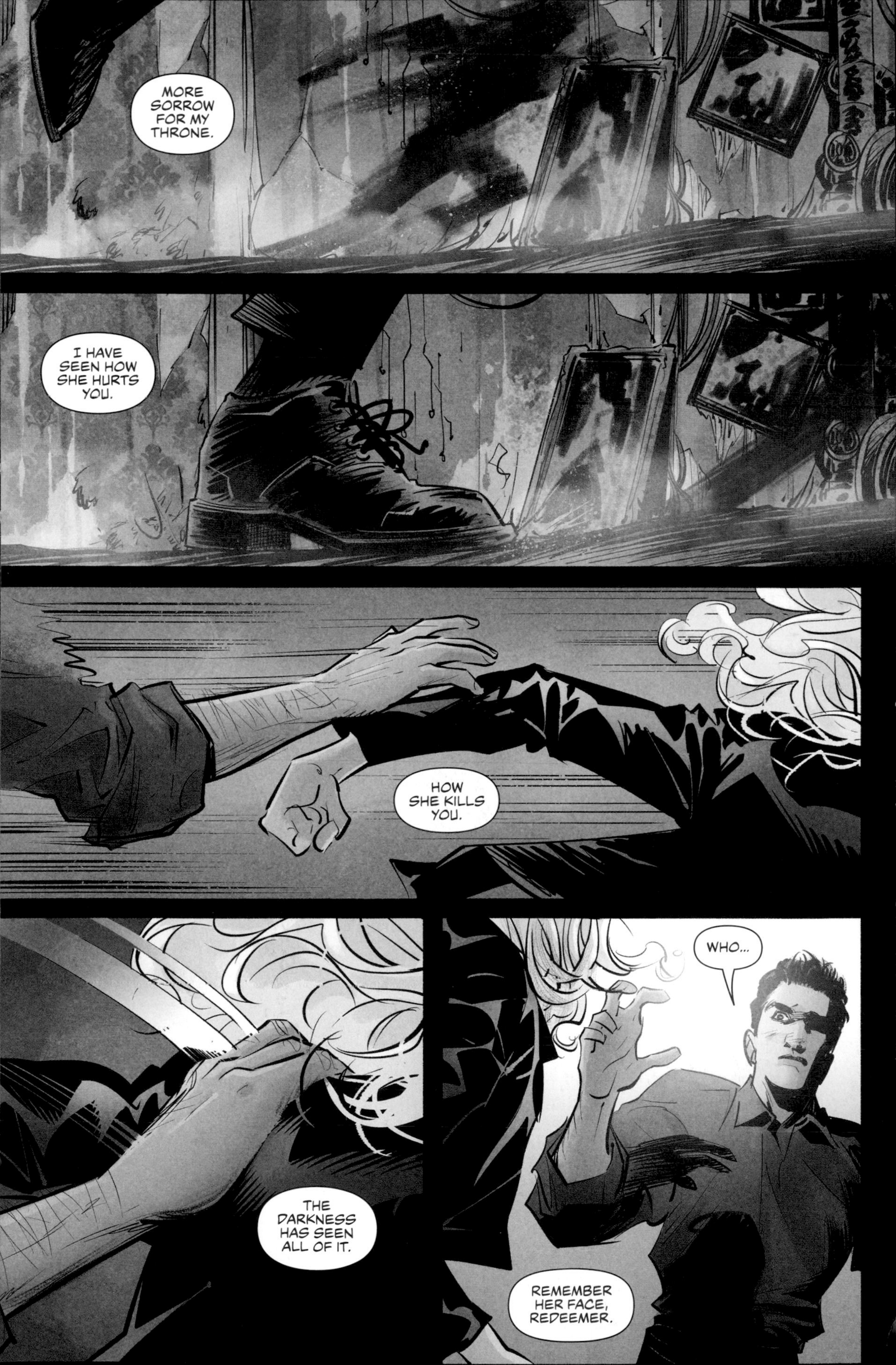
MORE SORROW FOR MY THRONE.
I HAVE SEEN HOW SHE HURTS YOU.
HOW SHE KILLS YOU.
THE DARKNESS HAS SEEN ALL OF IT.
WHO...
REMEMBER HER FACE, REDEEMER.

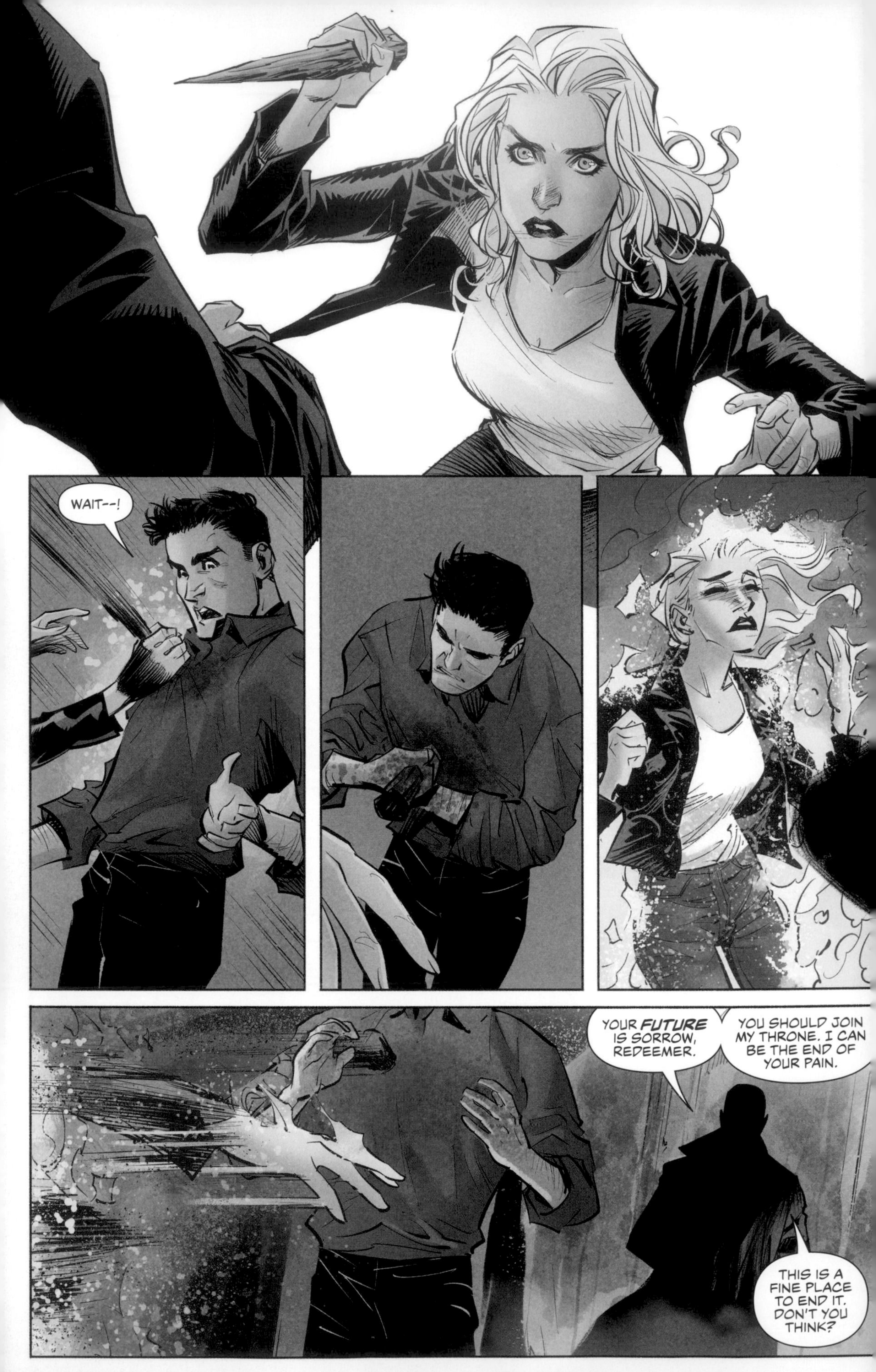
WAIT--!
YOUR FUTURE IS SORROW, REDEEMER.
YOU SHOULD JOIN MY THRONE. I CAN BE THE END OF YOUR PAIN.
THIS IS A FINE PLACE TO END IT. DON'T YOU THINK?

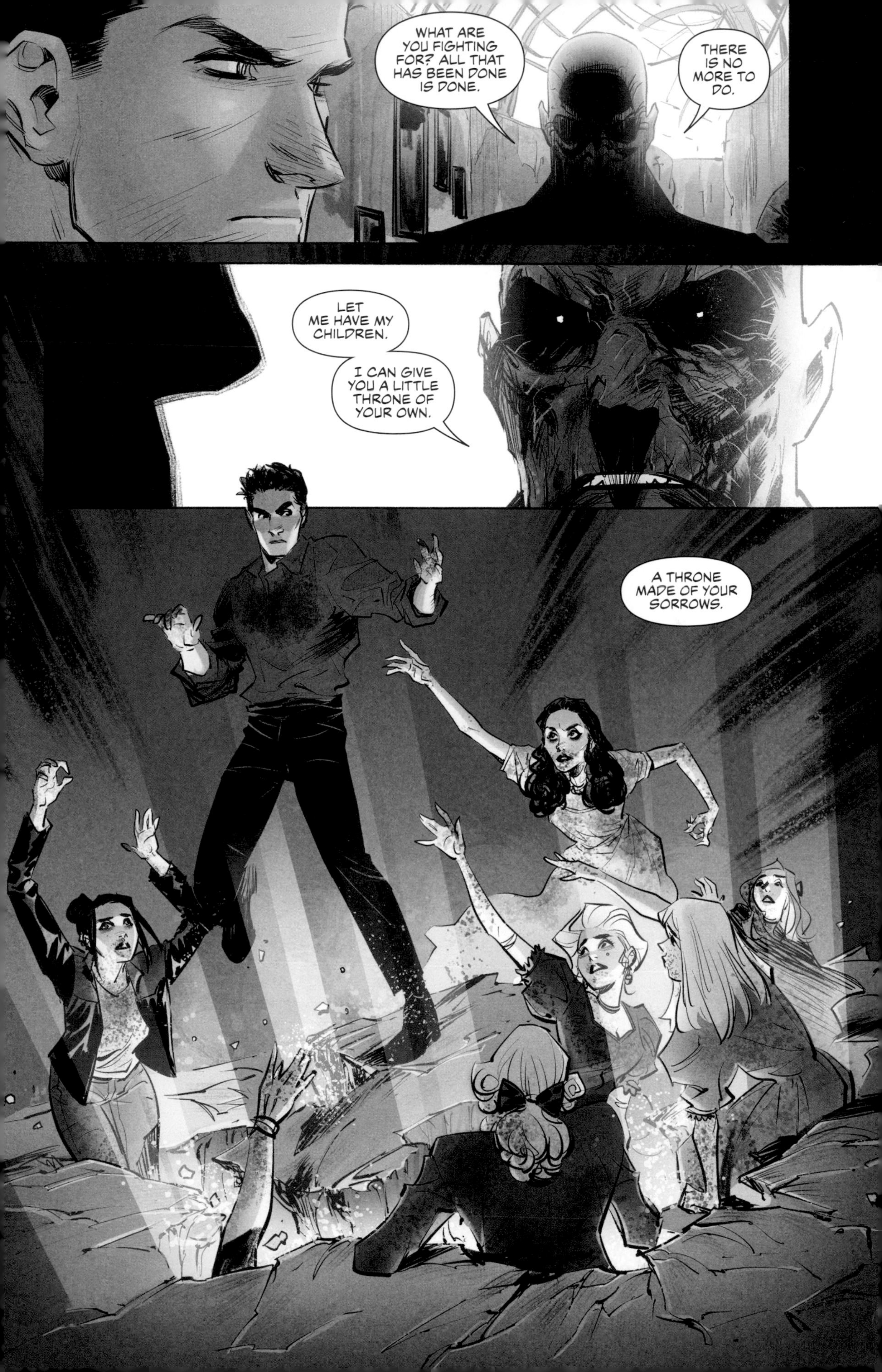
WHAT ARE YOU FIGHTING FOR? ALL THAT HAS BEEN DONE IS DONE.
THERE IS NO MORE TO DO.
LET ME HAVE MY CHILDREN.
I CAN GIVE YOU A LITTLE THRONE OF YOUR OWN.
A THRONE MADE OF YOUR SORROWS.

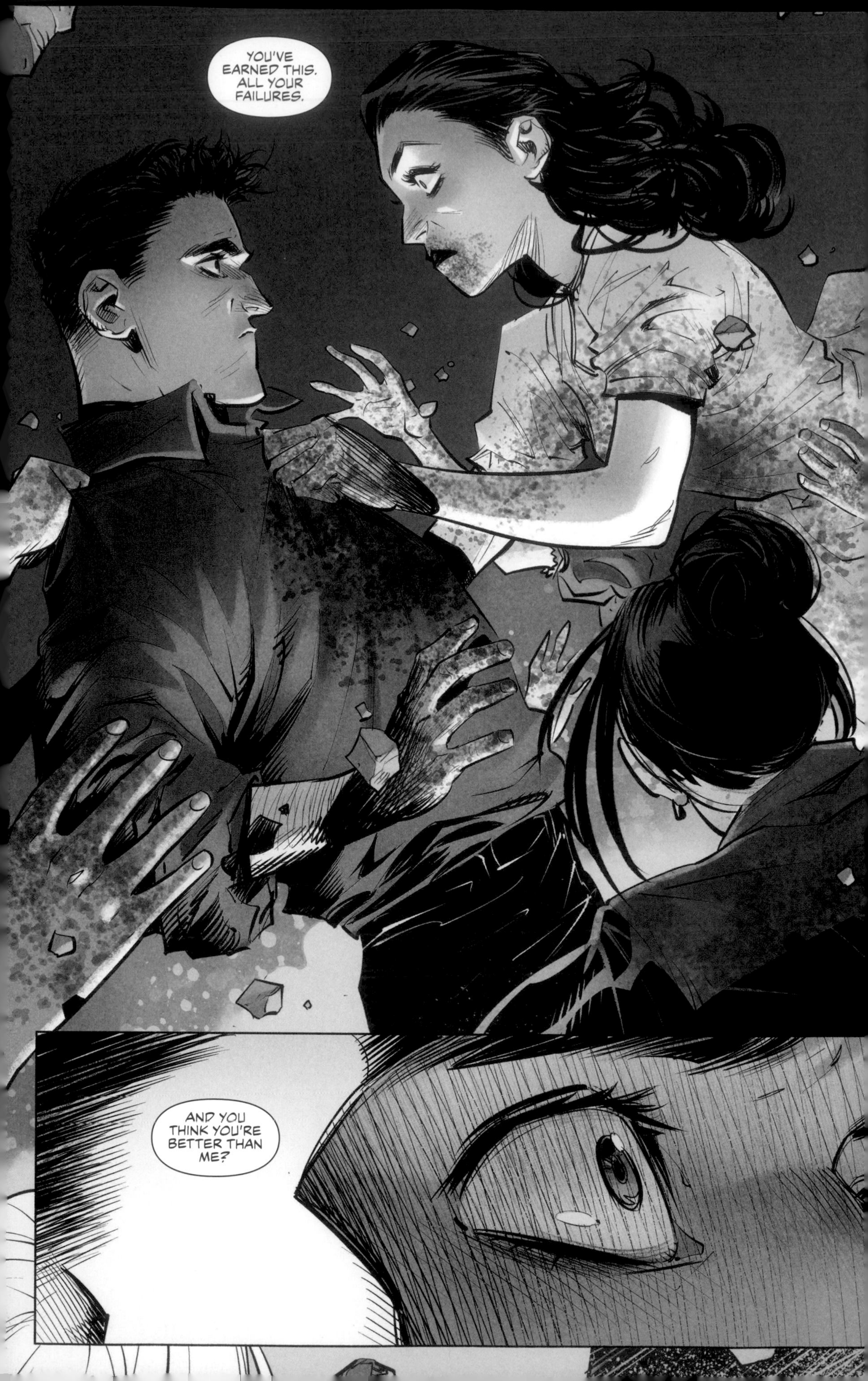
YOU'VE EARNED THIS. ALL YOUR FAILURES.
AND YOU THINK YOU'RE BETTER THAN ME?

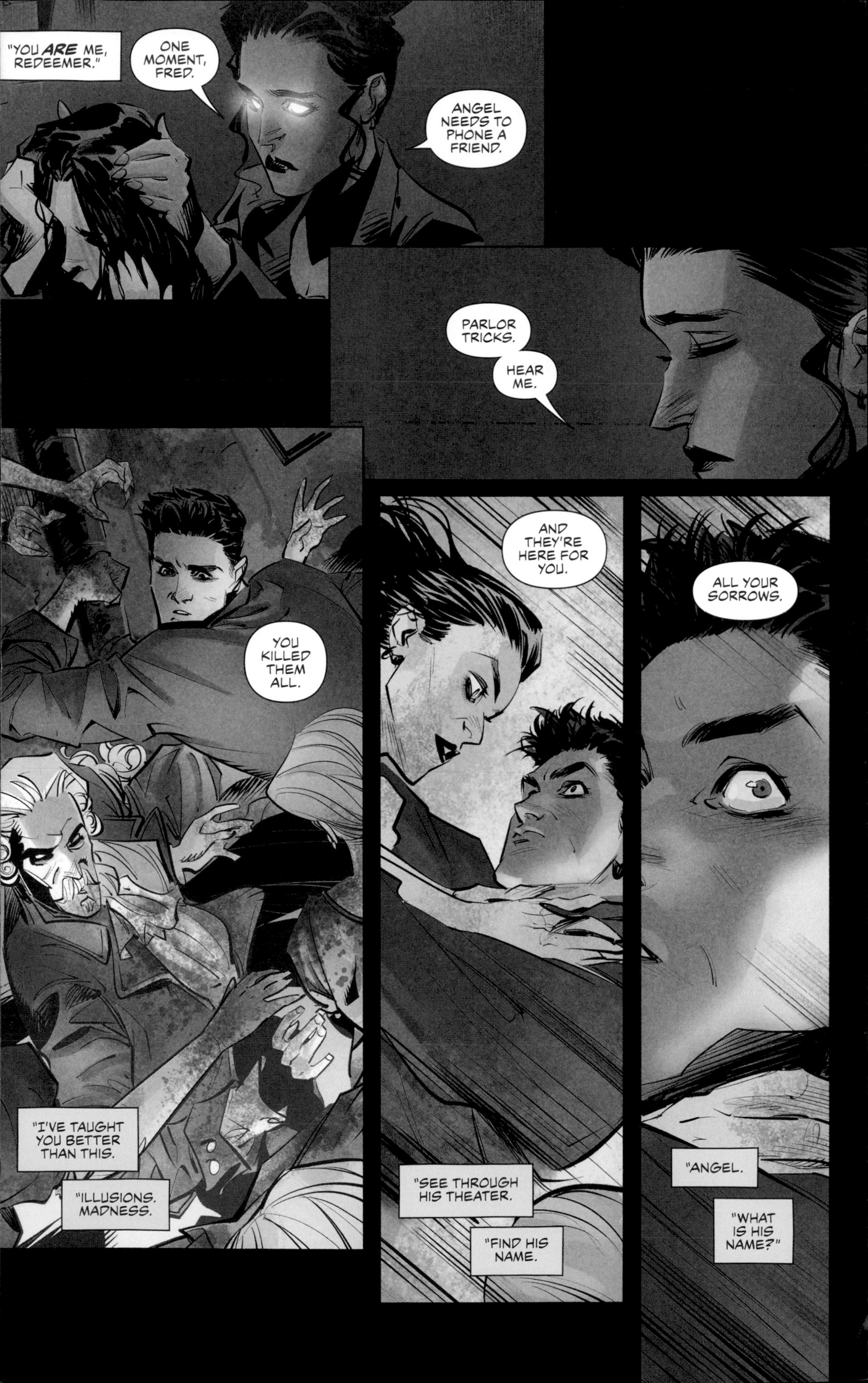
"YOU ARE ME, REDEEMER."
ONE MOMENT, FRED.
ANGEL NEEDS TO PHONE A FRIEND.
PARLOR TRICKS.
HEAR ME.
YOU KILLED THEM ALL.
"I'VE TAUGHT YOU BETTER THAN THIS.
"ILLUSIONS. MADNESS.
AND THEY'RE HERE FOR YOU.
"SEE THROUGH HIS THEATER.
"FIND HIS NAME.
ALL YOUR SORROWS.
"ANGEL.
"WHAT IS HIS NAME?"

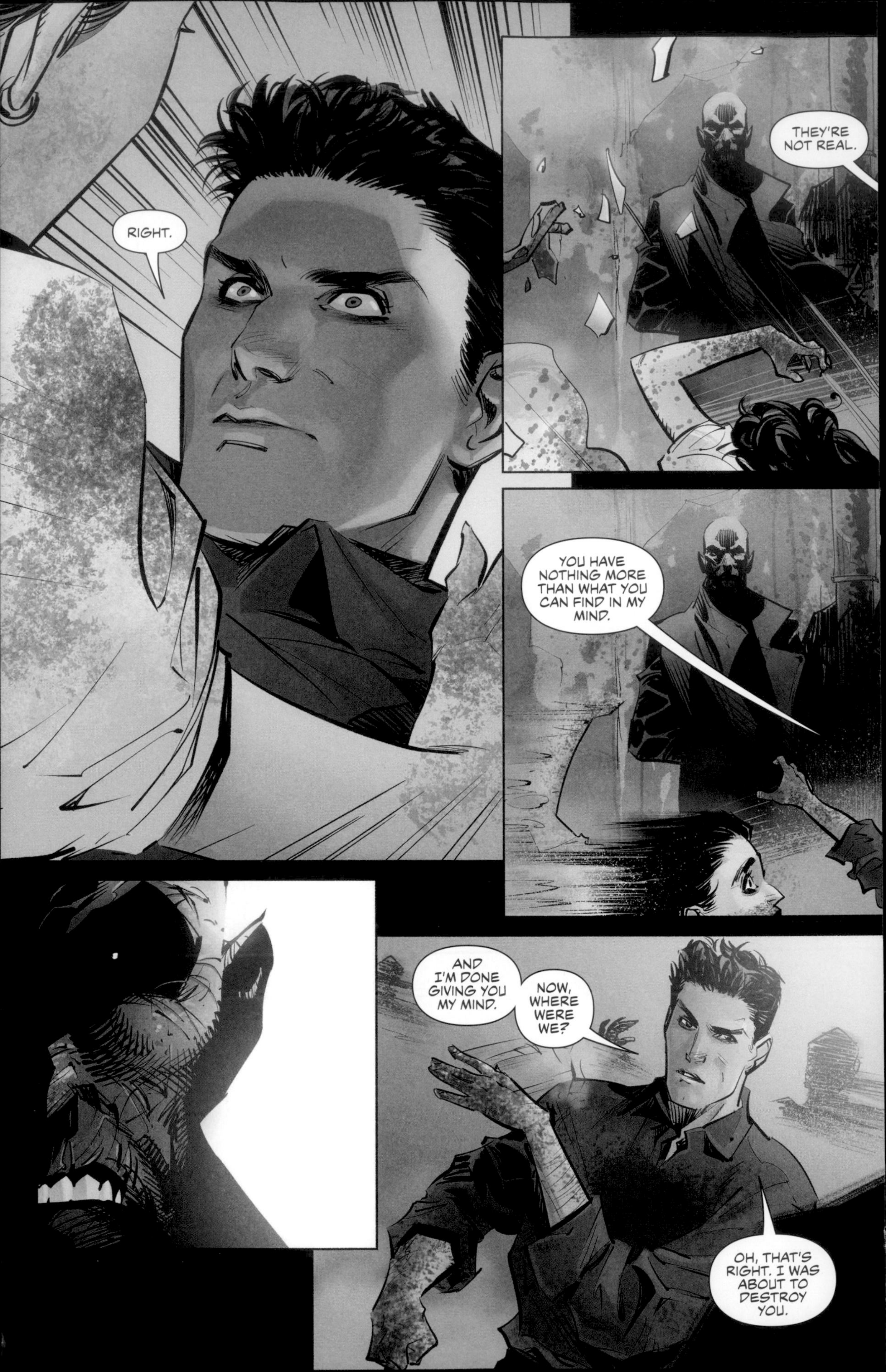
RIGHT.
THEY'RE NOT REAL.
YOU HAVE NOTHING MORE THAN WHAT YOU CAN FIND IN MY MIND.
AND I'M DONE GIVING YOU MY MIND.
NOW, WHERE WERE WE?
OH, THAT'S RIGHT. I WAS ABOUT TO DESTROY YOU.

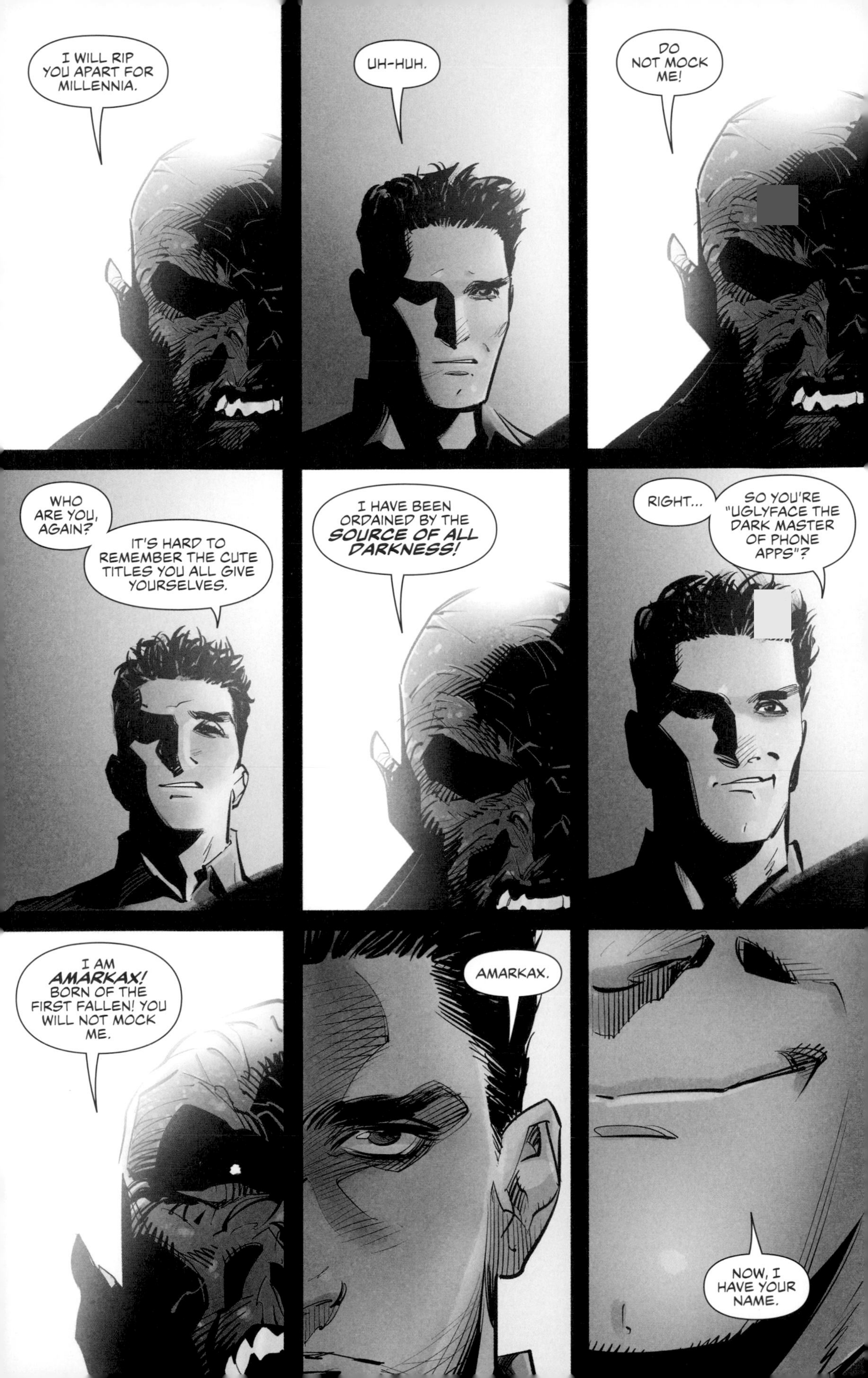
I WILL RIP YOU APART FOR MILLENNIA.
UH-HUH.
DO NOT MOCK ME!
WHO ARE YOU, AGAIN?
IT'S HARD TO REMEMBER THE CUTE TITLES YOU ALL GIVE YOURSELVES.
I HAVE BEEN ORDAINED BY THE *SOURCE OF ALL DARKNESS!*
RIGHT...
SO YOU'RE "UGLYFACE THE DARK MASTER OF PHONE APPS"?
I AM *AMARKAX!* BORN OF THE FIRST FALLEN! YOU WILL NOT MOCK ME.
AMARKAX.
NOW, I HAVE YOUR NAME.

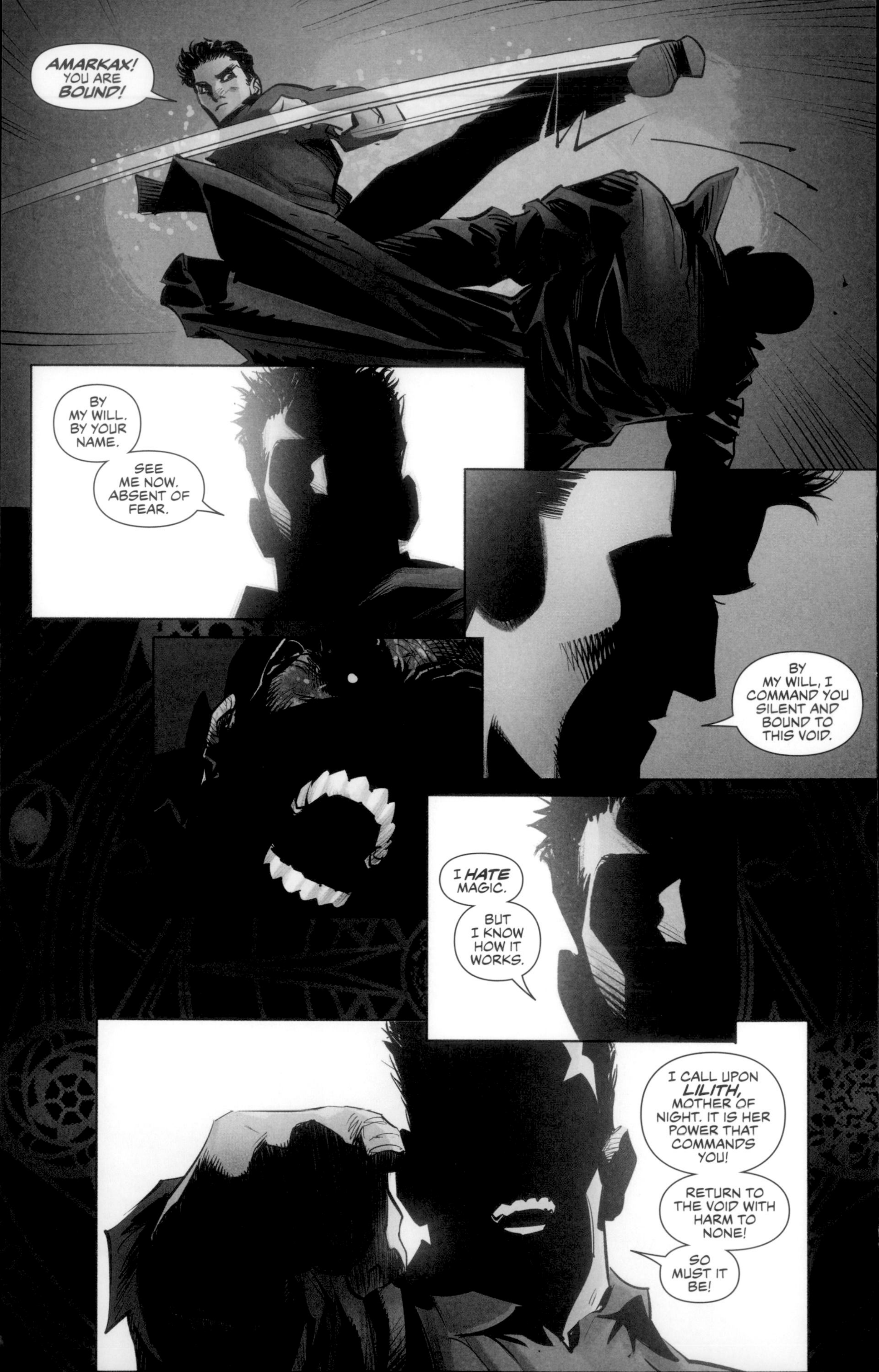
AMARKAX! YOU ARE BOUND!
BY MY WILL. BY YOUR NAME.
SEE ME NOW. ABSENT OF FEAR.
BY MY WILL, I COMMAND YOU SILENT AND BOUND TO THIS VOID.
I HATE MAGIC.
BUT I KNOW HOW IT WORKS.
I CALL UPON LILITH, MOTHER OF NIGHT. IT IS HER POWER THAT COMMANDS YOU!
RETURN TO THE VOID WITH HARM TO NONE!
SO MUST IT BE!

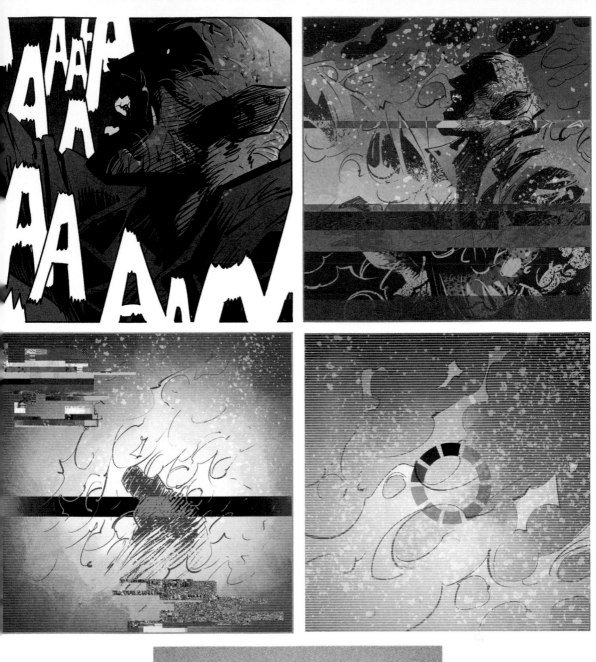

This account
is no longer
active.

"YOU'RE
BACK!"

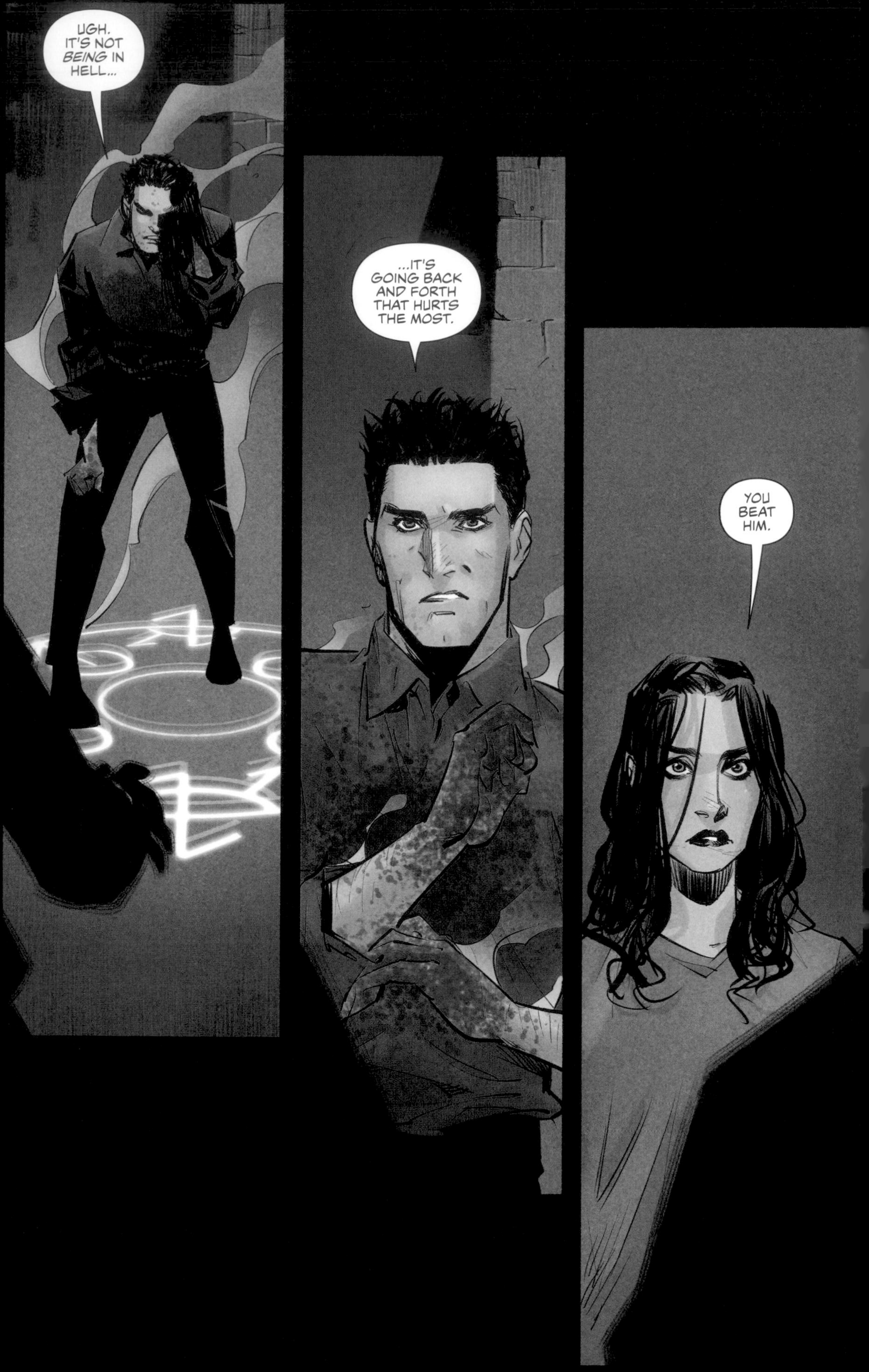
UGH. IT'S NOT *BEING* IN HELL...
...IT'S GOING BACK AND FORTH THAT HURTS THE MOST.
YOU BEAT HIM.

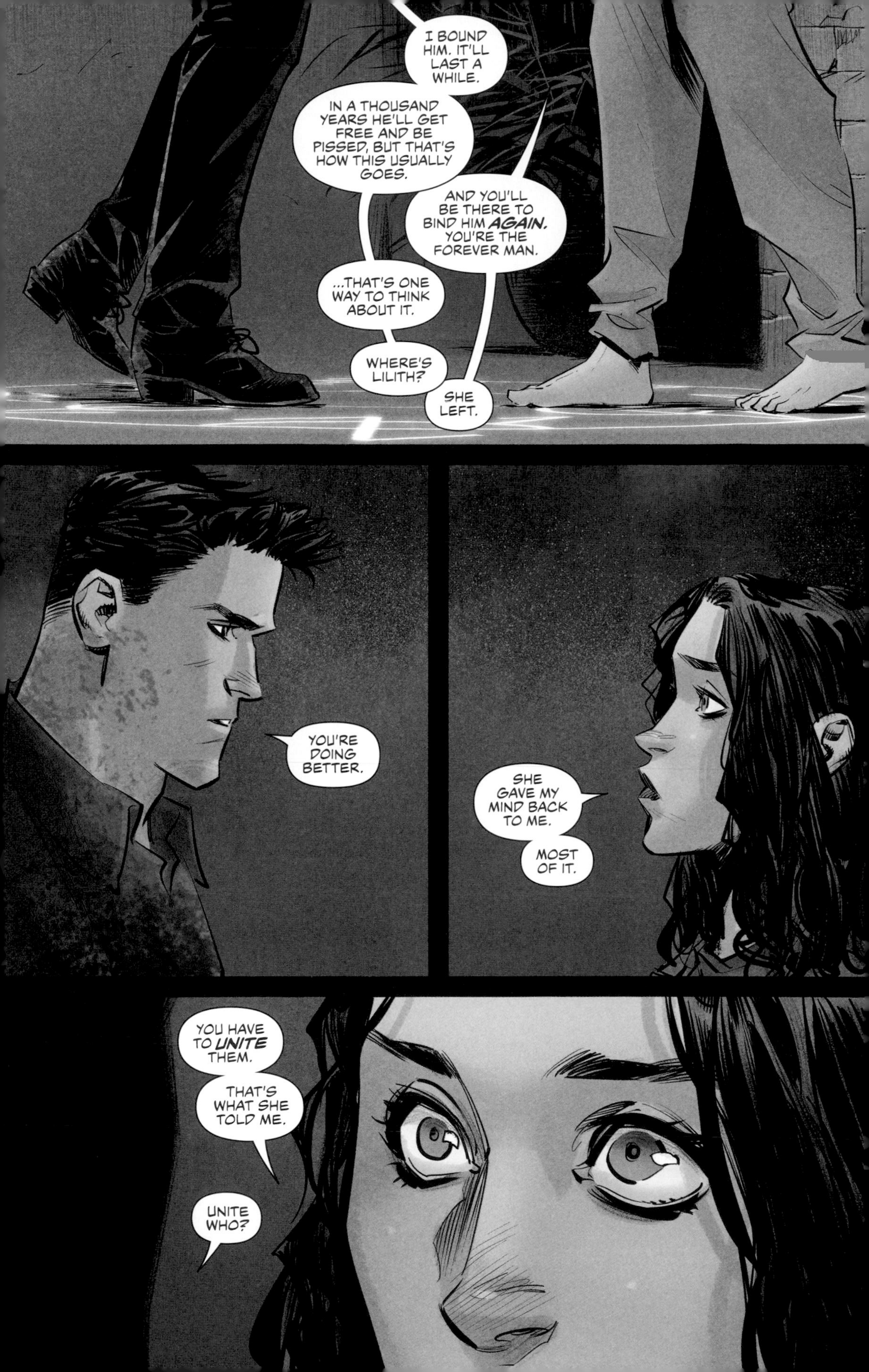
I BOUND HIM. IT'LL LAST A WHILE.
IN A THOUSAND YEARS HE'LL GET FREE AND BE PISSED, BUT THAT'S HOW THIS USUALLY GOES.
AND YOU'LL BE THERE TO BIND HIM *AGAIN.* YOU'RE THE FOREVER MAN.
...THAT'S ONE WAY TO THINK ABOUT IT.
WHERE'S LILITH?
SHE LEFT.
YOU'RE DOING BETTER.
SHE GAVE MY MIND BACK TO ME.
MOST OF IT.
YOU HAVE TO ***UNITE*** THEM.
THAT'S WHAT SHE TOLD ME.
UNITE WHO?

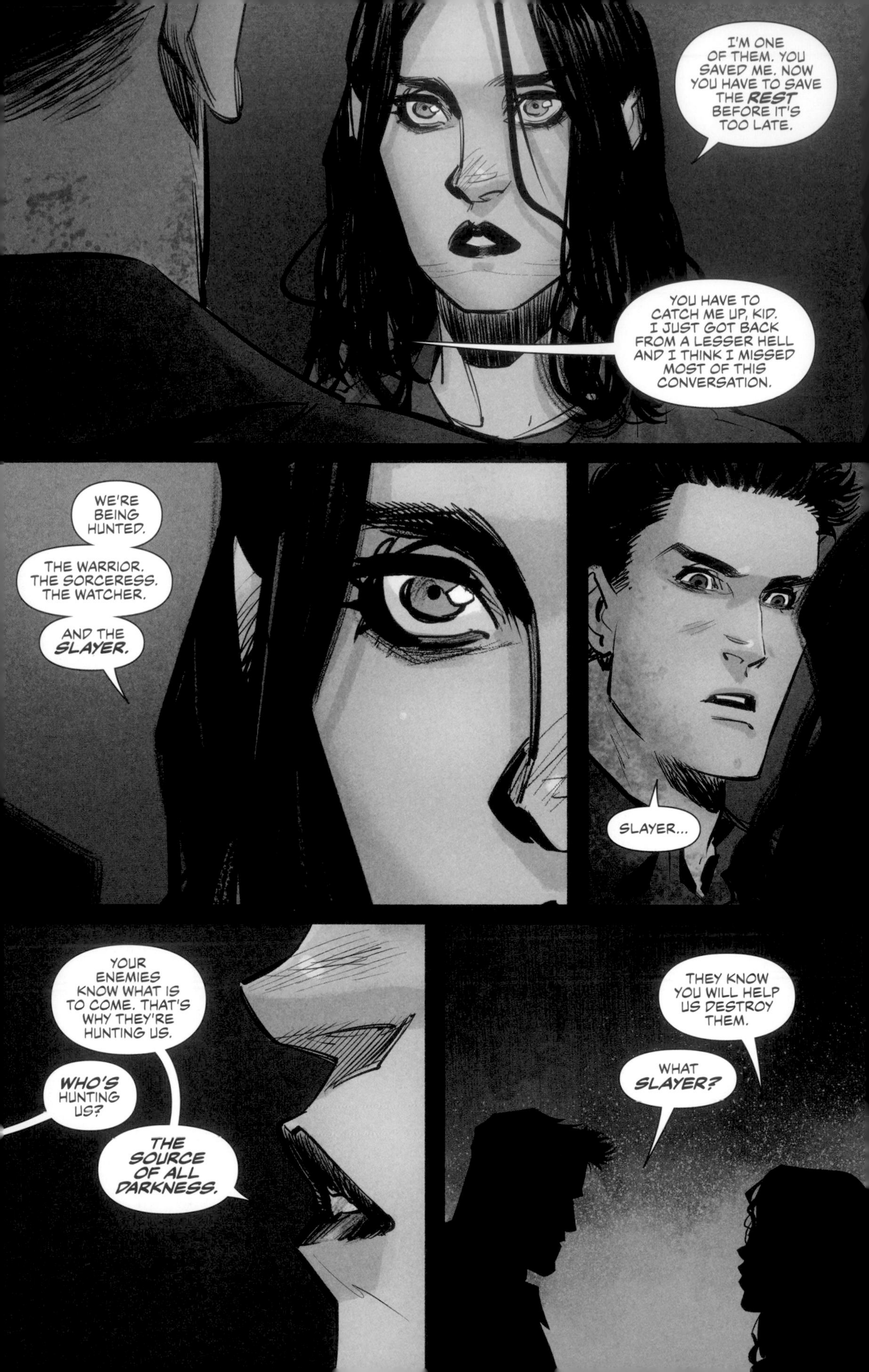
I'M ONE OF THEM. YOU SAVED ME. NOW YOU HAVE TO SAVE THE REST BEFORE IT'S TOO LATE.
YOU HAVE TO CATCH ME UP, KID. I JUST GOT BACK FROM A LESSER HELL AND I THINK I MISSED MOST OF THIS CONVERSATION.
WE'RE BEING HUNTED.
THE WARRIOR. THE SORCERESS. THE WATCHER.
AND THE SLAYER.
SLAYER...
YOUR ENEMIES KNOW WHAT IS TO COME. THAT'S WHY THEY'RE HUNTING US.
WHO'S HUNTING US?
THE SOURCE OF ALL DARKNESS.
THEY KNOW YOU WILL HELP US DESTROY THEM.
WHAT SLAYER?

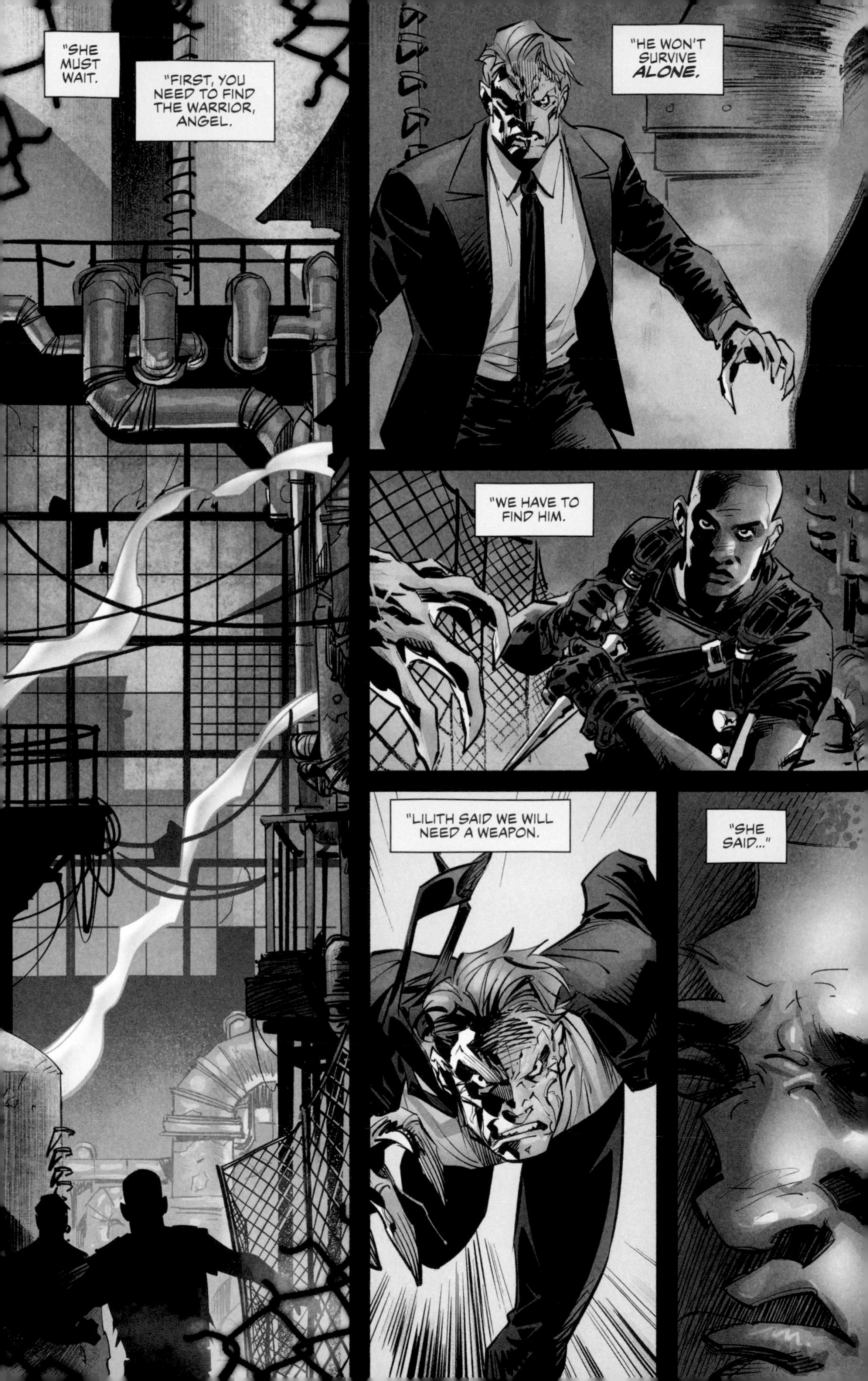
"SHE MUST WAIT.
"FIRST, YOU NEED TO FIND THE WARRIOR, ANGEL.
"HE WON'T SURVIVE *ALONE*.
"WE HAVE TO FIND HIM.
"LILITH SAID WE WILL NEED A WEAPON.
"SHE SAID..."

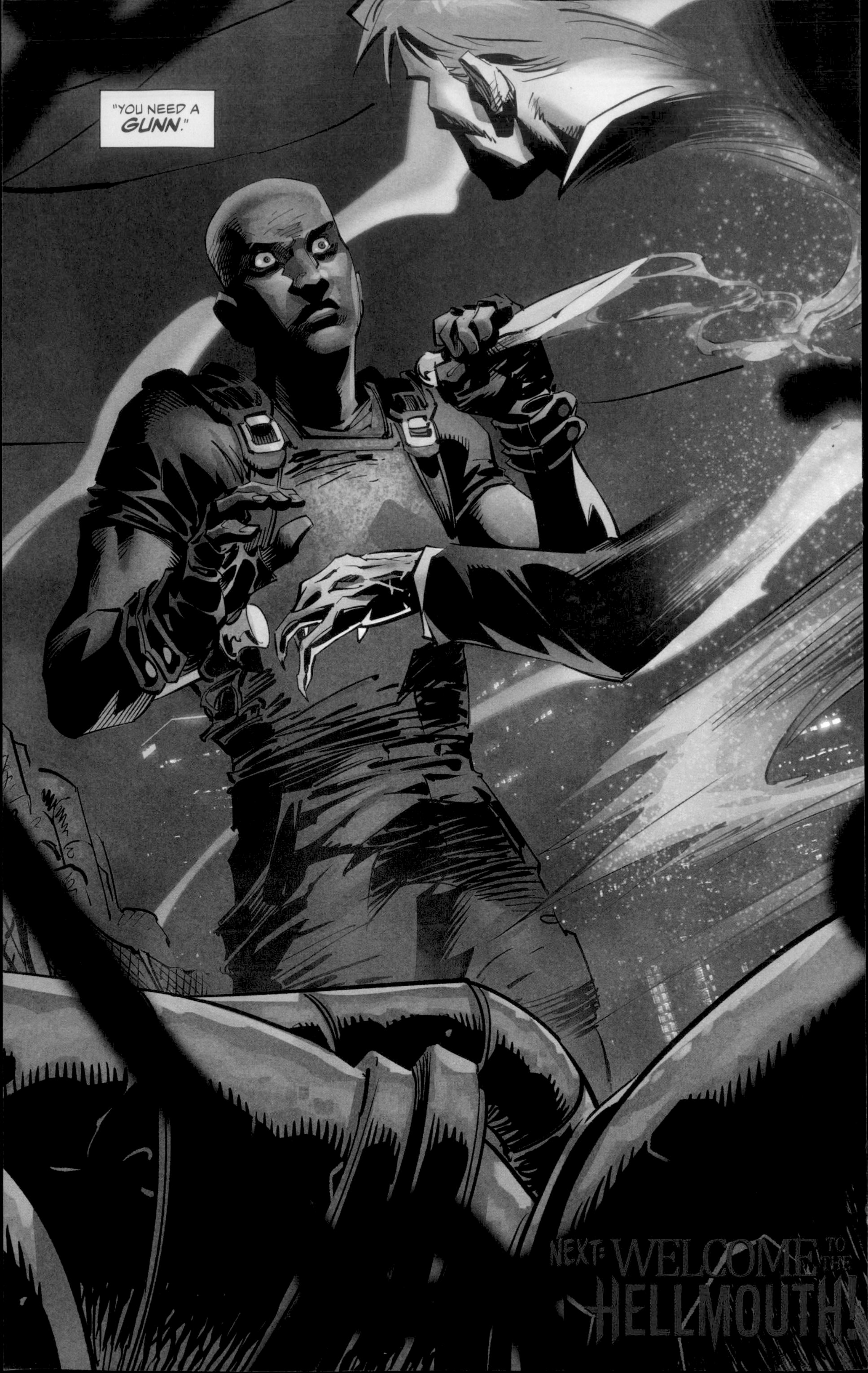
"YOU NEED A GUNN."
NEXT: WELCOME TO THE HELLMOUTH!

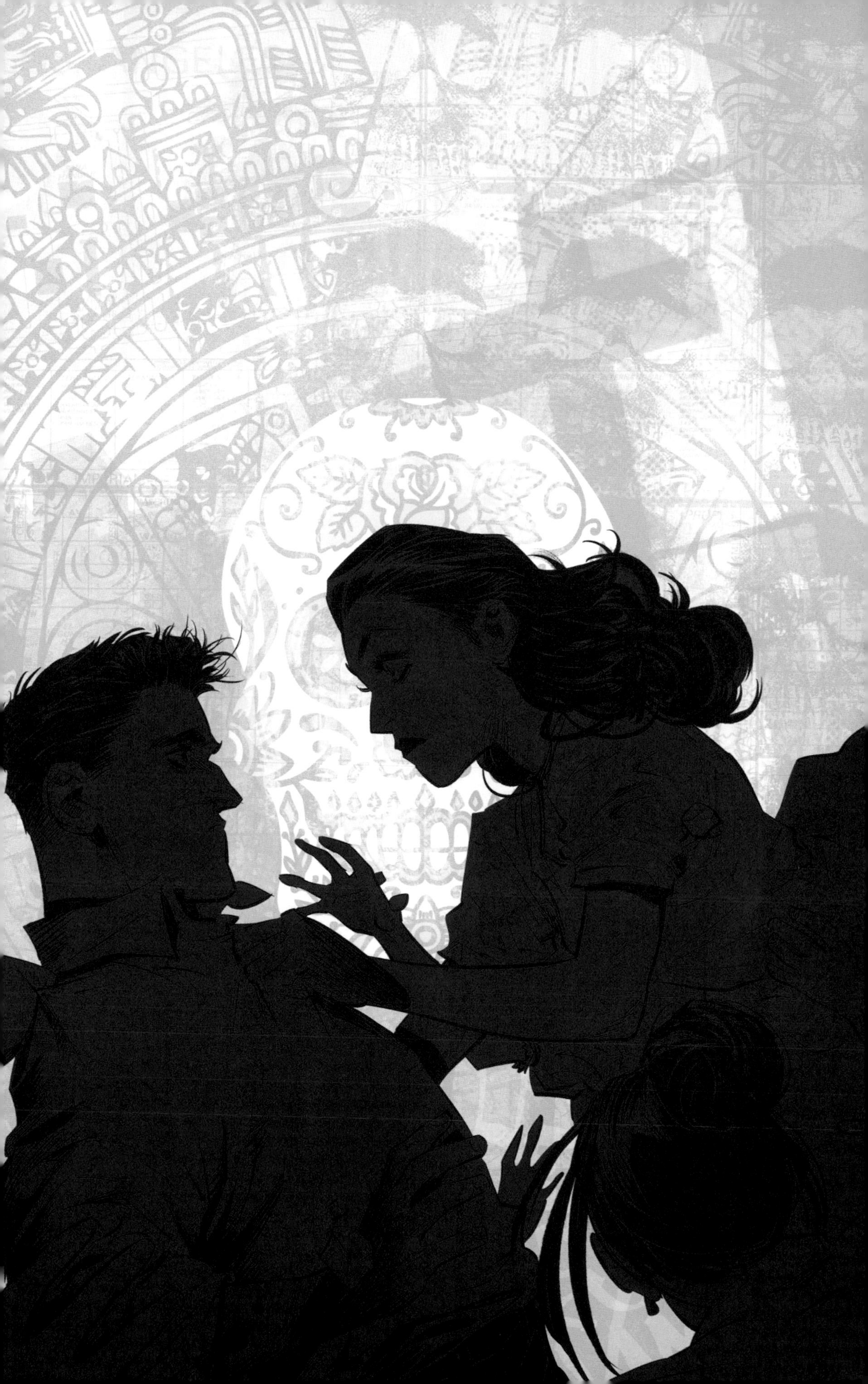

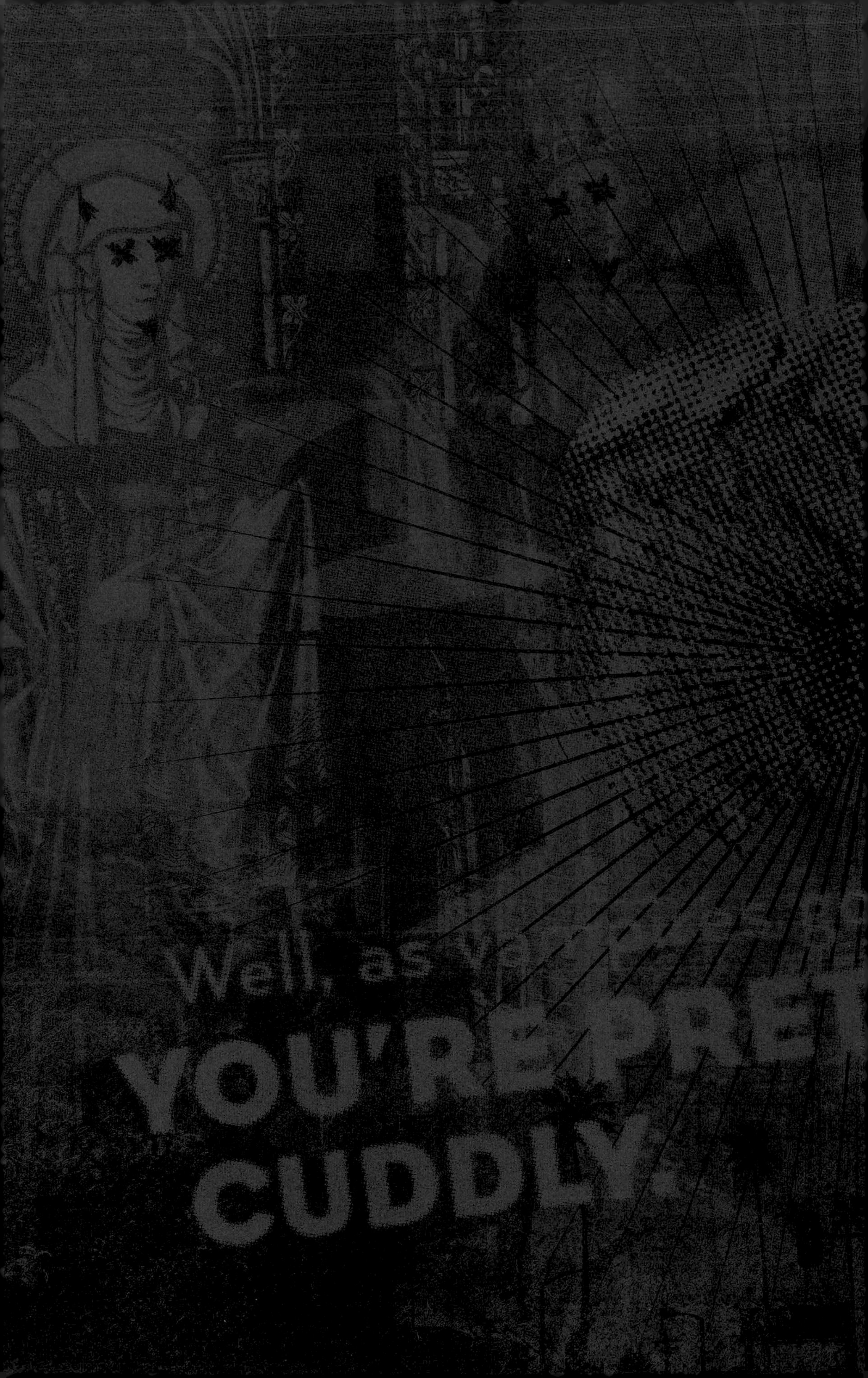
Well, as
YOU'RE PRE
CUDDLY.

COVER
GALLERY

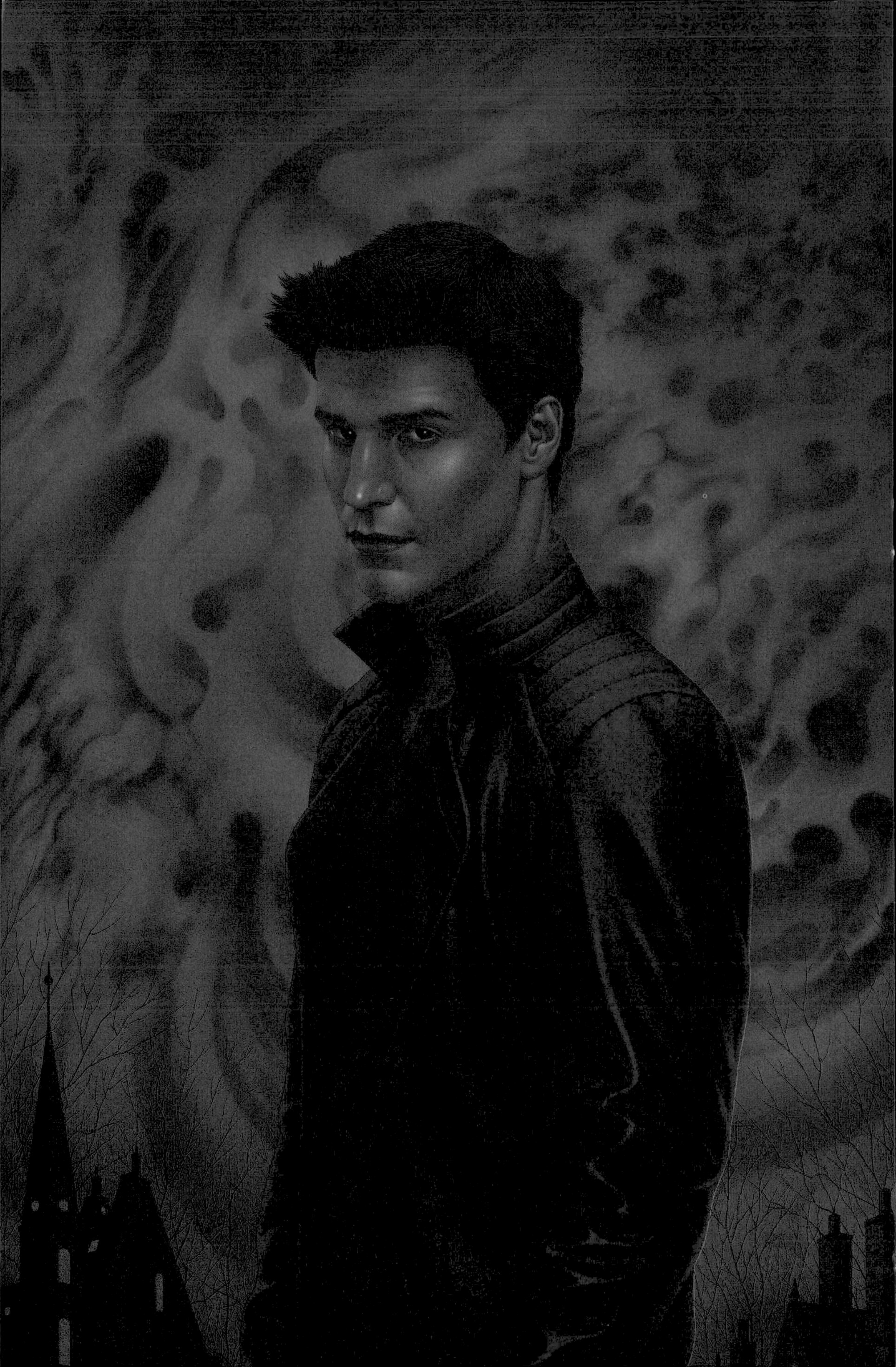
Angel #0 Cover by **Boris Pelcer**

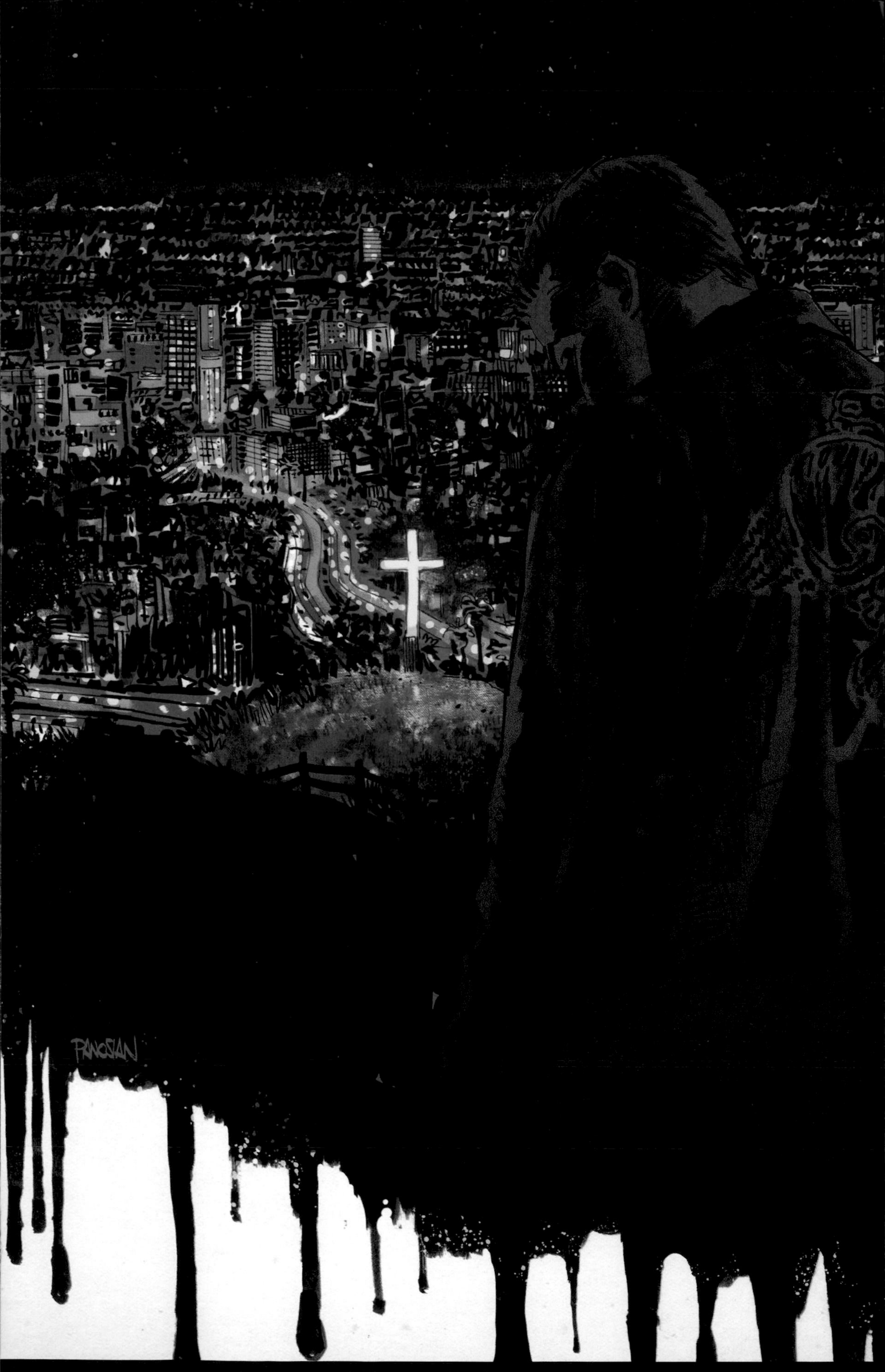
PANOSIAN

Angel #1 Cover by **Dan Panosian**

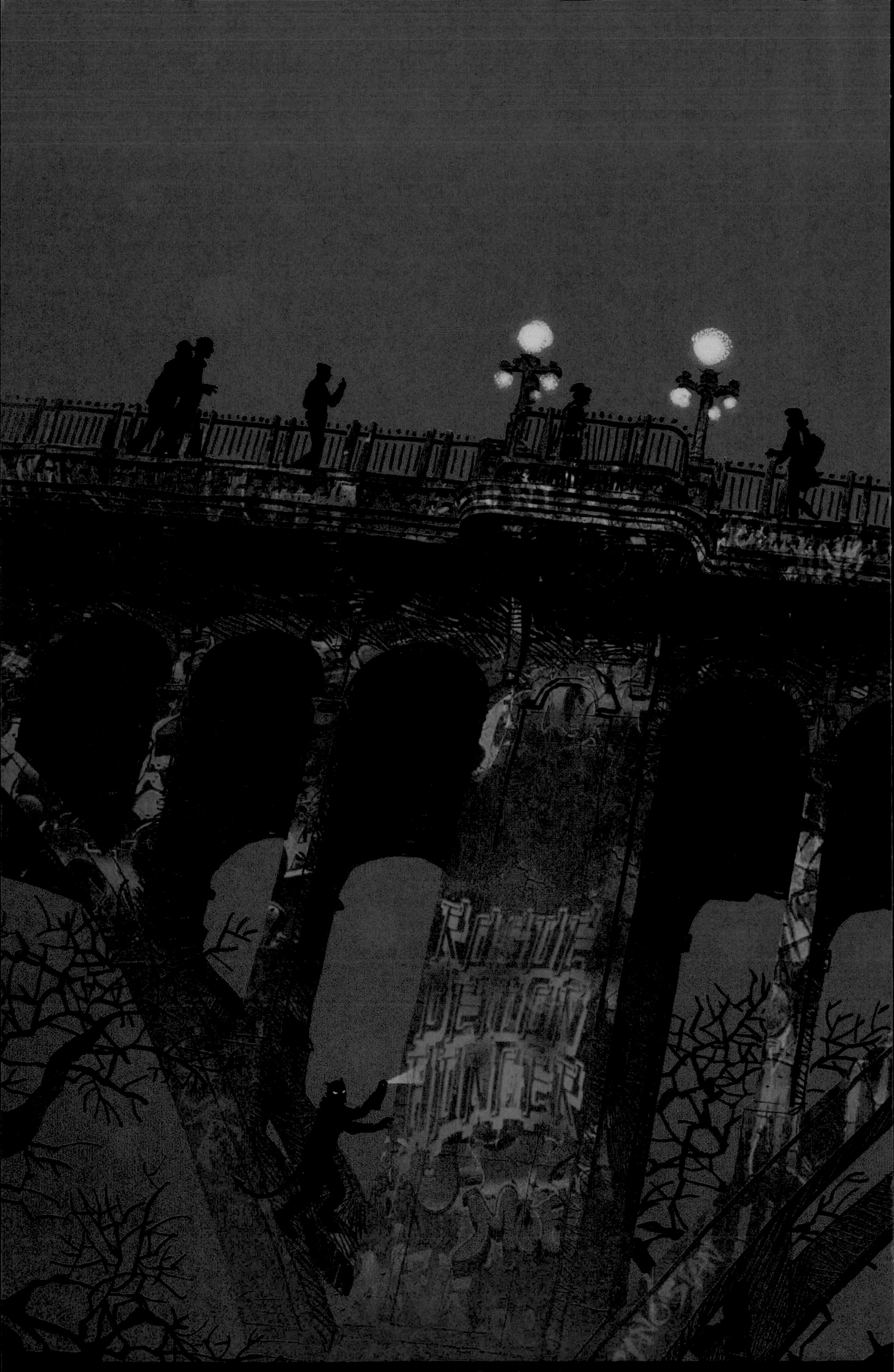

Angel #2 Cover by **Dan Panosian**

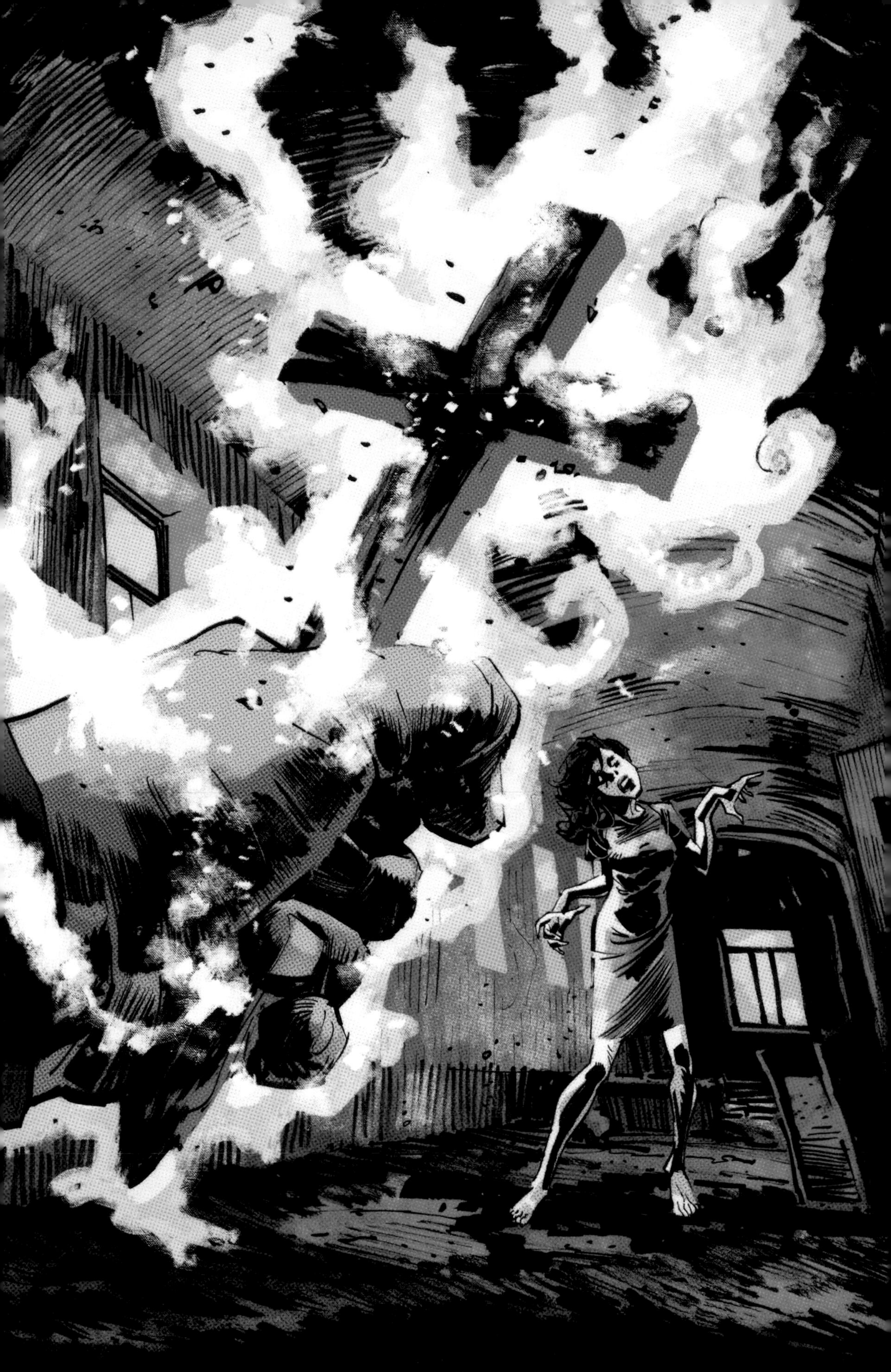

Angel #3 Cover by **Dan Panosian**

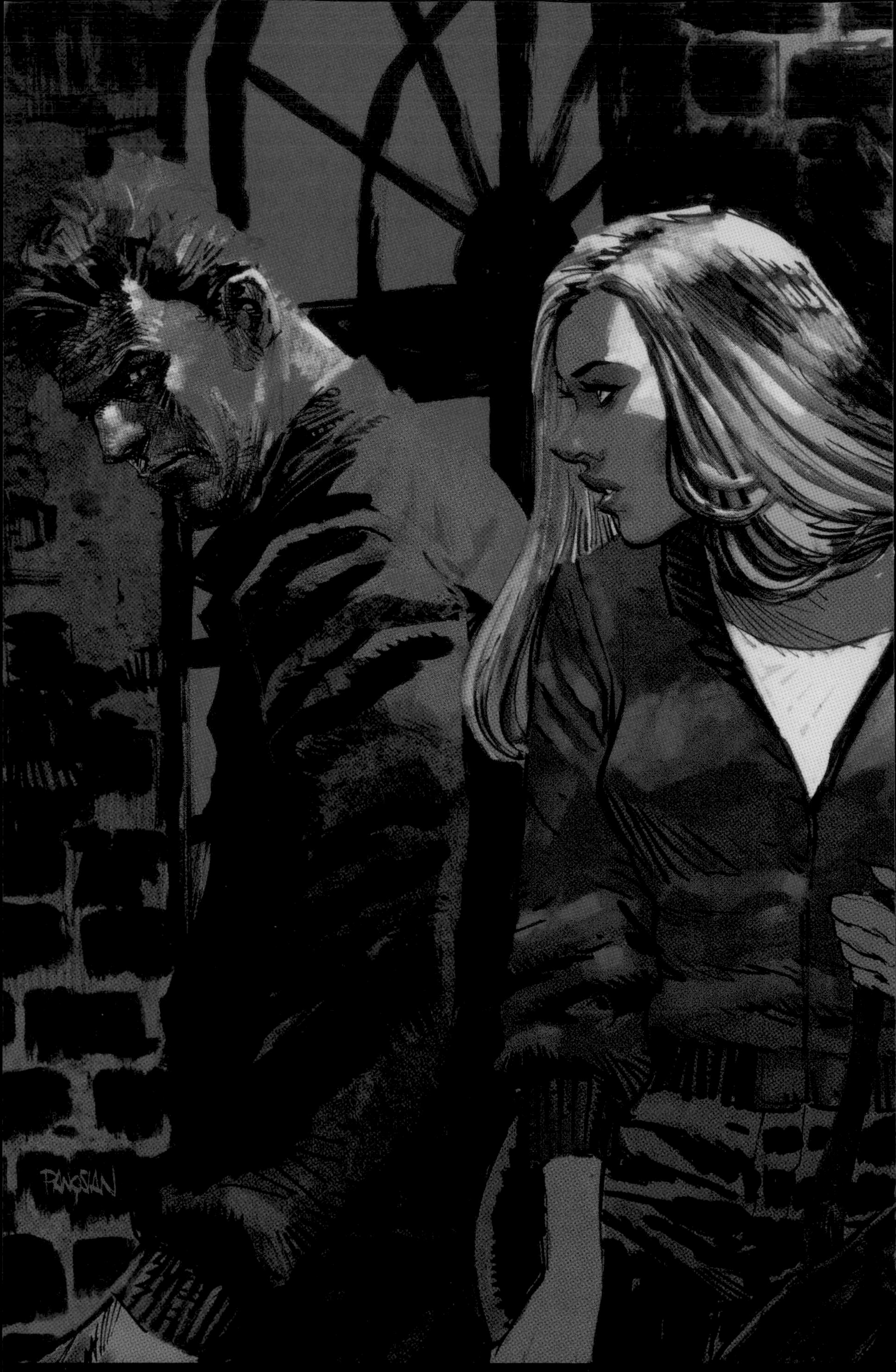
PANOSIAN

Angel #4 Cover by **Dan Panosian**

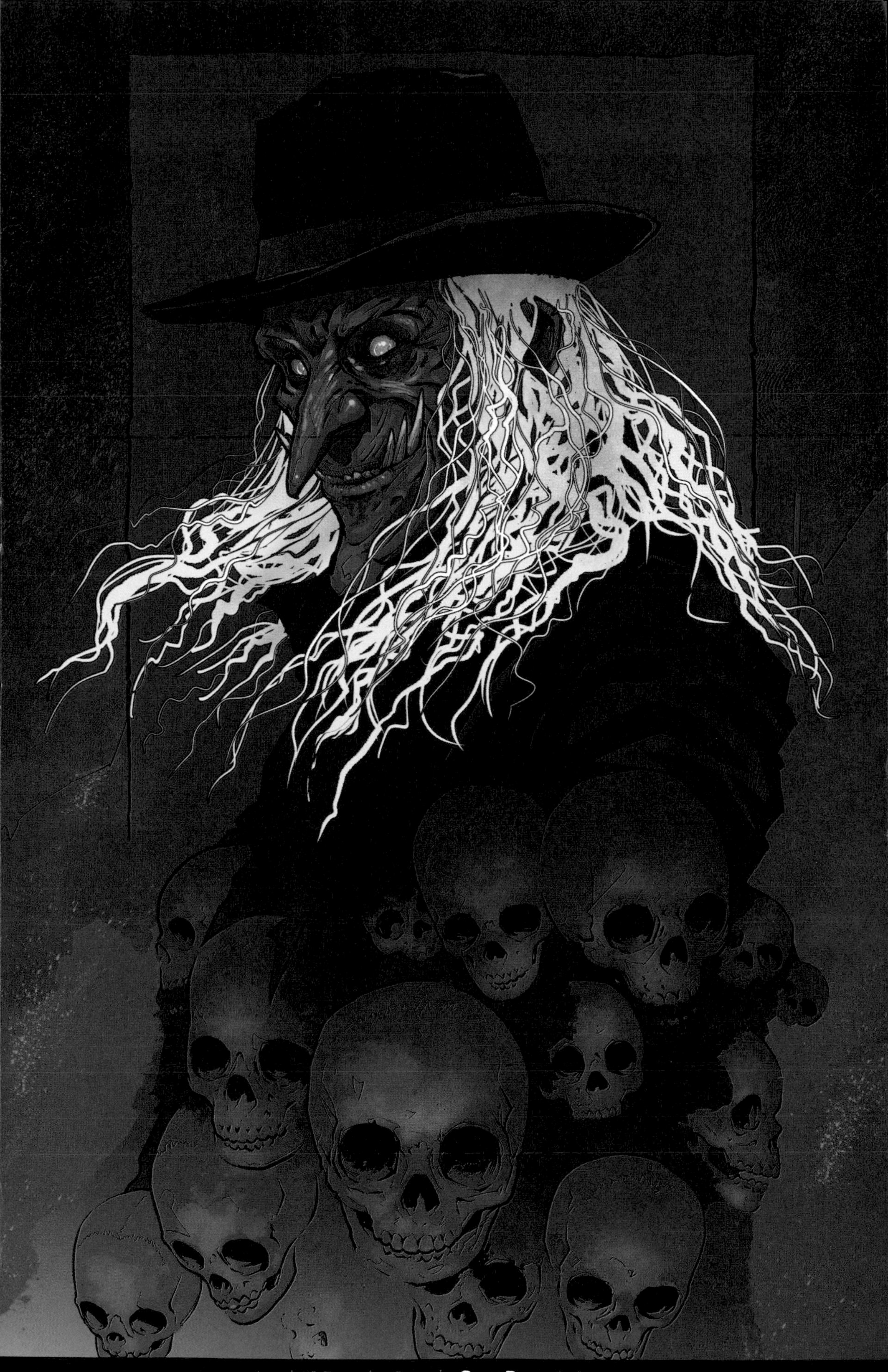

Angel #1 Preorder Cover by **Scott Buoncristiano**

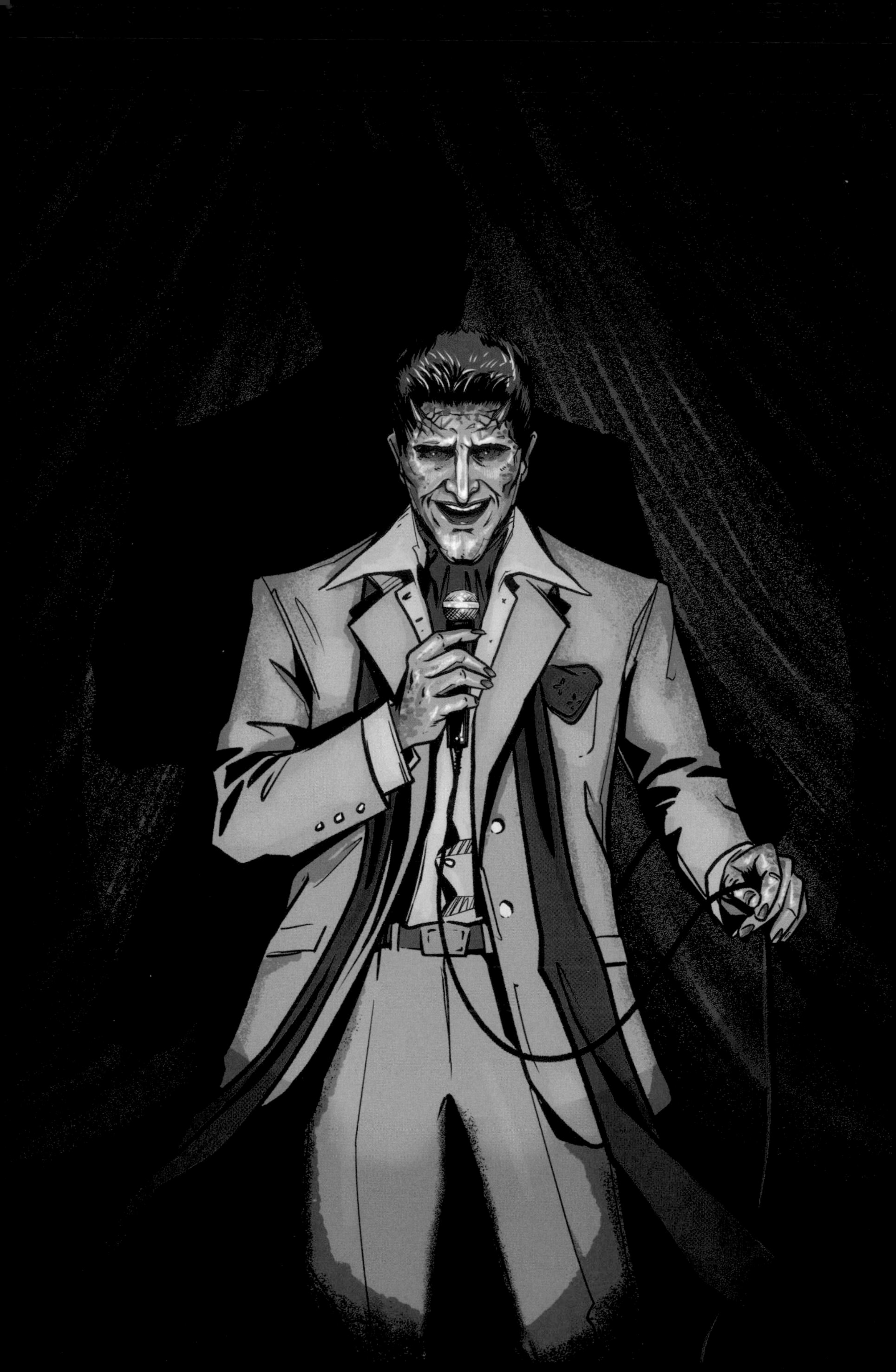

Angel #2 Preorder Cover by **Scott Buoncristiano**

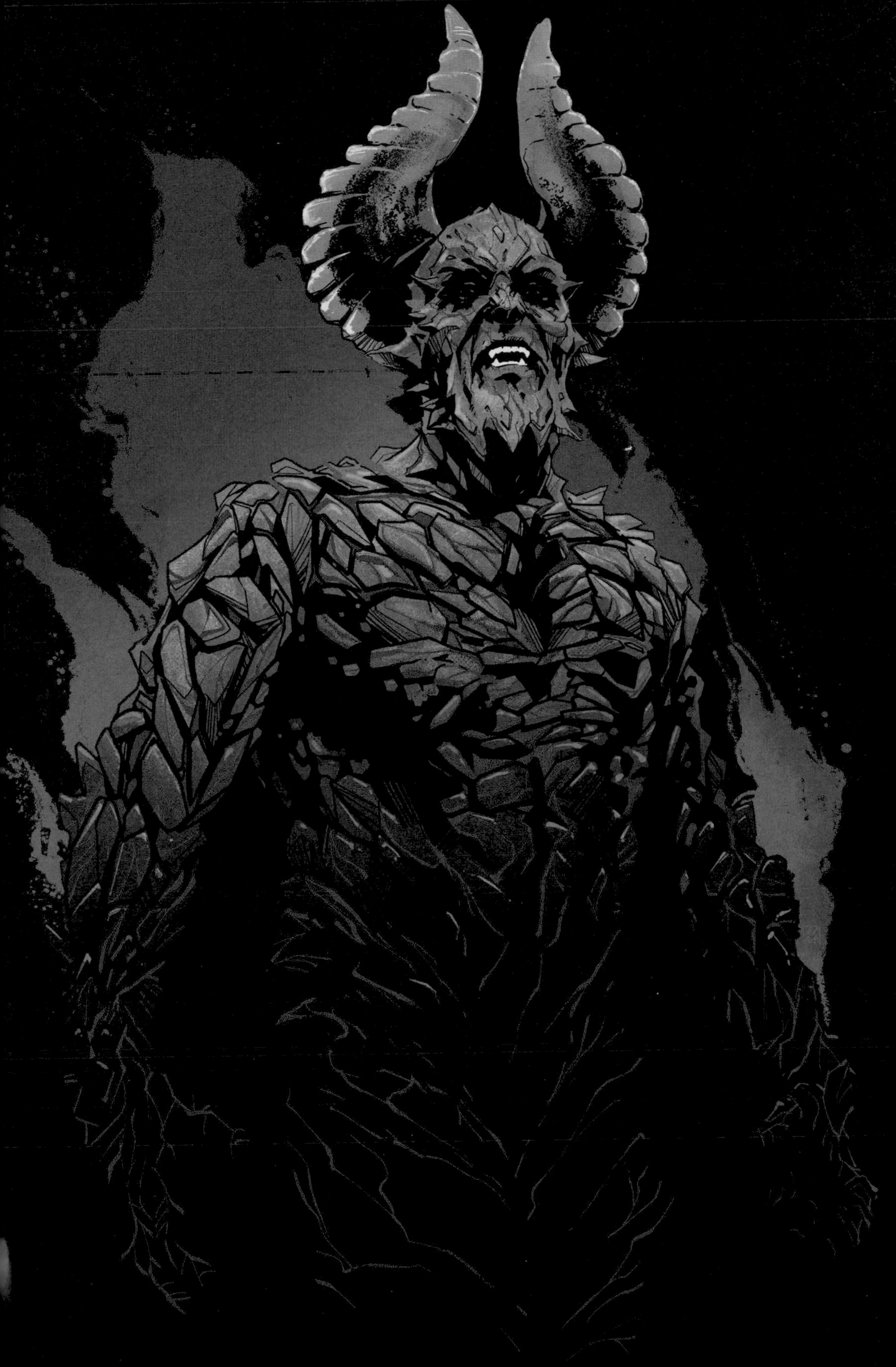

Angel #3 Preorder Cover by **Scott Buoncristiano**

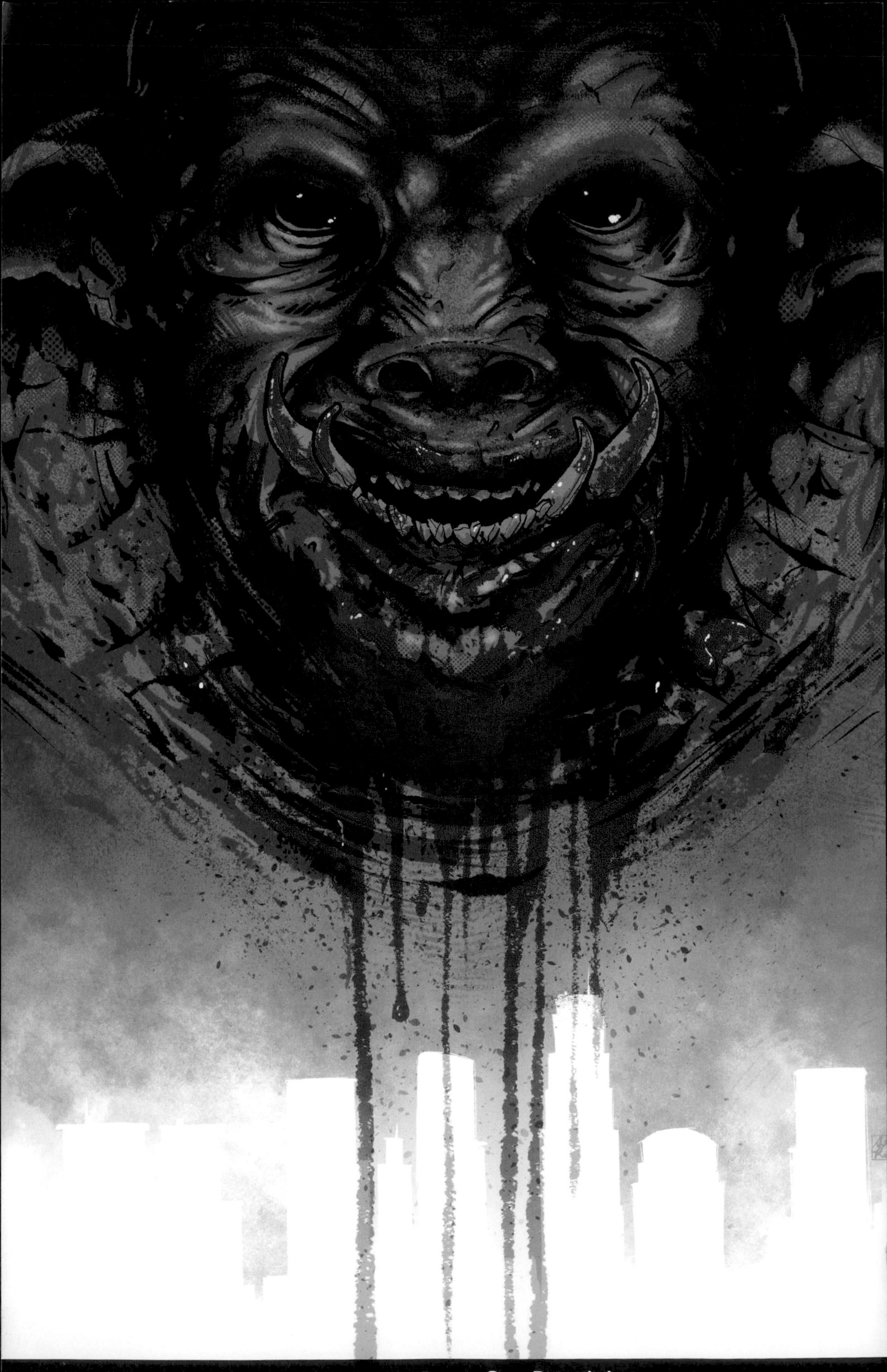

Angel #4 Preorder Cover by **Scott Buoncristiano**

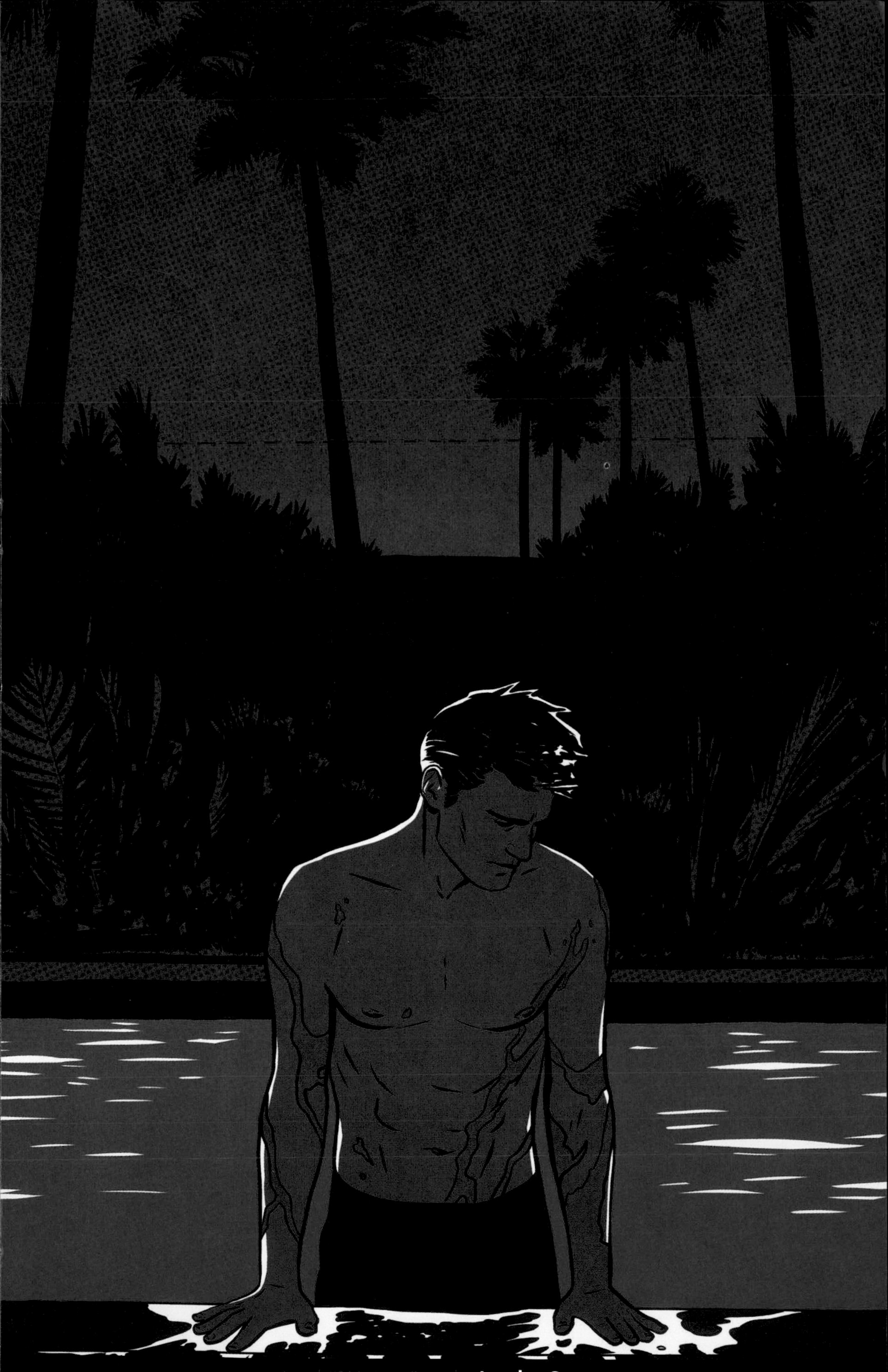

Angel #1 Variant Cover by **Jonathan Case**

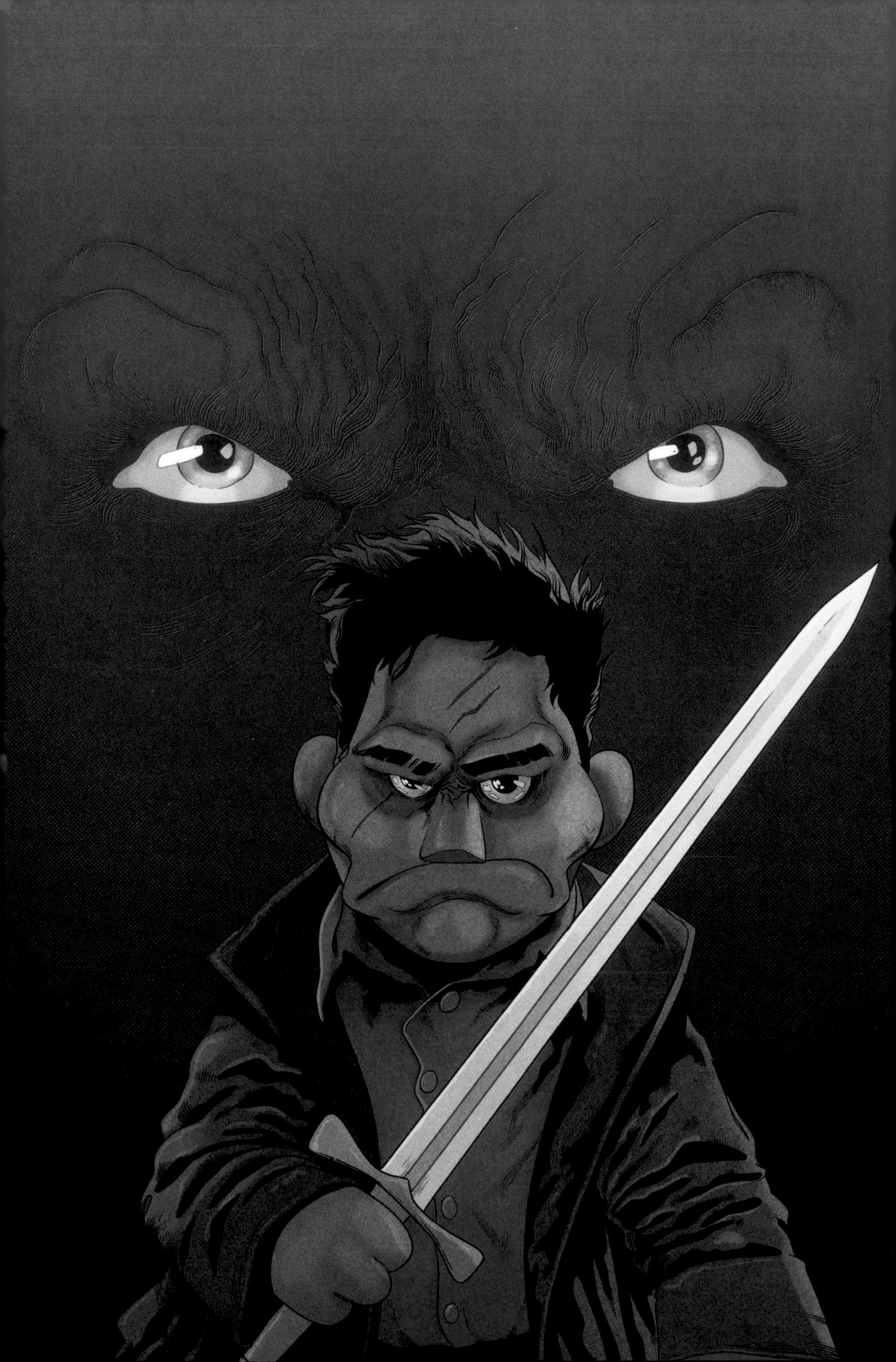

Angel #2 Variant Cover by **Will Sliney** with Colors by **Chris O'Halloran**

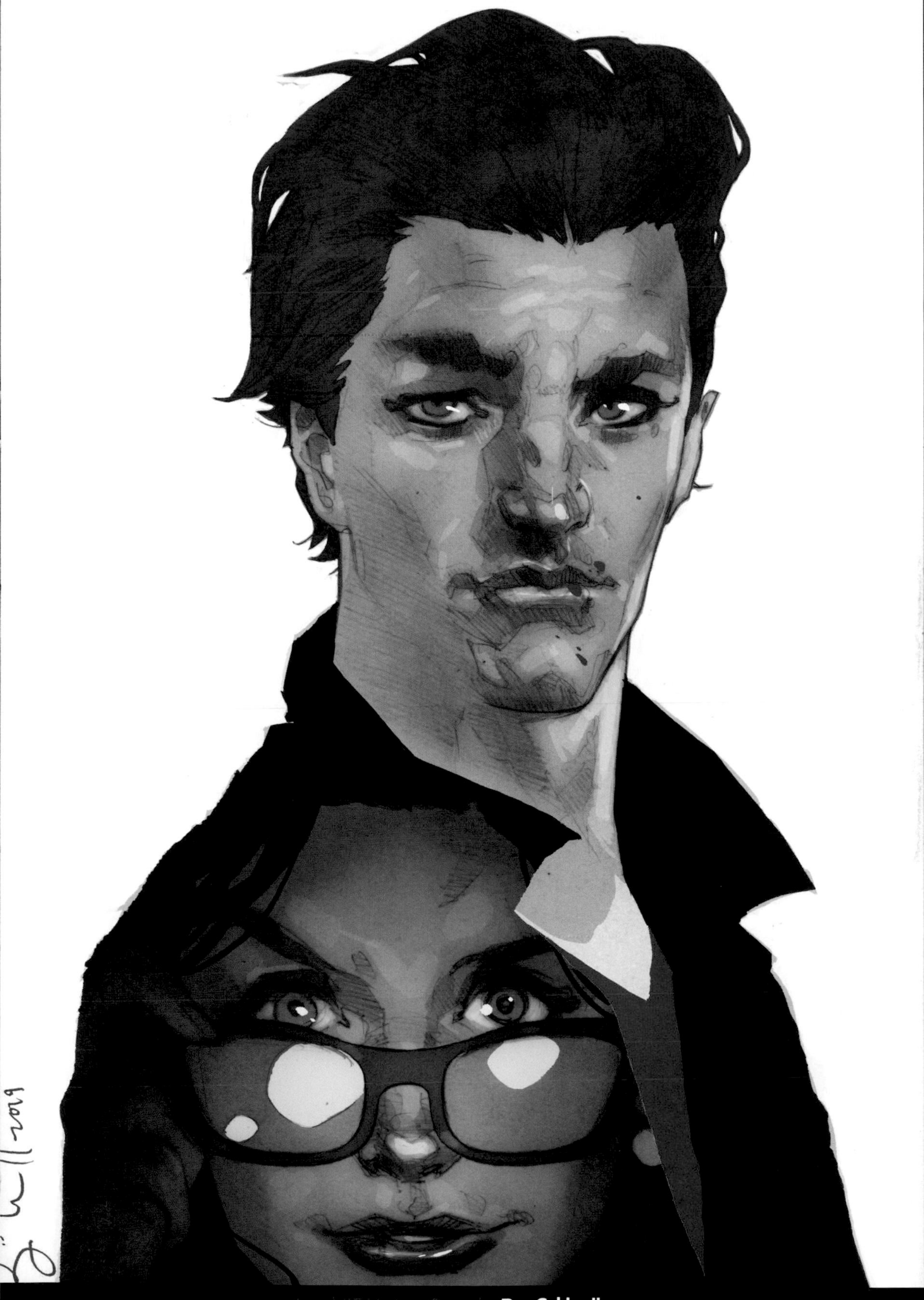

Angel #3 Variant Cover by **Ben Caldwell**

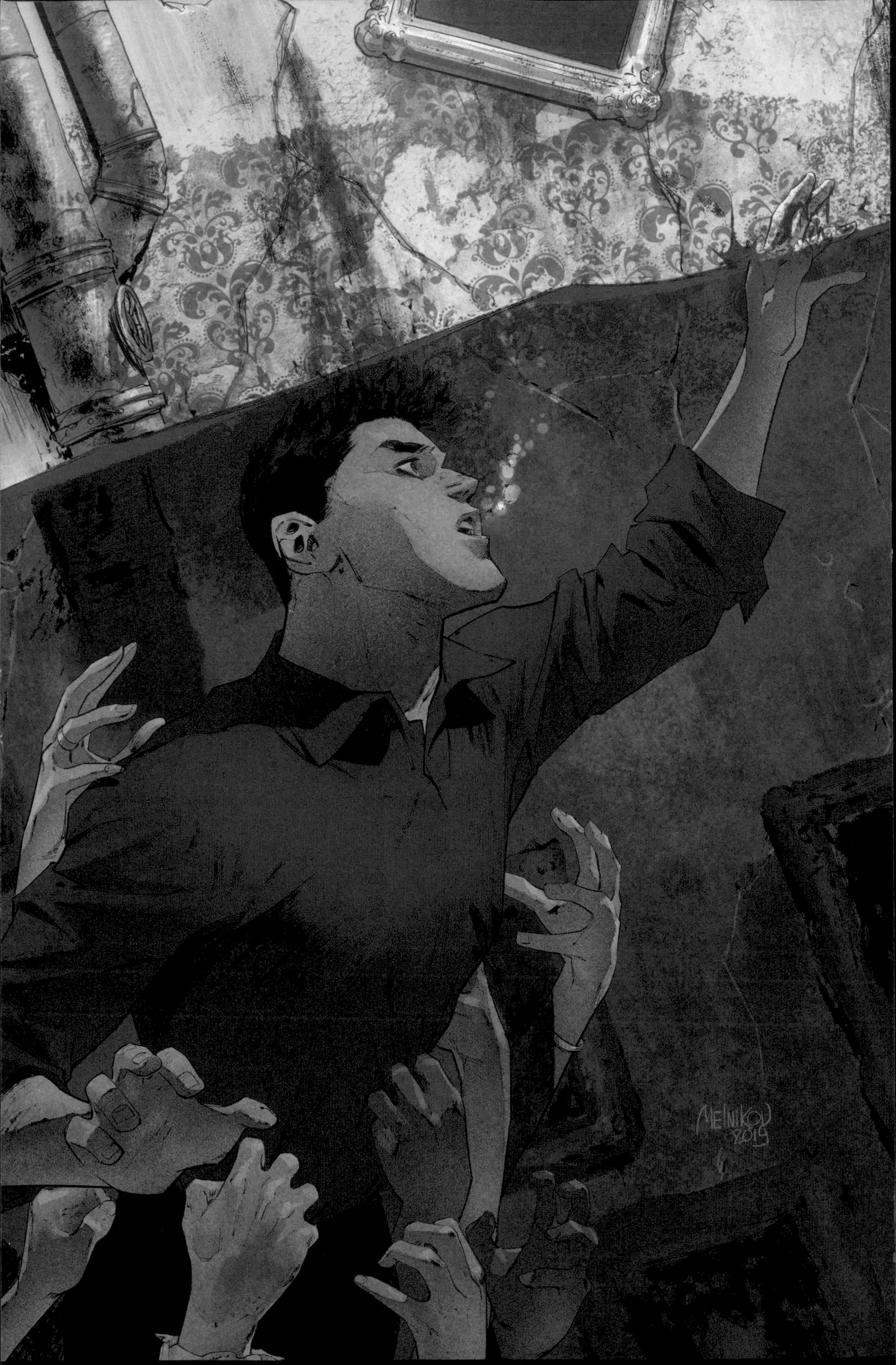
MELNIKOV
2019

Angel #4 Variant Cover by **Gleb Melnikov**

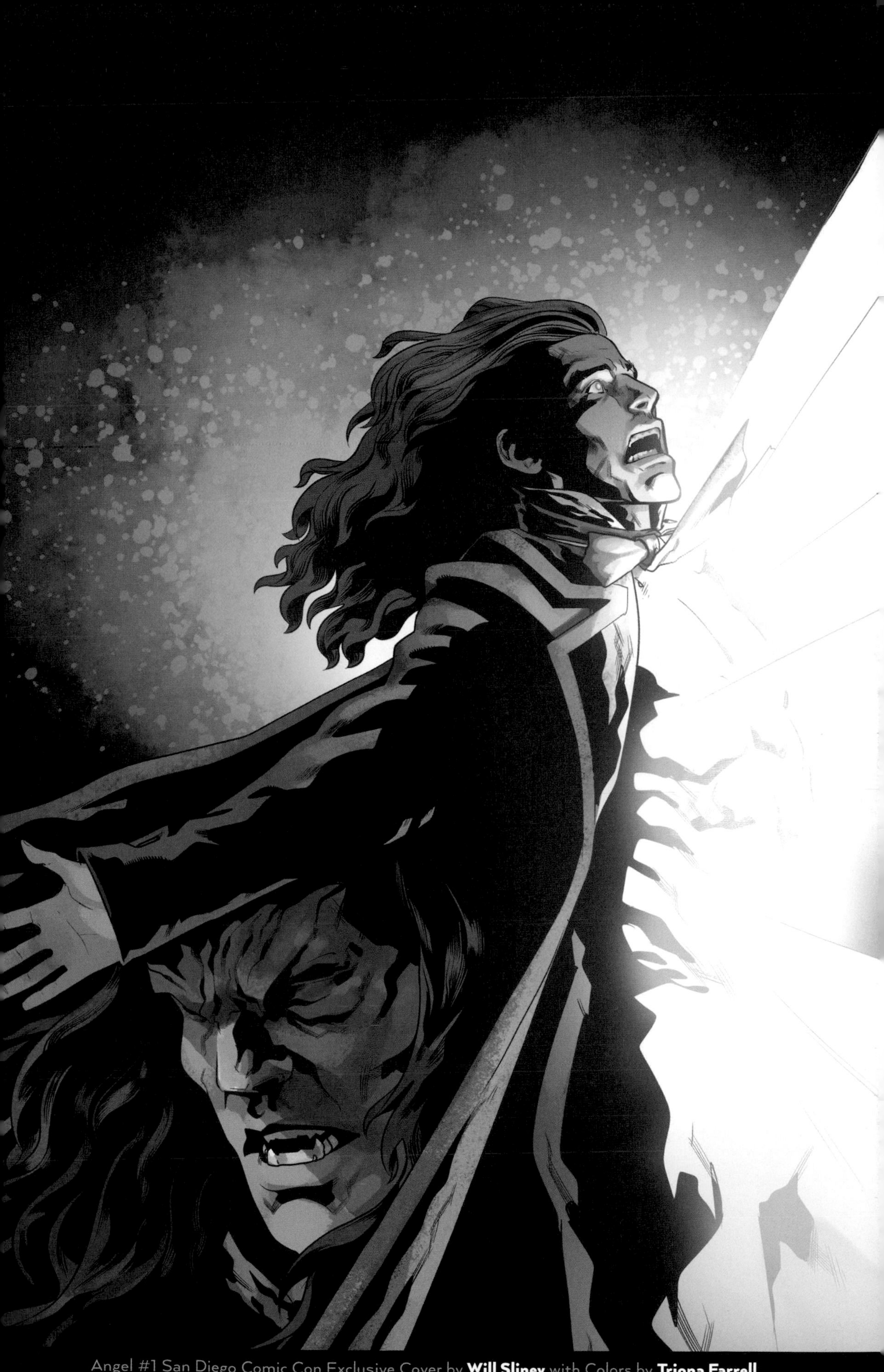

Angel #1 San Diego Comic Con Exclusive Cover by **Will Sliney** with Colors by **Triona Farrell**

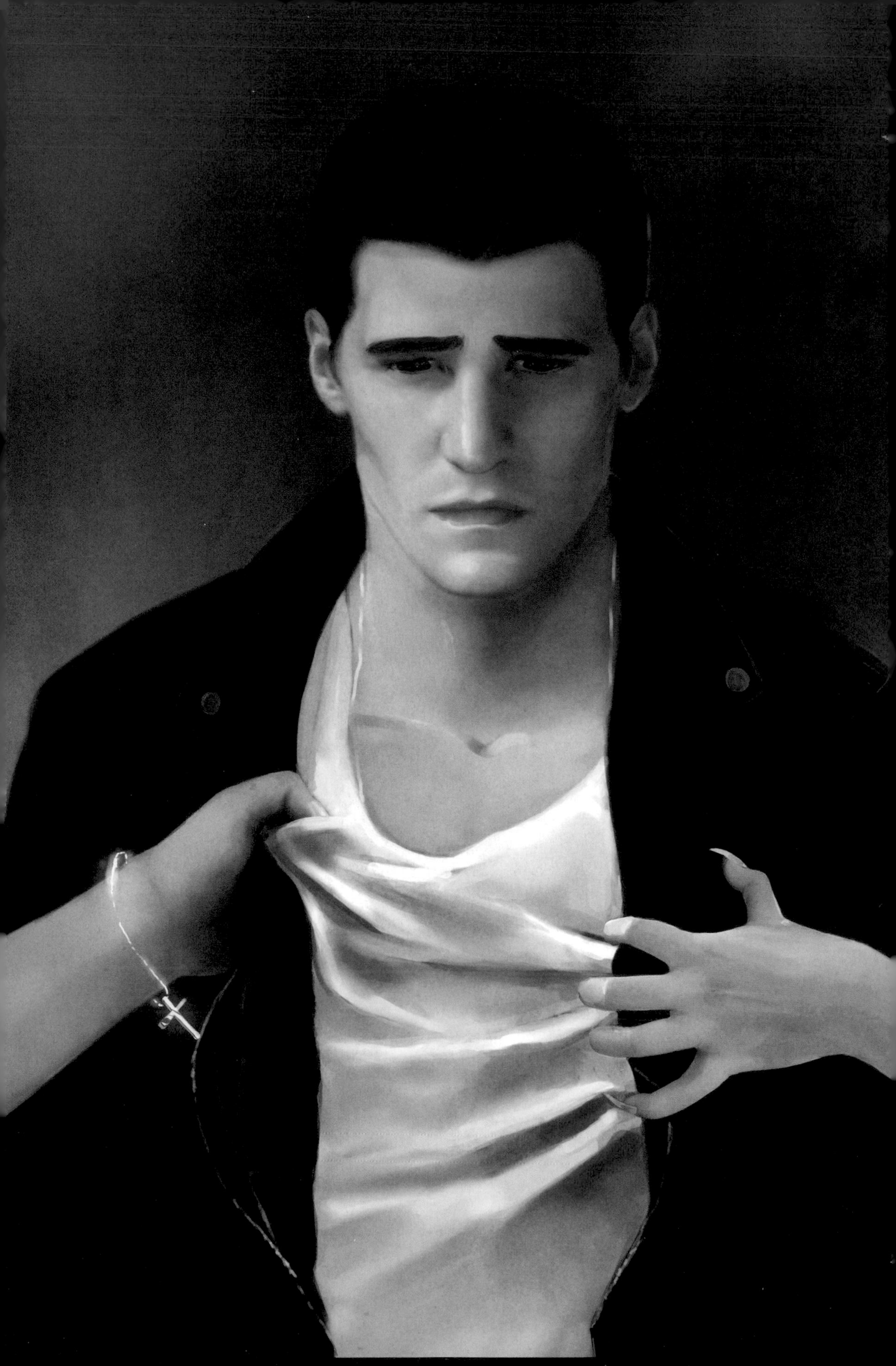

Angel #1 Connection Cover by **Kaiti Infante**